Lecture Notes in Artificial Intelligence 6251

Edited by R. Goebel, J. Siekmann, and W. Wahlster

Subseries of Lecture Notes in Computer Science

W0090817

Jürgen Dix   Cees Witteveen (Eds.)

Multiagent System Technologies

8th German Conference, MATES 2010
Leipzig, Germany, September 27-29, 2010
Proceedings

 Springer

Series Editors

Randy Goebel, University of Alberta, Edmonton, Canada
Jörg Siekmann, University of Saarland, Saarbrücken, Germany
Wolfgang Wahlster, DFKI and University of Saarland, Saarbrücken, Germany

Volume Editors

Jürgen Dix
Clausthal University of Technology
Department of Computer Science
Clausthal-Zellerfeld, Germany
E-mail: dix@tu-clausthal.de

Cees Witteveen
Delft University of Technology
Department of Software Technology
Delft, The Netherlands
E-mail: c.witteveen@tudelft.nl

Library of Congress Control Number: 2010935210

CR Subject Classification (1998): I.2, D.2, C.2.4, I.2.11, H.4, F.3

LNCS Sublibrary: SL 7 – Artificial Intelligence

ISSN	0302-9743
ISBN-10	3-642-16177-4 Springer Berlin Heidelberg New York
ISBN-13	978-3-642-16177-3 Springer Berlin Heidelberg New York

springer.com

© Springer-Verlag Berlin Heidelberg 2010
Printed in Germany

Typesetting: Camera-ready by author, data conversion by Scientific Publishing Services, Chennai, India
Printed on acid-free paper   06/3180

Preface

These are the proceedings of the 8th International Workshop on Multi Agent Systems Technologies (MATES 2010), held during 27–29 September in Leipzig, collocated with the 40th Annual Conference of the Gesellschaft fur Informatik e.V. (GI).

The main aim of the MATES conference series consists in bringing together researchers from around the world and providing a fruitful discussion basis for exchanging ideas and sharing the latest scientific results. Since its inception in 2003, MATES has been collocated with mainstream software engineering conferences like the NetObjectDays as well as with the German Artificial Intelligence Conference (KI) and has thus strived to address the full range of agent research topics from practical applications and tools for agent technology to the theoretical foundations of multi-agent systems. In addition to the broad range of topics covered by MATES, special areas of interest (hot topics) within the field of multi-agent systems have been identified in recent years and have influenced the conferences.

Multi-agent systems are communities of problem-solving entities that can perceive and act upon their environment in order to achieve both their individual goals and their joint goals. The work on such systems integrates many technologies and concepts from artificial intelligence and other areas of computing as well as other disciplines. In recent years, the agent paradigm has gained popularity, due to its applicability to a full spectrum of domains, such as search engines, recommendation systems, educational support, e-procurement, simulation and routing, electronic commerce and trade, etc.

These proceedings feature 18 regular papers (from a total of 34 papers submitted), as well as abstracts of two invited talks, given by Felix Brandt (TU München) and Michal Pěchouček (Czech Technical University in Prague).

Felix Brandt considered in his talk *Tournament Solutions and Their Applications to Multiagent Decision Making* the important problem of decision-making in multiagent systems. There are several broad areas, such as *adversarial, collective*, or *coalitional* decision making that have gained interest in the past years. It was shown in the talk how tournament solution concepts, based on binary dominance relations, can be applied. The overview was accompanied by a complexity analysis.

Michal Pěchouček talked about *Research Challenges in Simulation Aided Design of Complex Multi-Agent Systems*, based on joint research with Michal Jacob. In recent years more and more complex systems and infrastructures accompany and interact with us. These systems are based on complex networks with mutual interactions and feedbacks, giving rise to dynamic, non-linear emergent behavior. The following open research challenges were discussed during the talk: *(i)* automated construction, calibration, and synchronization of the simulation models, *ii)* scalability and fidelity of the simulation, *(iii)* introduction of mixed-mode simulation, and *(iv)* development and rapid prototyping support.

The regular papers of MATES 2010 have been classified in the following categories/sessions, in the order of their presentation at the conference.

Models and Specifications: This session consists of three papers. The first paper, by Inmaculada Ayala, Mercedes Amor, and Lidia Fuentes, *"A Model Driven Development of Platform-Neutral Agents,"* considers the problem of automatic transformation of software agent designs into implementations for different agent platforms. More specifically, they transform a particular agent metamodel into Malaca.

The second paper, by Mohamed Amin Laouadi, Farid Mokhati, and Hassina Seridi presents *"A Novel Formal Specification Approach for Real Time Multi-Agent System Functional Requirements."* The idea is to translate extended AUML diagrams describing RTMAS' functional requirements into a RT-Maude specification. This approach combines the advantages of the graphical modeling formalism Agent UML and the formal specification language RT-Maude.

The last paper in this session, by Joost Broekens, Maaike Harbers, Koen Hindriks, Karel van den Bosch, Catholijn Jonker, and John-Jules Meyer, *"Do You Get It? User-Evaluated Explainable BDI Agents,"* was about explaining to humans the behavior of autonomous agents. This is important for e.g., disaster training, tutor and pedagogical systems, agent development and debugging, gaming, and interactive storytelling.

Trust, Norms, and Reputation: We have three papers in this session. Miriam Heitz, Stefan König, and Torsten Eymann consider trust and reputation mechanisms in their paper *"Reputation in Multi Agent Systems and the Incentives to Provide Feedback."* Many transactions on the Internet are subject to fraud and cheating, so there is a need for incentive mechanisms to get users to report their experiences honestly.

Natalia Criado, Estefania Argente, and Vicent Botti extend BDI architectures by norms in *"Normative Deliberation in Graded BDI Agents."* This is done by adding both a recognition and a normative context so that agents can use norms in their decision making.

Roberto Centeno, Holger Billhardt, and Sascha Ossowski treat a similar problem in their paper *"Inducing Desirable Behavior through an Incentives Infrastructure"*: How can one make sure that heterogenous agents, possibly built on different platforms, act in a certain manner? The authors introduce an incentive infrastructure to formulate agents' preferences.

Models, Tools, and Architectures: In the first paper of this session, *"SONAR/OREDI: A Tool for Creation and Deployment of Organization Models"* by Michael Köhler-Bußmeier and Endri Deliu, a middleware concept for support of organizational teamwork is discussed using Sonar, a Petri-net based specification formalism for multi-agent organizations.

Christian Hahn, Sven Jacobi, and David Raber in their paper *"Enhancing the Interoperability between Multiagent Systems and Service-Oriented Architectures through a Model-Driven Approach"* present a model-driven approach for the integration of service-oriented architectures and multi-agent systems and provide a real-world industry scenario showing the relevance of their approach.

The final paper in this session, by Alexander Pokahr, Lars Braubach, and Kai Jander, titled *"Unifying Agent and Component Concepts - Jadex Active Components,"* discusses a new software concept called active components, a system architecture for them, and an implementation in the Jadex Active Component Infrastructure.

Applications I: There are three papers in this session. The first paper by Ferdi Grootenboers, Mathijs de Weerdt, and Mahdi Zargayouna, titled *"Impact of Competition on Quality of Service in Demand Responsive Transit"* deals with enhancing the QoS of transportation companies offering demand responsive transportation. The authors set up a multi-agent environment to simulate the assignment of rides to companies through an auction on QoS and the inserting of rides using an online optimization tool, showing that in this way service can be improved, while costs only increased moderately. Stefano Bromuri, Michael Schumacher, and Kostas Stathis in their contribution *"Towards Distributed Agent Environments for Pervasive Healthcare"* show how by applying the concept of agent environment, a pervasive GRID can be defined for roaming agents that monitor continuously the health status of patients.

Finally, Adriaan ter Mors, Cees Witteveen, Jonne Zutt, and Fernando Kuipers in their paper *"Context-Aware Route Planning"* show how conflict resolution in multi-agent traffic applications can be shifted from resolution during plan execution to resolution during the planning phase. They discuss a planning method where each agent is aware of the results of route planning by other agents.

Coordination and Learning: The first contribution is this session is the paper *"Social Conformity and Its Convergence for Reinforcement Learning"* by Juan A. Garcia-Pardo, Jose Soler, and Carlos Carrascosa. In this paper a social reinforcement mechanism is discussed that allows agents to adapt better to environmental changes. Here, social reinforcement enables an agent to take into account the opinion of other agents on its actions. The convergence of the approach is shown and the authors show that socially aware agents adapt better than traditional agents.

The second paper *"Colypan: A peer-to-Peer Architecture for a Project Management Collaborative Learning System"* by Hanaa Mazyad and Insaf Tnazefti-Kerkeni also deals with learning. Here, the authors focus on a project based learning environment where a multi-agent system supported by a peer-to-peer networking infrastructure constitutes a truly collaborative learning environment.

In the third paper titled *"Preference Generation for Autonomous Agents,"* Umair Rafique and Shell Ying Huang deal with the problem of learning preferences. They discuss a preference generation method that allows an agent to learn new preferences about an object based on its existing preferences about similar objects.

In the last paper of this session Robert Junges and Franziska Klügl deal with learning in a very general setting. In their paper *"Agent Architectures for a Learning-Driven Modeling Methodology in Multiagent Simulation,"* they introduce a learning-driven methodology that exploits learning architectures for generating suggestions for agent behavior models based on a given environmental model. They discuss several criteria that such a suitable learning agent architecture must fulfill.

Applications II: We have two papers in this second session about applications of multi-agent systems. First, Juan M. Alberola, Ana Garcia-Fornes, and Agustín Espinosa in their paper *"Price Prediction in Sports Betting Markets"* discuss an agent approach where an agent participates in the sport market focusing on the task of learning the price movements in order to make predictions of future prices. The agent then tries to identify and learn pattern price movements in order to predict the price movements of new events using an underlying case based reasoning system.

In their paper *"Modelling Distributed Network Security in a Petri Net and Agent-Based Approach,"* Simon Adameit, Tobias Betz, Lawrence Cabac, Florian Hars, Marcin Hewelt, Michael Köhler-Bußmeier, Daniel Moldt, Dimitri Popov, José Quenum, Axel Theilmann, Thomas Wagner, Timo Warns, and Lars Wüstenberg discuss an approach aiming to provide a novel way of handling and managing distributed network security through the means of agent-based software. Their model is based on the Paose (Petri net-based and agent-oriented software engineering) software development approach of the Herold research project. This project aims to provide a novel way of handling and prototyping distributed network security.

We thank all the authors of submissions for MATES 2010 for submitting papers and for revising their contributions to be included in these proceedings. We are very grateful to the members of the MATES 2010 steering committee, program committee, and the additional reviewers. Their service ensured the high quality of the accepted papers.

A special thank-you goes to the local organizers in Leipzig for their help and support. We are very grateful to them for handling the registration and a very enjoyable social program. A special thank-you to Mrs. Alexandra Gerstner for her continual and enduring support and availability in all organizational matters.

July 2010   Jürgen Dix
                                                                                              Cees Witteveen

Organization

Program Co-chairs

Jürgen Dix   Clausthal University of Technology, Germany
Cees Witteveen   Delft University of Technology, The Netherlands

Doctoral Consortium Chair

Ingo J. Timm   Goethe-Universität Frankfurt, Germany

Steering Committee

Matthias Klusch   DFKI, Germany
Winfried Lamersdorf   Universität Hamburg, Germany
Jörg P. Müller   Technische Universität Clausthal, Germany
Paolo Petta   University of Vienna, Austria
Rainer Unland   Universität Duisburg-Essen, Germany
Gerhard Weiss   University Maastricht, The Netherlands

Program Committee

Klaus-Dieter Althoff   Universität Hildesheim, Germany
Federico Bergenti   Università degli Studi di Parma, Italy
Ralph Bergmann   Universität Trier, Germany
Vicent Botti   Universidad Politécnica de Valencia, Spain
Lars Braubach   Universität Hamburg, Germany
Longbing Cao   TU Sydney, Australia
Torsten Eymann   Universität Bayreuth, Germany
Klaus Fischer   DFKI, Germany
Maria Ganzha   Elblag University of Humanities and Economy,
                            Poland
Paolo Giorgini   Università degli Studi di Trento, Italy
Christian Guttmann   Monash University, Australia
Koen Hindriks   TU Delft, The Netherlands
Benjamin Hirsch   Technische Universität Berlin, Germany
Stefan Kirn   Universität Hohenheim, Germany
Franziska Klügl   Örebro University, Sweden
Gabriela Lindemann   Humboldt Universität zu Berlin, Germany
Stefano Lodi   Università di Bologna, Italy
Beatriz López   Universitat de Girona, Spain

Viviana Mascardi	Università degli Studi di Genova, Italy
Mirjam Minor	Universität Trier, Germany
Daniel Moldt	Universität Hamburg, Germany
Jörg P. Müller	Technische Universität Clausthal, Germany
Peter Novák	Czech Technical University, Czech Republic
Andrea Omicini	Università di Bologna, Italy
Sascha Ossowski	Universidad Rey Juan Carlos, Spain
Marcin Paprzycki	Polish Academy of Sciences, Poland
Adrian Paschke	Freie Universität Berlin, Germany
Alexander Pokahr	Universität Hamburg, Germany
Alessandro Ricci	Università di Bologna, Italy
Abdel Badeh Salem	Ain Shams University, Egypt
Amal El Fallah Seghrouchni	University Pierre and Marie Curie, France
Ingo J. Timm	Goethe-Universität Frankfurt, Germany
Rainer Unland	Universität Duisburg-Essen, Germany
Wiebe van der Hoek	University of Liverpool, UK
László Zsolt Varga	MTA SZTAKI, Hungary
Yingqian Zhang	Erasmus University Rotterdam, The Netherlands

Additional Reviewers

Rehab Alnemr
Estefanía Argente
Kerstin Bach
Kamel Barkaoui
Tristan Behrens
Daniel Briola
Roberto Centeno
Sebastian Hudert

Régis Newo
Christoph Niemann
Miguel Rebollo
Daniel Schmalen
Adriaan ter Mors
Matteo Vasirani
Jiří Vokřínek

Table of Contents

Applications I

Coordination and Learning

Applications II

Tournament Solutions and Their Applications to Multiagent Decision Making

Felix Brandt

Institut für Informatik
Technische Universität München
brandtf@in.tum.de

Abstract. Given a finite set of alternatives and choices between all pairs of alternatives, how to choose from the entire set in a way that is faithful to the pairwise comparisons? This simple, yet captivating, problem is studied in the literature on tournament solutions. A tournament solution thus seeks to identify the "best" elements according to some binary dominance relation, which is usually assumed to be asymmetric and complete. As the ordinary notion of maximality may return no elements due to cyclical dominations, numerous alternative solution concepts have been devised and axiomatized.

Many problems in multiagent decision making can be addressed using tournament solutions. For instance, tournament solutions play an important role in *collective decision-making* (social choice theory), where the binary relation is typically defined via pairwise majority voting. Other application areas include *adversarial decision-making* (theory of zero-sum games) and *coalitional decision-making* (cooperative game theory) as well as multi-criteria decision analysis and argumentation theory.

In this talk, I will present an overview of some of the most common tournament solutions such as the uncovered set, the minimal covering set, and the bipartisan set and analyze them from an algorithmic point of view.

J. Dix and C. Witteveen (Eds.): MATES 2010, LNAI 6251, p. 1, 2010.
© Springer-Verlag Berlin Heidelberg 2010

Research Challenges in Simulation Aided Design of Complex Multi-agent Systems

Michal Pěchouček and Michal Jakob

Agent Technology Center, Department of Cybernetics,
Czech Technical University in Prague
pechoucek@fel.cvut.cz
http://www.agents.cz

In today's world, we are increasingly surrounded by and reliant on complex systems and infrastructures. Often, these systems behave far from the optimum or even highly undesirable. Roads in our cities are congested, plane trips frequently delayed, computer networks routinely overrun by worms and electricity grids fail in split-second cascade reactions. Our systems have become massively interwoven and interdependent making both highly positive and negative chain reactions possible in critical systems. The systems that surround us, that provide us with communication, energy resources and support our safety and comfort are increasingly decentralized, interconnected and autonomous, with more and more decisions originating at the level of individual subsystems rather than being imposed top-down. These systems are characterized by large numbers of geographically dispersed active entities with a complex network of mutual interactions and feedbacks, together giving rise to dynamic, non-linear emergent behavior which is very difficult to understand and even more difficult to control.

Creation of mechanisms controlling the operation of above described *massively connected autonomous systems* cannot be on intuition alone - we need tools and techniques which could provide us with foresight regarding the effect on the control mechanism and policies we want to put in place. Scalable, high-fidelity agent-based modeling simulation is the right modeling framework using which such foresight can be obtained. Such simulations will provide experimental computational environment supporting the analysis, design, construction, validation and deployment of multi-agent control systems that are tightly connected with real-world heterogeneous distributed systems. *Simulation-aided design* of such systems will not only accelerate the development of such system, but will also provide the researchers with a laboratory environment for studying problems and concepts of the future, for which current technology and society is not ready yet.

Before the vision of simulation-aided design can be made a reality realized, however, the following open research challenges need to be addressed and will be discussed during the talk: (*i*) automated construction, calibration and synchronization of the simulation models, (*ii*) scalability and fidelity of the simulation, (*iii*) introduction of mixed-mode simulation and (*iv*) development and rapid prototyping support.

J. Dix and C. Witteveen (Eds.): MATES 2010, LNAI 6251, p. 2, 2010.
© Springer-Verlag Berlin Heidelberg 2010

A Model Driven Development of Platform-Neutral Agents

Inmaculada Ayala, Mercedes Amor, and Lidia Fuentes

E.T.S.I. Informática, Universidad de Málaga
{ayala,pinilla,lff}@lcc.uma.es

Abstract. The automatic transformation of software agent designs into implementations for different agent platforms is currently a key issue in the MAS development process. Recently several approaches have been proposed using model driven development concepts to specify generic agent metamodels and/or define a set of transformation rules from the design phase for different agent implementation platforms. Although for some systems this is acceptable, in the context of Ambient Intelligence, this could be a serious limitation because of the variety of devices involved in these systems ranging from desktop computers to lightweight devices. In this paper we propose to transform PIM4Agents, a generic agent metamodel used at the design phase, into Malaca, an agent specific platform-neutral metamodel for agents. With only one set of transformations it is possible to generate a partial implementation in Malaca, which can be deployed in any kind of device and can interact with any FIPA compliant agent platform.

Keywords: AOSE, MDD, Malaca, Code generation, AmI.

1 Introduction

There are plenty of proposals that try to bridge the classical gap between design and implementation of multiagents systems (MAS) [1, 2, 4]. The most relevant ones have been published recently, showing that this is still a hot and open issue. What characterizes the majority of these proposals is that they generate code for a single Agent Platform (AP)[2] (or as much for a small and predetermined set of APs[1]). While for some systems this is acceptable, in the context of other booming research areas such as Ambient Intelligence (AmI) this could be a serious limitation as is shown later.

The main characteristic of AmI and similar environments is the variety of devices involved in these systems that range from desktop computers to devices with limited set of resources (e.g. sensors, PDAs, mobile phones). In order to face the resource limitations of devices present in AmI environments, several classical APs already provide efficient versions specially well suited for running in lightweight devices typical of AmI environments (e.g. LEAP[5], µFIPA-OS[6]). Due to the boom of AmI systems, it is expected that new lightweight devices and adequate APs for these new devices for will appear in the next few years. Consequently, code generation processes for APs must be extensible to incorporate new APs developed for new devices and operating systems.

This also means that agents of an AmI system must be able to communicate and cooperate with agents running on devices with different APs. Concretely in

J. Dix and C. Witteveen (Eds.): MATES 2010, LNAI 6251, pp. 3–14, 2010.

this paper we will analyse the case study of the Vehicular Ad-Hoc Network (VANET) systems. In AmI environments, and specifically in VANET systems, where standardization is not yet possible, it is not reasonable to suppose that all the devices will have the same AP installed, since traffic sensors, external services dynamically discovered on the road, mobile phones belonging to different users and so on, will normally bring their own operating system or AP. On the other hand, even when different versions of the same platform are used, like JADE and JADE-LEAP, it is not guaranteed that the same agent can be executed in all of them. If an agent was developed for JADE without considering the possibility of porting it to the CLDC/MIDP environment, it could contain a JADE API or even standard Java code not supported in the CLDC/MIDP profile. Therefore, the development of MAS for AmI environments is not affordable using the traditional agent development processes that normally consider the generation of agents for a single AP.

Model Driven Development (MDD) [7] is an advanced software technology that can naturally address the generation of agents for diverse APs, by means of transformations between platform independent models (PIM) and platform specific models (PSM). Several recent works already apply MDD to automate the generation of agent implementations, but only DSML4MAS [2] defines a generic metamodel from which agents are generated for different APs. But as we will show in the next section, the effort of including a new platform is considerable.

In order to deal with the diversity of APs in AmI environments we propose to use Malaca [8], a platform-neutral agent architecture, able to be executed in different APs and devices. We have defined a MDD process that using only one set of transformations rules, automatically generates agents capable of running on different APs. In our approach we use the PIM4Agents metamodel [2] as a PIM and Malaca as PSM. We have chosen PIM4Agents since it is rich enough to represent the domain specific concepts of different application domains, including the AmI environments. In this context, the main advantage of having platform neutral agent architecture is that the model driven process is significantly simplified since we only have a single target metamodel. The choice of the AP used by each agent of the MAS is postponed until the deployment phase, and additionally the interoperability between Malaca agents is guaranteed.

The structure of the paper is as follows: Section 2 presents our motivating case study, it provides a brief overview of our approach, describes the VANET case study and how it is modelled using PIM4Agents. Section 3 shows the transformation rules implemented in ATL to transform agents from the PIM4Agents metamodel to Malaca, we illustrate how to use them with the VANET case study and describe the deployment process. Section 4 discusses the results of our approach and compares it with the PIM4Agents approach. Finally, Section 5 provides related work and Section 6 draws some conclusions.

2   Motivating Case Study

2.1 Our Approach

As stated before, several approaches already apply MDD to derive agents for different platforms, normally following a similar schema to the one shown on the left hand side of Fig. 1. One of the most representatives is the DSML4MAS approach, which provides a set of mapping functions to transform PIM4Agents models to JACK and JADE in two steps. This means that other APs, which have emerged recently for AmI systems are not currently covered by this proposal. Furthermore, including a new AP in this proposal is a very complex task, since it requires defining a new set of transformation rules, transforming PIM4Agents into the metamodel of the new AP, and another set transforming the new AP metamodel into code.

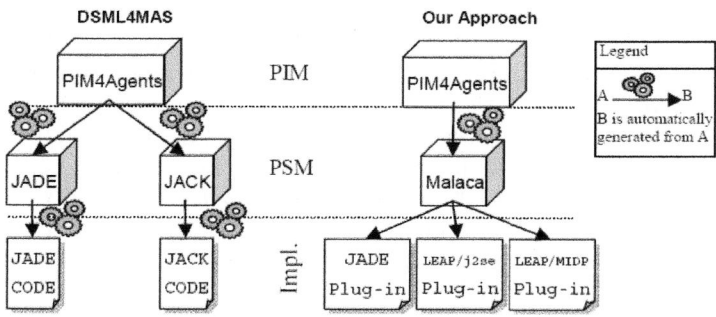

Fig. 1. The overall picture: From PIM4Agents metamodel to Malaca metamodel.

As shown in the right hand side of Fig. 1, the process proposed in this paper has substantially simplified the MDD process by using Malaca, a platform-neutral agent architecture as the single target metamodel (i.e. PSM). For the PIM we studied the feasibility of using one of the works proposed recently [1, 3]. Finally we decided to use PIM4Agents since this metamodel meets the following requirements: (i) it is possible to represent concepts from different agent types (e.g. BDI, reactive agents), (ii) it is easy to specify MAS for different domains, such as AmI; (iii) the DDE tool [13] helps to specify different views of MAS.

We would like to emphasize that in our proposal, the set of transformations rules was implemented only once, since the Malaca model is not modified for each new AP. This is because Malaca applies *aspect-orientation*[1] to separate the delivery of messages and depending on the AP used, a *distribution aspect* is implemented using an external plug-in. So, the integration of a new AP in our proposal is performed by developing a new plug-in including agent platform-specific code, requiring less effort and no expertise on specific transformation languages (perhaps) unfamiliar to programmers.

Another distinctive feature of Malaca is that the agent internal architecture is described explicitly, using the domain specific language MaDL [8], based on XML. This means that once a Malaca agent is generated, it is possible to configure deployment-specific information using the MaDL language. One example of this configuration information is the choice of the AP for each MAS agent, which is required by heterogeneous AmI environments. Another example is the configuration of a functional component of the Malaca architecture as a Web service. So, access to Web services, which normally occurs in many AmI environments, is integrated naturally into the Malaca architecture.

---

[1] Aspect-Oriented Software Development (AOSD), http://aosd.net

2.2 Case Study

To illustrate our approach we will use a VANET application as the use case scenario. A VANET is a form of Mobile ad-hoc network, which provides communication to vehicles on the road and between these vehicles and nearby fixed equipment, usually referred to as *on road equipment*.

Vehicles are equipped with a network interface, GPS receiver, different sensors and an on-board computer. Integrating these elements into a motor vehicle allows comfort-related applications to be developed, whose purpose is to provide valuable and useful services for the vehicle occupants during a road trip; information such as, for example, the weather forecast at a particular destination or where the closest gas station is. In most cases, this information is obtained from different information sources, external to the vehicle, which can be deployed in different kinds of devices and locations. For instance, in the case study the driver application is provided with information on the weather and the location of gas stations. Specifically for this paper, part of the application (the user interface and some functionality) is executed in a lightweight device (an on-board computer – if available, a PDA or a mobile phone). The weather forecast is provided by a web service running on a web server accessible via the Internet. Locating gas stations in the vicinity requires retrieving such information from devices near the current location of the vehicle. These devices may be either a PC or a lightweight device.

The case study has been modeled as a MAS including two kinds of agents: agents for vehicles (*VehicleAgent*) and agents for gas stations (*GasStationAgent*). A *VehicleAgent* is executed in the vehicle and it provides the user with weather forecast information and it locates gas stations in the vicinity. A *GasStationAgent* is the agent that represents a gas station and it interacts with an agent in the vehicles to negotiate the provision of the service following an interaction protocol.

2.3 Multi-agent System Design with the DDE Tool

In this section, the first step of our approach (to model a system in PIM4Agens using the DSML4MAS approach) is shown. An overview of the design of the VANET system is provided and the concepts of the PIM4Agents metamodel are explained. PIM4Agents is structured into several aspects each focusing on a specific viewpoint of a MAS and these viewpoints are represented in the DDE Tool.

The first viewpoint in the design process of our application is MAS viewpoint, which specifies the main building blocks of the MAS and their relationships. Fig. 2 shows the MAS viewpoint of the VANET system in the DDE Tool. The representation of the agents, organizations and roles is straightforward in the PIM4Agents model. In order for agents to interact, they must be members of an *Organization*. Agents involved in the services exchange (*GasStationAgent* and *VehicleAgent*) are members of the *OnRoadServiceOrganization*. This service has two roles; to model the service providers and the clients. To model the agent execution environment, PIM4Agents has two kinds of elements: (i) *Environment* includes the set of object that can be accessed by the agent (*OnRoadServices* in Fig. 2); (ii) *SOAEnvironment*, a special kind of *Environment* to model a web services that the agent can access (*ForecastService* to model the weather forecast web service).

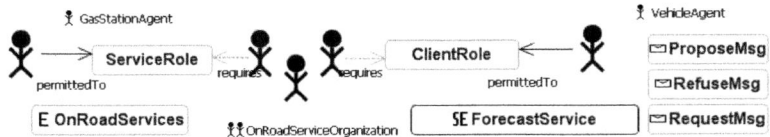

Fig. 2. PIM4Agents Multi-Agent system diagram in DDE Tool

The agent viewpoint is the second step in the design process and it deals with related agent issues. An agent in PIM4Agents is an entity which can perform particular roles and behaviours and the agent has certain capabilities that represent a set of behaviours. This viewpoint shows how agents are associated to the roles performed in the organization and their plans. For the VANET case study, *GasRequestPlan* and *GasResponsePlan* are the plans used by the MAS agents to request the refuelling and to negotiate the service provision. Moreover, *GetForecastPlan* is a plan to get the weather forecast information in the *VehicleAgent*.

The collaboration and organization viewpoints deal with the design of interactions, but for space reasons, this paper is only focused on the design of the interaction protocol itself. The design of the protocol is done using the interaction viewpoint. This involves a set of actors interacting within a protocol and a set of message flows specifying how the exchange of messages takes place. Fig. 3 shows the protocol diagram of the *RequestResponseProtocol*, which covers the interaction between the *Requester* and *Responder* actors in the location of a gas station according to the user preferences. *Requester* sends a *Request* that can be answered by *Responders* with a *Propose* or a *Refuse* message. At run-time, the *Requester* is performed by *VehicleAgent*, while the *GasStation*Agent acts as *Responder*.

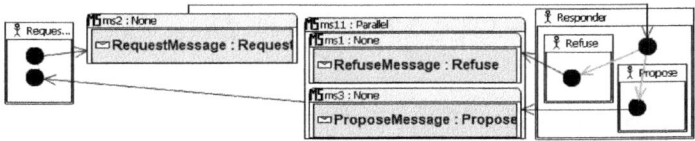

Fig. 3. *RequestResponseProtocol* in DDE Tool

The *behaviour* viewpoint describes the plans. Plans are composed of simple atomic tasks like sending messages using complex control structures and they show how information flows between those constructs. This viewpoint is represented by plan diagrams in the DDE Tool. As an example, the plan for requesting a gas station (*GasRequestPlan*) is presented in Fig. 4. This plan is executed by the *VehicleAgent* when the user decides to make a gas request and also represents the execution of the *RequestResponseProtocol* for this agent. The plan starts with the agent preparing request data, and then it sends a *Request,* which contains user preferences, to agents for gas stations. The next step is to wait for agents' responses, if the answer is a *Propose* message, then this is processed by *ProcessProposeResponse*, otherwise it is

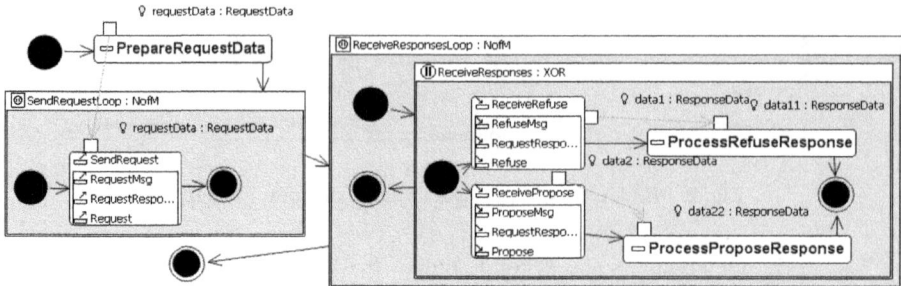

Fig. 4. *GasRequestPlan* in DDE Tool

processed by *ProcessRefuseResponse*. The VANET system also includes plan diagrams for getting the weather forecast and responding to a gas request.

3   Generation and Deployment of Malaca Agents

3.1   Generation of a Multi-agent System for VANETs

In the Malaca metamodel two main parts can be distinguished: the specification of the agent architecture in an agent description language (MaDL) and the specification of interaction protocols using a specific high level language (ProtDL). Table 1 summarizes the main mappings between PIM4Agents concepts and MaDL concepts and Table 2 does the same for ProtDL concepts. The mapping rules list included is not an exhaustive one. Detailed information about these rules can be found in [9]. We have only included those that help readers to comprehend the most relevant model mappings required for the use case scenario. Some mapping rules are applied automatically (simple ATL rules), while others must be invoked by other rules (ATL lazy rules).

Table 1. Mapping process between the PIM4Agents concepts and MaDL concepts

Target	Source	Explanation
R1:*AgentDescription*	*Agent*	Each *Agent* in PIM4Agents is mapped to an *Agent* in MaDL.
R2:*Functionality*	*InternalTask*	Each *InternalTask* from a *Plan* associated to an *Agent* in PIM4Agents is a *componentDescription* in *Functionality*.
R3:*Coordination*	*Protocol*	Each *Protocol* associated to an *Agent* by means of a *Collaboration* is mapped to a *Coordination*.
R4:*RuntimeDirectives*	*AgentInstance*	Each *AgentInstance* with its *agentType* is mapped to an MaDL description with the same name in *RuntimeDirectives*.
R5:*Distribution*		JADE-mts by default.
R6:*Representation*		FIPA-ACL by default.

Table 2. Mapping process between the PIM4Agents concepts and ProtDL concepts

Target	Source	Explanation
R7:_Protocol_	_Protocol_	Each _Protocol_ from PIM4Agents is mapped to a _Protocol_ in ProtDL.
R8:_Actor_	_RoleDescription_	Each _Actor_ is mapped to a _RoleDescription_ associated to a specific _Protocol_
R9:_MessageFlo, MessageFlow_	_StateTransitionRule_	From two _MessageFlow_ concepts this rule creates a _StateTransitionRule_ that begins in the first _MessageFlow_ and ends in the second one.
R10:_MessageFlo w, MessageFlow_	_TransitionDescription_	From two _MessageFlow_ concepts this rule creates a _TransitionDescription_ that begins in the first _MessageFlow_ and ends in the second one.
R11:_Plan, String_	_RoleDescription_	Creates a _RoleDescription_ from a _Plan_ and a _String_ that is the name for the _Role_.
R12:_Activity, Activity_	_StateTransitionRule_	From two _Activity_ concepts this rule creates a _StateTransitionRule_ that begins in the first _MessageFlow_ and ends in the second one.
R13:_Activity, Activity_	_TransitionDescription_	From two _Activity_ concepts this rule creates a _TransitionDescription_ that begins in the first _Activity_ and ends in the second one.
R14:_InternalTask_	_ProcessComponent_	Each _InternalTask_ is mapped to a _ProccesComponent_ that has an _AtomicProcess_ whose type is _DoActionType_.
R15: _InvokeWS_	_ProcessComponent_	Each _InternalTask_ is mapped to a _ProccesComponent_ that has an _AtomicProcess_ whose type is _DoActionType_.
R16:_Split_	_ProcessComponent_	Each _Split_ is mapped to a _ProccesComponent_ that has a _CompositeProcess_ whose type is _SplitType_.
R17:_Protocol, Organization_	_Protocol_	Each _Protocol_ which is from an _Organization_ is mapped to a _Protocol_.

With the data provided in diagrams presented in Section 2.3, transformation rules have the necessary information to generate MaDL and ProtDL specifications for _VehicleAgent_ and _GasStationAgent_. The first applied rule is **R1**; it generates the basic structure of a Malaca agent that is named _AgentDescription_. This concept contains elements related to the agent architecture: _Functionality, Interaction, InitialContext_ and _RuntimeDirectives_. _InitialContext_ contains information about agent knowledge and actions to be performed by agents on start up. With the information provided by the design phase, this concept has to be completed using the MAD Tool[2]. _RuntimeDirectives_ contains information on the agent name and on whether the protocols are used on demand or on startup. If users wish to make a deployment diagram in the DDE Tool, **R4** maps _name_ in _AgentInstance_ to _agentName_ in _runtimeDirectives_. _Functionality_ has the information about the components that an agent can use during its execution. This concept is derived using **R2**, but the only information provided by DSML4MAS is component name, so this is the only information about the component that is derived by **R2**. The _Interaction_ concept has

---

[2] http://caosd.lcc.uma.es/softwareAgents/malacaTools.htm

the necessary information to make interaction between agents possible, in other words, how to represent and to distribute messages, and the interaction protocols. To get the *Interaction* field, **R3**, **R5** and **R6** are applied. **R5** and **R6** are used to provide information by default and **R3** generates the necessary information to link the ProtDL specification that will be generated by the rules from Table 2. Fig. 5 (left side) shows a partial view of the generated MaDL specification for *VehicleAgent*, the figure has a caption which indicates rules used to generate it.

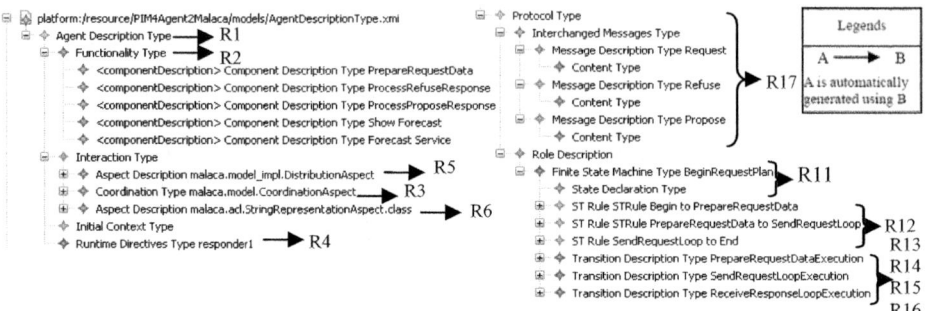

Fig. 5. MaDL specification for *VehicleAgent* and ProtDL specification for *RequestResponse*

Fig. 3 shows the protocol diagram of the *RequestResponseProtocol*, which covers the interaction between the *Requester* and *Responder* actors in the location of a gas station according to the user preferences. The first applied rule is **R17**; this rule generates an empty ProtDL specification and calls other rules to complete it. A ProtDL specification is composed of a set of message descriptions and a set of role descriptions that describe an agent protocol execution using a finite state machine. The role description structure is mapped using **R11**; it takes a name of role and a plan associated to this and then calls **R12** and **R13** which generate the finite state machine. A finite state machine in ProtDL consists of transitions rules and executions. Transitions rules are generated by **R12** and executions by **R13**, executions are very similar to the PIM4Agents plan so the mapping between these two concepts is straightforward. A partial view of the generated code is shown in Fig. 5 (right side).

3.2 Deployment

As a result of the MDD process we obtained a set of MaDL and ProtDL descriptions. Finally, the deployment phase takes each agent architecture description to add agent-specific implementation details, with the aid of the MAD tool.

In Malaca, the deployment phase consists of configuring the appropriate components and aspects implementations. This means that now we have to bind the component and aspect types to specific implementations. Since Malaca is implemented as an aspect-oriented and component-based framework, this encourages the reuse of pre-built components and aspects from a repository. This means that some of the component and aspect implementations needed may be already available in a repository. Otherwise the agent developer must implement the necessary agent building blocks, and add them to the repository in order to facilitate their later reuse.

Going back to our example, first we need to configure the distribution aspect for each agent. Configuring the *distribution aspect* implies deciding which AP to use. For the *VehicleAgent* agent we select the JADE LEAP/MIDP and for the *GasStationAgent* agent the JADE LEAP/J2SE. For the rest of the aspects, the Malaca framework provides a default implementation, which could be modified if necessary.

Secondly, we need to select the components implementations that provide the agent functionality. In our example, the developer has to configure the suitable implementation for the components services tagged as *<componentDescription>* (see Fig. 5). In this case, part of the services are provided by a component implemented as a Java class (*vanet.service.GasServiceComponent*), while the services related to the provision of the weather forecast are provided by accessing a (external) web service (accessible at *http://map.lcc.uma.es:19592/WeatherWS/WeatherWSService?WSDL*). This selection completes the agent description in MaDL (see

Fig. 6 for the complete description of the weather forecast services).

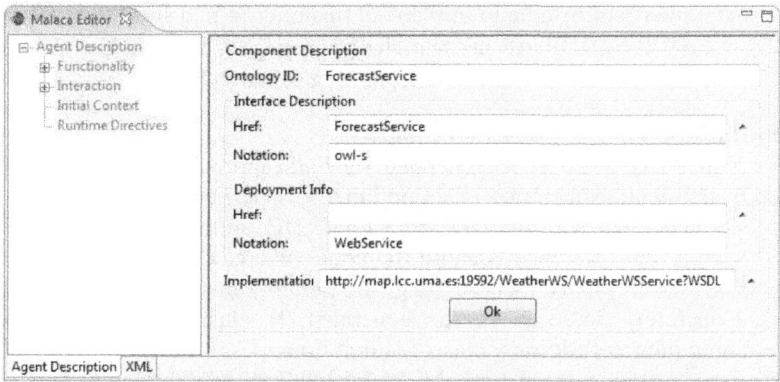

Fig. 6. MaDL description of the ForecastService component (MaDTool snapshot)

4 Discussion

This section evaluates the contributions of this paper and provides a critical discussion of the benefits of our approach comparing with current MDD agent generation processes, focusing on the DSML4MAS process.

(1) Cost of including a new agent platform
Let us consider the scenario of extending a DSML4MAS-like process with a new AP. In first place the metamodel of the target AP must be available. Otherwise, the developer must specify this metamodel in a variant of MOF. This effort could be considerable; requiring very in-depth knowledge of the internal architecture of the new AP. Secondly, the set of mappings from the PIM4Agents to the new AP metamodel must be implemented in a transformation language like ATL. Normally, programmers are still not familiar with these kinds of languages, so additional learning time/effort could be necessary. Finally, the generation of executable code in

the target AP must be accomplished by implementing a second set of mapping rules. These mapping rules must be implemented in a model-to-text transformation language, like MOFScript. As can be seen, the effort of including a new AP is considerable, especially because the developer must acquire knowledge both in agent models and in many novel MDD languages (e.g. MOF, ATL, MOFScript).

On the other hand, in our approach the developer (or normally, we, the Malaca providers) must implement a new plug-in in charge of instantiating the corresponding platform-dependent communication subsystem (which uses the specific Message Transport Service (MTS) provided by the AP), and related data, for example the classes representing ACL messages. This plug-in receives the incoming messages and delivers outgoing messages to an AP, hiding platform specific dependencies. The development of this plug-in consists of implementing a high-level interface *MTSAdapter* to send and receive messages. After creation, this plug-in gets a valid ID and registers the agent in the corresponding AP. Then every time it is required, the plug-in uses the MTS of the AP to send and receive messages. In our approach any expert programmer will be able to implement this plug-in in a short time (for instance, the JADE-LEAP for MIDP AP takes us half a day). So, we consider that the effort and skills necessary to incorporate a new platform is much lower in our approach.

(2)   Optimization of the generated code
Now we will analyse the code generated by both approaches. Normally, the code obtained by automatic generation is not optimized. Specifically, for this case study, 91 classes were generated with the DDE tool for JADE, and only 9 classes for Malaca. There is such a big difference because the code generated by DDE includes several dummy classes with empty methods (e.g. the *action()* method of behavioural JADE classes). Concretely 34.06 % of the generated 91 classes is dummy code. One negative consequence of dummy classes is that it increases the number of indirections required for example to invoke a behavioural method. In lightweight devices where memory and computation resources are scarce, this is not acceptable since the code must be highly optimized to consume the least amount of resources. Since in our approach we do not generate code, we only have to concentrate on Malaca framework optimization, whose code can be optimized independently of the execution AP.

(3)   Limitations for the AmI domain
An AmI environment is often made up of different devices, which could contain agents running on top of different APs. With Malaca it is possible to generate agents cooperating in the same MAS for different AP where the interoperability is guaranteed. Also, agents generated with a DSML4MAS-like process for a general purpose AP (e.g. JADE) may not be executable in other versions of the platform for lightweight devices (e.g. JADE LEAP for CLDC/MIDP device profile). For example, in DSML4MAS the transformation rules related with organizations and the ontology must be redefined for the MIDP profile, since LEAP uses a different set of classes. Then, the code for the same agent must be generated by a different set of transformation rules and completed by the agent designer several times for each AP, which is not desirable. Finally, the web services often needed in AmI environments are naturally integrated in Malaca, which is not the case of other approaches.

5 Related Work

There are some approaches that apply MDD concepts to AOSE in different contexts. The Gaia methodology [9] defines a specific mapping to JADE as PSM, but it is not an automatic process. Different agent oriented methodologies, such as MaSE [10] support a complete tool-aided life cycle process from early requirements to code generation. Moreover, in some of them, such as INGENIAS [12], the life-cycle is an MDD process. MDD is also approached for agents in mobile devices in [1]. It takes Agent-π, a metamodel for mobile devices. It also applies MDD and provides transformations to two mobile-specific PSMs, Andromeda and JADE-Leap for Android. However, this metamodel can not be considered generic since it does not contain important agent concepts like organization in MAS. Additionally, target APs do not make interoperability possible between agents in different kinds of devices.

In general, although the intention of these approaches was to cover the implementation phase, they have the same disadvantages as PIM4Agents approach: (i) a different transformation is needed for every PSM; (ii) the generation code process does not take into account the integration with web services although the target AP has constructions for this issue (JADE); and (iii) the implementation of agents in JADE and other OO agent architectures is difficult to maintain and reuse. The problem is that normally the agent internal architecture consists of a collection of highly-coupled objects, making it difficult to extend.

6 Conclusions

MDD is the most natural approach to automate the derivation of agent implementations from high level agent models, considering different target APs. The process presented in this paper significantly simplifies this process by using Malaca, a platform-neutral agent architecture. This enhancement is particularly important for AmI environments, since new devices are continuously appearing and this is expected to continue. With Malaca it is possible to configure agents to be executed in different target APs for different mobile and lightweight devices, as required by most AmI environments. We have evaluated our proposal by comparing it with a DSML4MAS-like process, concluding that (1) in our approach including a new AP requires less effort and user skills, (2) generated agents are more optimized than in other approaches (3) Malaca agents are interoperable even with different profiles of AmI devices (e.g. MIDP). We have used PIM4Agents as the PIM, but we plan to extend this metamodel with new properties like context-awareness and learning, which are very useful for AmI environments and are already present in the Malaca architecture.

Acknowledgments. This work has been supported by the Spanish Ministry Project RAP TIN2008-01942 and the regional project FamWare P09-TIC-5231.

References

1. Agüero, J., Rebollo, M., Carrascosa, C., Julián, V.: Agent Design Using Model Driven Development. In: PAAMS'09, AISC, vol. 55, pp. 60–69 (2009)
2. Molesini, A., Denti, E., Omicini, A.: From AO Methodologies to MAS Infrastructures: The SODA Case Study. In: Artikis, A., O'Hare, G.M.P., Stathis, K., Vouros, G.A. (eds.) ESAW 2007. LNCS (LNAI), vol. 4995, pp. 300–317. Springer, Heidelberg (2008)

3. Hahn, C., Madrigal-Mora, C., Fischer, K.: A platform-independent metamodel for multiagent systems. Auton Agent Multi-Agent Syst. 18, 239–266 (2009)
4. Amor, M., Fuentes, L., Vallecillo, A.: Bridging the gap Between Agent–Oriented Design and Implementation Using MDA. In: Odell, J.J., Giorgini, P., Müller, J.P. (eds.) AOSE 2004. LNCS, vol. 3382, pp. 93–108. Springer, Heidelberg (2005)
5. Federico, B., Agostino, P.: Leap: a FIPA platform for handheld and mobile devices. In: Agent Theories, Architectures, and Languages, ATAL-2001 (2001)
6. Tarkoma, S., Laukkanen, M.: Supporting software agents on small devices. In: Proceedings of the (AAMAS'02), New York, USA, pp. 565–566 (2002)
7. Stephen, J., Mellor, A.N., Clark, T.F.: Guest Editors' Introduction: Model-Driven Development. IEEE Software 20(5), 14–18 (2003)
8. Amor, M., Fuentes, L.: Malaca: A component and aspect-oriented agent architecture. Information and Software Technology 51, 1052–1065 (2009)
9. Ayala, I., Amor, M., Fuentes, L.: Towards the automatic derivation of Malaca agents using MDE. In: 11th International Workshop on AOSE, pp. 61–72 (2010)
10. Moraitis, P., Spanoudakis, N.I.: The Gaia2Jade process for multi-agent systems development. Applied Artificial Intelligence 20(2-4), 251–273 (2006)
11. DeLoach, S.A., Wood, M.: Developing Multiagent Systems with agentTool. In: 7th International Workshop on Agent Theories, Architectures, and Languages (2000)
12. Pavón, J., Gómez-Sanz, J., Fuentes, R.: Model Driven Development of Multi-Agent Systems. In: Rensink, A., Warmer, J. (eds.) ECMDA-FA 2006. LNCS, vol. 4066, pp. 284–298. Springer, Heidelberg (2006)
13. Warwas, S., Hahn, C.: The DSML4MAS development environment. In: 8th International Conference on Autonomous Agent and Muliagent Systems (2009)

A Novel Formal Specification Approach for Real Time Multi-Agent System Functional Requirements

Mohamed Amin Laouadi[1], Farid Mokhati[2], and Hassina Seridi-Bouchelaghem[1]

[1] Computer Science Department, Badji Mokhtar University, Annaba,
Algeria. LabGED Laboratory
Laouadiamin@yahoo.fr, seridi@labged.net
[2] Computer Science Department, Oum El-Bouaghi University, Algeria
mokhati@yahoo.fr

Abstract. A novel formal functional requirements specification approach for real-time multi-agent system is presented in this paper. The methodology of our approach consists in translating extended AUML diagrams describing RT-MAS' functional requirements into a RT-Maude specification. The proposed approach considers jointly functional, static and dynamic aspects of real-time multi-agent systems. The functional aspects are described by a temporal AUML use case diagram and the static aspects are represented using a temporal AUML class diagram. Whereas the dynamic aspects are described using state chart (individual behavior) and an extended AUML protocol (collective behavior) diagrams. The aims of this approach are, on the one hand, to combine the advantages of the graphical modeling formalism Agent UML and the formal specification language RT-Maude in a single technique, and, on the other hand, to integrating the formal validation of the consistency of the models, since the analysis phase. The approach is illustrated using a concrete example.

Keywords: Formal specification, Real-time Multi-Agent System, Functional Requirements, Agent UML, RT-Maude, Supply Chain Management (SCM).

1 Introduction

A recent trend in the development of distributed real-time systems is the use of real-time multi-agent system. In contrast to conventional MAS, the real time MAS reflect intrinsic real-time systems characteristics, more precisely, the time constraints. For many years, MAS designers have development methodologies and modeling language without reflects the different temporal restrictions that these systems may have. Moreover, even the proposed methodologies for the development of real time MAS as: 'RT-Message' [1], 'BDI-ASDP extended for real time' [2] and 'Development Method of Lichen Zhang' [3], are inadequate. They have certainly made important responses in the development process of real-time MAS. However, the methodological aspect is not yet mastered. Indeed, none of these methodologies takes into account the functional requirements formalization of the future system.

J. Dix and C. Witteveen (Eds.): MATES 2010, LNAI 6251, pp. 15–27, 2010.

Formalizing the functional requirements of real-time MAS is in our opinion, an importance way for verification and validation activities. Furthermore, the MAS design requires the involvement with software engineering techniques. The main objective of this work is to offer a generic approach for a use case oriented specification of real time MAS functional requirements. Among these techniques: UML [4] is probably the best known and most widely used languages for object-oriented modeling. The MAS developers have recently the same facilities in particular the language Agent UML [5] [6]. However, there is currently no work applying Agent UML to real-time MAS specification and both to real time applications.

The proposed methodology differs from other modeling methodologies by the use of the AUML language extensions presented in [6] [7] [8], which have an agent-oriented development view inspired from object-oriented development. The AUML language is from our own point of view the future industry standard for agents oriented systems development. AUML models describe several complementary views of the same system but suffer as UML of a lack of formal semantics. AUML models may therefore contain inconsistencies which are difficult to detect manually.

Formal methods represent an interesting solution to this problem. The formal specifications will have the effect of eliminating the ambiguities in the models interpretation. The Agent UML combination with the RT-Maude formal specification language will formally validate developed AUML models.

This work takes place in the context of Software Engineering and Distributed Artificial Intelligence and aims to support the verification and validation of real-time MAS as an important discipline of Agent Based Software Engineering. Therefore, the main interest in this work is to describe, as a first step, the functional requirements of real time MAS using the graphical modeling formalism Agent UML, and translate these descriptions in RT-Maude.

The remainder of this paper is organized as follows: In section 2 we give a brief overview of major related works. Section 3 is devoted to the formal specification language RT-Maude. In section 4, we present the AUML extensions. Section 5 gives the proposed translation process. Section 6 illustrates the translation and validation processes using a case study. Finally, we give a conclusion and some future work directions in section 7.

2   Related Works

Several methodological proposals for software development exist and can be applied to agents systems. Inspired from knowledge based systems domain [9], or directly focusing the agents' properties [10], or object-oriented development methodologies and languages extensions as UML [6] but only a few of these methodologies are taking into account the agent temporal behavior [2].

Among these methodologies that directly addressing the design of real-time multi-agent systems, we are interested by: the Methodology RT-Message [1], the extended BDI-ASDP methodology for real time [2] and the development method of Lichen Zhang [3]. For a description of real-time agents, these three methodologies use different models namely: domain model, role model, and timed model (Table 1.)

Table 1. Real-Time Agent identification Approaches

	Domain Model	Role Model	Timed Model	Functional Requirements
The RT- Message Methodology [1]	✓	✓	✓	
Extended BDI ASDP methodology for real time [2]	✓		✓	
Zhang development method[3]	✓		✓	

The RT-Message methodology [1], uses a domain model to define the concepts inherent to the environment where agents are located. The main result of this model is a domain diagram which is basically a class diagrams containing all the relevant variables and entities in the development process, like it was proposed in Zhang [3]. However, in the extended BDI-ASDP methodology for real time [2], a symbolic model of the environment is defined based on the decomposition of the problem with Beliefs, desires and intentions that represent agent's information, motivations and decisions.

The concept of role is only present in RT-Message [1], where the roles are identified independently of the agent system. Regarding the modeling of temporal constraints of real-time agents, each methodology offers an approach: for the RT-Message case, extensions made on the different models imported from the MESSAGE method [11] [12] allow analyzing the MAS for real-time environments. For example, "the Goal / Task model" has been modified to incorporate a taxonomy of goals (Goal taxonomy) which takes into account temporal criteria. When specifying the goal's different types, it is necessary to extend the goal and task patterns of the method "message" for integrating the real-time features. The artifacts obtained are a set of 'implications diagrams' showing the relationship between goals and tasks. Subsequent, in extended BDI-ASDP for real time, proposed by Melián et al. [2], the temporal constraints modeling is done through "the timing diagrams" specified in UML 2.0. To satisfy the need to model real-time systems by the agent approach, Zhang [3] proposed to extend UML by introducing a new stereotype, called <<agents>>. The timing characteristics are specified as an instance of this stereotype called <<TimeAspect>>. This stereotype uses a timed model developed independently, according to the principle of AOP (Aspect Oriented Programming), to express the temporal aspect of a real-time system.

However, the real-time MAS modeling is frequently linked to functional specifications in the sense that those specifications provide a basis for describing the functional requirements of agents, applying a set of software engineering techniques. These functional descriptions are often modeled by UML that is the most widely deployed standard, providing multiple notations. This concept has been neglected in these analyzed methodologies (Table 1).

In fact, these methodologies don't focus on the real time MAS functional requirements formalization during their development process. Hence, it is important that they will supplemented by methods that strongly encourage the formalization of the functional requirements captured in the analysis for the upstream phases of software engineering process.

3 Real Time Maude

Real-Time Maude is a programming language (an extension of Maude [13]) that was designed to exploit the concepts of the real-time rewrite theory. A real-time rewrite theory is a Maude rewrite theory, which also contains the specification of [14]:

- sort *Time* to describe the time domain,
- sort *GlobalSystem* with a constructor '{ _ }": { _ } : *System -> GlobalSystem*
- And a set of tick rules that model the elapsed time in the system that have the following form: {t} => {t'} in time if condition μ

Where μ is a term which may contain variables, of sort *Time* that denotes the length of the rule, and the terms t and t' are terms of sort *System*, which denotes the state of the system. The rewriting rules that are not tick rules are rules supposed to take a time instant zero. The initial state must always have the form {t"}, where t'' is a term of sort *System*, so that the form of tick rules ensures that time flows uniformly in all parts of the system. Real-time rewrite theories are specified in Maude as timed modules or timed object-oriented modules.

4 Extended Agent UML

We present in this section some extensions to AUML diagrams in order to describe functional requirements of real-time MAS.

4.1 Temporal AUML Use Case Diagrams

Given that, the analysis based on use cases proven in specifying the requirements of MAS [15], [16], [17]. This motivated us to apply these same techniques but with some modifications on real-time multi-agent system modeling. By using the extension mechanism of "stereotyping" offered by the language Agent UML, use case diagrams will be enriched by the following 'five stereotypes':

- The stereotypes « Agent Use Case » (Fig. 1.a) and « Temporal Agent Use Case » (Fig. 1.b) are used to denote respectively, a use case that represent a functionality performed by agents and a use case that interact with real-time agents.

(a)   (b)

Fig. 1. Stereotyped use cases

- The stereotypes « Agent » (Fig 2.a), « External Agent » (Fig 2.b) and « Real Time Agent » (Fig. 2.c) describe in this order: the agents within the system, external agents to the system and real time agents which are internal agents.

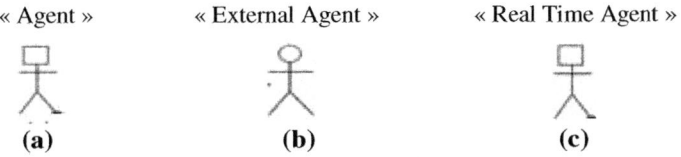

Fig. 2. Agent notations

4.2   Temporal AUML Class Diagrams

The two levels of abstraction proposed by Huget [8] are studied, when designing class diagrams: "the conceptual level and implementation level". The first level is unchanged and gives a high view of MAS, while 'second level' gives in detail the agents contents and modified as follows: to all compartments proposed in [8], a new compartment called "temporal constraints" is added (Fig. 3).

« Real Time Agent »
role1, role2, ..., rolen
Temporal constraint1 (soft/hard).....
statechart1 ...statechartn
attribut1......attributn
operation1 ...operationn
protocol1 : role...protocoln : role

Fig. 3. The used AUML class diagram

To describe agents' individual and collective behaviors we use respectively the AUML state-chart and protocol diagrams.

5   The Proposed Approach

The proposed translation process aims to translate the AUML diagrams described above (Section 4) for describing real time MAS functional requirements to RT-Maude formal specifications. This process is divided into three major steps (Fig. 4): (1) Description of real-time multi-agent system functional requirements using AUML diagrams, (2) inter-diagrams validation, and (3) Generation of RT-Maude formal description.

The first step is the usual analysis phase of software development process. The second step aims to validate the coherence between the designed models. The last step is the systematic generation of RT-Maude source code from the considered AUML diagrams. The formal framework proposed (Fig. 5) is composed of several modules: nine functional modules, seven object-oriented modules, and four timed object-oriented modules. For reason of limitation of space, we present only the main modules of the proposed framework. The Module STATE describes agents' states; the ACTION module describes the actions types that an agent can use. These two last modules and the CONDITION module (which is used to define the type *Condition*) are imported into STATE-OPERATIONS module to define the operations related to agent's states.

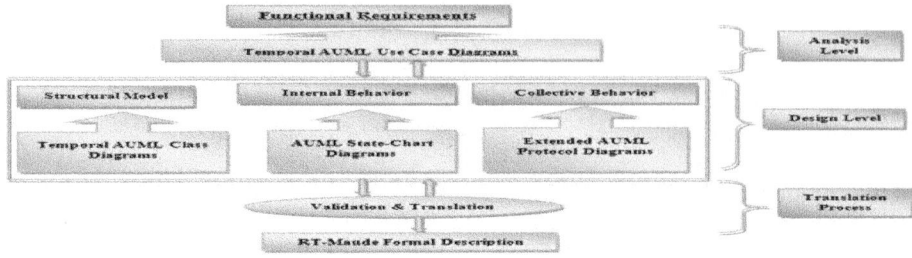

Fig. 4. Methodology of the approach

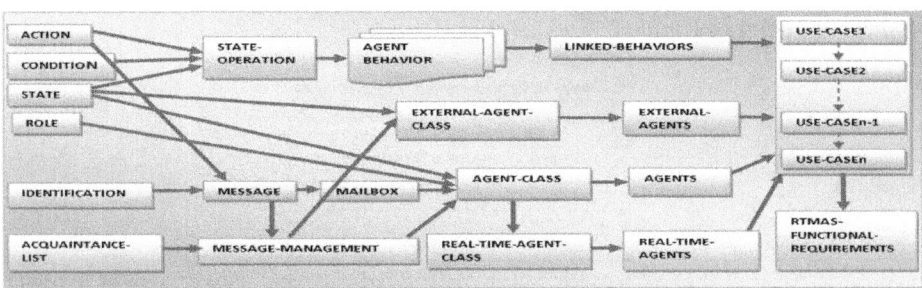

Fig. 5. Generated Modules

AGENTi-BEHAVIOR modules that import STATE-OPERATIONS module are used to illustrate the behavior of individual agents. In order to respect interactions between the different agents, connections between them are performed through the LINKED-Behavior module, which reuses AGENTi-BEHAVIOR modules. The identification mechanism for agents is defined by the IDENTIFICATION module, and message structure description exchanged between the various agents is done via MESSAGE module that imports the IDENTIFICATION, and ACTION modules.

Communicating agents are generally endowed with a Mailbox containing the received messages of other agents and a list of its acquaintances. For that, we define the functional modules MAILBOX and ACQUAINTANCE-LIST to manage respectively Mailboxes and acquaintance lists of agents. Agents' roles are defined in the module ROLE. To describe the sending/ receiving operations, we define module MESSAGE-MANAGEMENT which imports AQUAINTANCE-LIST and MESSAGE modules.

The object oriented module EXTERNAL-AGENT-CLASS (Fig. 6) is used to define the base class of external agents, with attributes *CurrentState* and *AcqList* (line [1])

```
(omod EXTERNAL-AGENT-CLASS   is

protecting  STATE . protecting   MESSAGE-MANAGEMENT .

 class ExtAgent | CurrentState : State, AcqList :
AcquaintanceList .          ---[1]    endom)
```

Fig. 6. The O.O Module EXTERNAL-AGENT-CLASS

which represent the agent's current state and its acquaintances list. This module imports STATE, and MESSAGE-MANAGEMENT modules.

In the object oriented module AGENT-CLASS (Fig. 7), we define the internal agents' base class structure. This class (line [1]) has as attributes: *PlayRole*, *CurrentState*, *MBox* and *AcqList* to contain in this order: the role played by the agent, its current state, its mailbox and its acquaintances list. This module imports all the modules: STATE, ROLE, MAILBOX, and MESSAGE-MANAGEMENT.

```
(omod AGENT-CLASS is protecting STATE. protecting ROLE.

protecting MAILBOX .  protecting MESSAGE-MANAGEMENT .

 class Agent | CurrentState : State, PlayRole : Role,
AcqList: AcquaintanceList, MBox : MailBox .--[1] endom)
```

Fig. 7. The O.O Module AGENT-CLASS

To describe the real-time agents, we have defined the *RealTimeAgent* class with the attribute *Clock* (line [1]) in the timed object oriented module REAL-TIME-AGENT-CLASS (Fig. 8) as a subclass of *Agent* Class (line [2]).

```
(tomod REAL-TIME-AGENT-CLASS is extending AGENT-CLASS .

class RealTimeAgent | Clock : Time . ---[1]

subclass RealTimeAgent  < Agent .    ---[2]   endtom)
```

Fig. 8. The Timed O.O Module REAL-TIME-AGENT-CLASS

To each use case is associated one timed O.O module USE-CASEi (Fig. 9), which has the same name as the corresponding use case. In each module USE-CASEi are defined the rewriting rules describing the different interaction scenarios between the agents defined in the different AUML Protocol diagrams, instances of the use case. Note that these rules may be instantaneous rules or tick rules, conditional or unconditional.

```
(tomod USE-CASEi is inc EXTERNAL-AGENTS . inc AGENTS .

including REAL-TIME-AGENTS. including LINKED-BEHAVIORS.

rl [1] : Configuration1 => Configuration2. ...

rl [m] : Configuration 2m-1 =><Configuration2m. endtom)
```

Fig. 9. The Timed O.O Module USE-CASEi

Once generated, all USE-CASEi modules are imported in the timed object oriented module RTMAS-FUNCTIONAL-REQUIREMENTS (Fig. 10) which describes all system's functional requirements.

```
(tomod  RTMAS-FUNCTIONAL-REQUIREMENTS   is

including USE-CASE1. …  including USE-CASEm.    endtom)
```

Fig. 10. The Timed OO Module RTMAS-FUNCTIONAL-REQUIREMENTS

The tick rule used to ensure the progress of time in the system is given in Fig. 11, where we have defined the message *Timer* to change the real time agent clock defined by the attribute *Clock* (line [1]). Obviously, this change also depends on the agent's current state: if the agent is in its *wait* state and the Timer has not reached the value zero, the clock is incremented by 1, until that this condition will no longer be valid.

```
crl [tick] :{Timer(TimeOut) < A : RealTimeAgent |
CurrentState : S, Clock : T, PlayRole: Initiator> --[1]
REST:Configuration} => { Timer(TimeOut monus 1)

< A : RealTimeAgent |CurrentState: S, Clock : T plus 1>
REST:Configuration }   in time 1

if (TimeOut > zero)and(S==AgentState(WaitI, ordinary)).
```

Fig. 11. The Tick Rule

6   Case Study: Supply Chain Management (SCM)

The supply chain management has been realized using a multi-agent system [18]. The agent decomposition that we select for this application is as follows (Fig. 12): different types of agents are involved in this application, there are two external agents: (1) the Client who passes, modifies and deletes the orders, (2) the Provider of materials for the

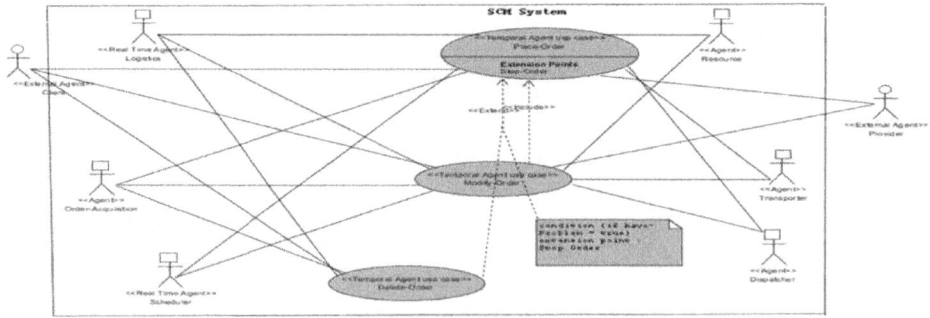

Fig. 12. AUML Use Case Diagram of SCM

realization of products, and six internal agents (Order-Acquisition, Dispatcher, Resource, Transporter, Logistics and Scheduler). Logistics and Scheduler are real time agents. These agents interact with the three temporal agent use cases: Place Order, Modify Order, and Delete Order. The use case Place Order is linked to the use case-Modify Order by the relationship "Include" and to Delete-Order use case by the relationship "Extend".

Fig.13. illustrates the temporal AUML Class diagram of the SCM. This diagram gives a detailed view of agents and their relationships. For example in the Real Time Agent 'Logistics' class, the following six compartments are defined: Role (Logistics), Attributes (Acqlist, MBox), Operations (Request-Plan), Protocols (Create-Order, Modify- Order, and Delete-Order), statecharts (Logistics), Temporal Constraint (Time of Negotiation).

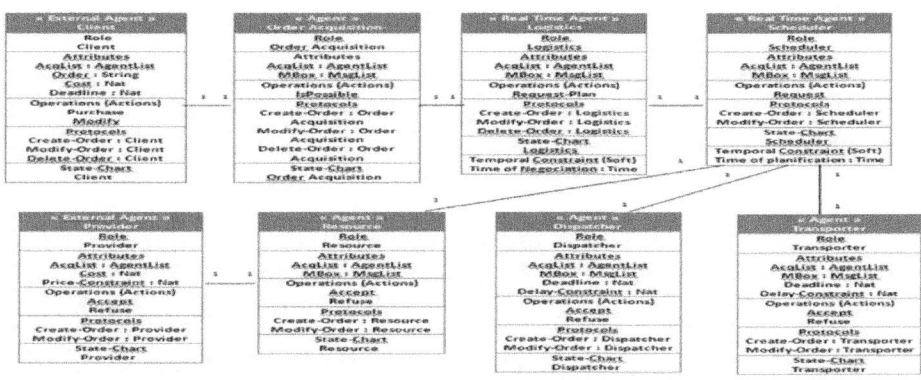

Fig. 13. AUML class diagram of SCM

As example of state-chart of real-time agents, we give in the Fig.14 the internal behavior of the real-time agent Logistics.

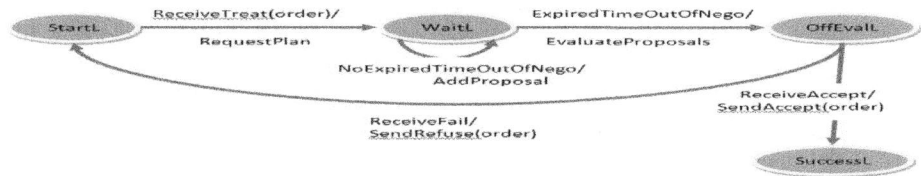

Fig. 14. AUML State-Chart diagram of the real time agent Logistics

The different interaction scenarios that implement the three above use cases are described using AUML protocol diagrams. We only present the protocol diagram of the use case Place-order (Fig.15), where different interaction modes are used (AND, exclusive OR) and the notions of reference and alternate (Alt, Ref).

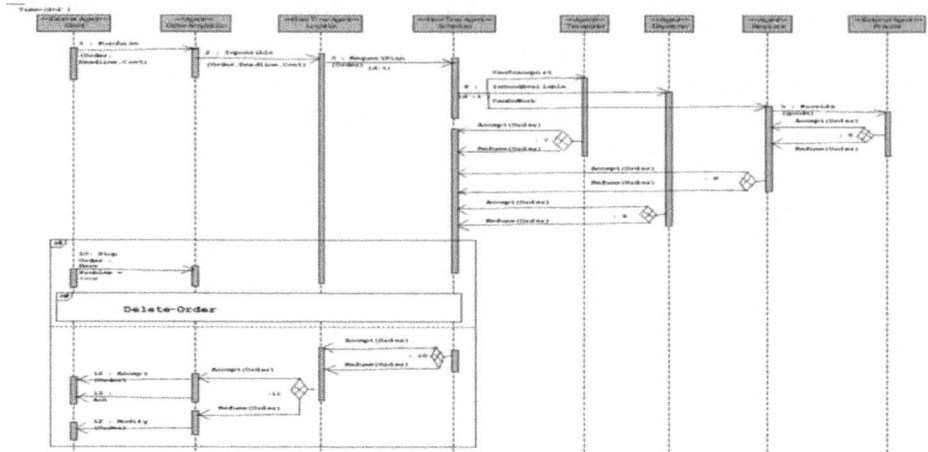

Fig. 15. AUML protocol diagram corresponding to use case Place-Order

6.1 Translation Process Application

The generated description implies the modules STATE, ACTION, CONDITIONS, STATE-OPERATION, MESSAGE-MANAGEMENT, IDENTIFICATION, MESSAGE, MAILBOX, ACQAINTANCE-LIST, EXTERNAL-AGENT-CLASS-AGENT-CLASS, and REAL-TIME- AGENT-CLASS, which remain unchanged with the definition of the other modules: EXTERNAL-AGENTS (Fig. 16), AGENTS (Fig. 17), 'PLACE-ORDER' (Fig. 18), RTMAS-FUCTIONAL-REQUIREMENTS (Fig. 19) ... etc.

```
(omod EXTERNAL-AGENTS is

extending EXTERNAL-AGENT-CLASS. inc STRING. inc NAT.

subclass Client   Provider   <   ExtAgent .

class Client |Order : String, Deadline: Nat. Cost: Nat.

class Provider |PriceConstraint: Nat,Cost : Nat. endom)
```

Fig. 16. The OO Module EXTERNAL-AGENTS

```
(omod AGENTS is extending AGENT-CLASS. inc STRING. Inc
NAT. subclass Transporter Dispatcher < Agent.

class Transporter |DelayConstraint : Nat,Deadline: Nat.

class Dispatcher| DelayConstraint: Nat, Deadline : Nat.
endom)
```

Fig. 17. The OO module AGENTS

```
(tomod PLACE-ORDER is inc EXTERNAL-AGENTS . inc AGENTS .
inc REAL-TIME-AGENTS. inc LINKED-BEHAVIORS.  ...  endtom)
```

Fig. 18. The Timed O.O Module PLACE-ORDER

```
(tomod RTMAS-FUNCTIONAL-REQUIREMENTS is inc PLACE-ORDER
inc MODIFY-ORDER . inc DELETE-ORDER .  endtom)
```

Fig. 19. The Timed O.O Module RTMAS-FUNCTIONAL-REQUIREMENS

6.2 Generated Description Validation

The RT-Maude offers a great flexibility in terms of simulation of a specification, in particular, concerning the choice of the initial configuration. This choice plays a primordial role in the validation of the description of a system. Using all the system's description, we can validate a part of the system without involving the rest. In this example of' SCM, we considered : (1) the behavior that starts by passing an order by the external agent *Client* and finishes by satisfying the requirements of the other agents, (2) the decision taken by the client for deleting a passed order, and (3) the incapacity of internal agents to treat a passed order. Fig. 20 illustrates the timed O.O module SUPPLY-CHAIN-MANAGEMENT, which imports the module RTMAS-FUNCTIONAL-REQUIREMENTS and contains an initial configuration. This later describes agents in their initial states with empty mail boxes. Real time agents' clocks are initialized to zero. Two messages are defined *TimerOfNeg*, and *TimerOfSched,* with the event *Event("client", AgentState(StartC),IsInitialized)* that starts the SCM process.

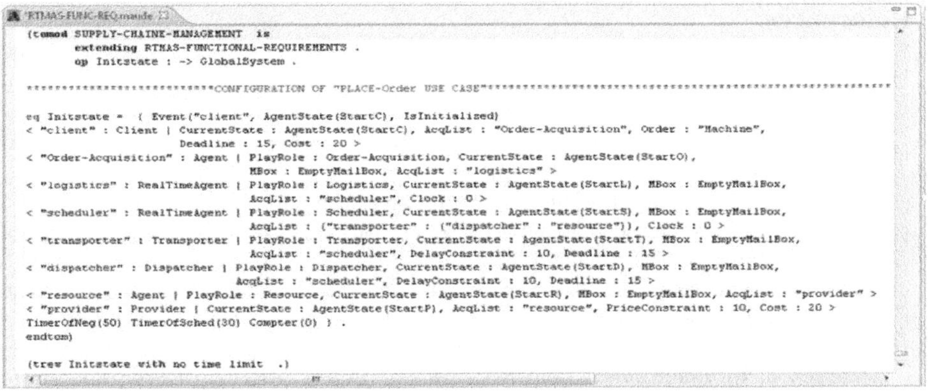

```
(tomod SUPPLY-CHAINE-MANAGEMENT  is
       extending RTMAS-FUNCTIONAL-REQUIREMENTS .
       op Initstate : -> GlobalSystem .

*************************CONFIGURATION OF "PLACE-Order USE CASE"**************************************************

eq Initstate =  { Event("client", AgentState(StartC), IsInitialized)
< "client" : Client | CurrentState : AgentState(StartC), AcqList : "Order-Acquisition", Order : "Machine",
                      Deadline : 15, Cost : 20 >
< "Order-Acquisition" : Agent | PlayRole : Order-Acquisition, CurrentState : AgentState(StartO),
                                MBox : EmptyMailBox, AcqList : "logistics" >
< "logistics" : RealTimeAgent | PlayRole : Logistics, CurrentState : AgentState(StartL), MBox : EmptyMailBox,
                                AcqList : "scheduler", Clock : 0 >
< "scheduler" : RealTimeAgent | PlayRole : Scheduler, CurrentState : AgentState(StartS), MBox : EmptyMailBox,
                                AcqList : ("transporter" : ("dispatcher" : "resource")), Clock : 0 >
< "transporter" : Transporter | PlayRole : Transporter, CurrentState : AgentState(StartT), MBox : EmptyMailBox,
                                AcqList : "scheduler", DelayConstraint : 10, Deadline : 15 >
< "dispatcher" : Dispatcher | PlayRole : Dispatcher, CurrentState : AgentState(StartD), MBox : EmptyMailBox,
                              AcqList : "scheduler", DelayConstraint : 10, Deadline : 15 >
< "resource" : Agent | PlayRole : Resource, CurrentState : AgentState(StartR), MBox : EmptyMailBox, AcqList : "provider" >
< "provider" : Provider | CurrentState : AgentState(StartP), AcqList : "resource", PriceConstraint : 10, Cost : 20 >
TimerOfNeg(50) TimerOfSched(30) Compter(0) } .
endtom)

(trew Initstate with no time limit  .)
```

Fig. 20. Initial Configuration

The result of the unlimited rewriting (with no time limit) of such a configuration is illustrated by Fig.21. This result configuration shows the agents in their success states which explains that the constraints imposed by the client have been accepted. Subsequently, the client also passes to its success state.

Fig. 21. Result of the unlimited rewriting of the initial configuration

7 Conclusion and Future Work

Using formal notations to specify RT-MAS' requirements makes it possible to produce precise descriptions. This also offers a better support to their verification and validation processes. In this paper, we presented a novel and generic approach supporting the formal description and validation of RT-MAS' functional requirements. The proposed approach allows translating functional aspect (described by extended AUML use case), static aspects (described by extended AUML class diagram), and dynamic aspects (described by AUML protocol diagrams together with AUML state-chart diagrams) of RT-MAS into a RT-Maude formal specification. As future work directions, we plan to extend our approach by integrating possibilities offered by RT-Maude to verify some properties of the specification of RT-MAS' functional requirements.

References

1. Julián, V., Soler, J., Moncho, M.C., Botti, V.: Real-Time Multi-Agent System Development and Implementation (2004)
2. Melián, S.F., Marsá, I., Ukrania, M., Miguel, D.-R., Carmona, A.-L.: Extending the BDI ASDP methodologie for Real Time (2005)
3. Zhang, L.: Development Method for Multi-Agent Real Time Systems. Faculty of Computer Science and Technology Guangdong University of Technology. International Journal of Information Technology 12(6) (2006)
4. Booch, G., Rumbaugh, J., Jacobson, I.: The Unified Modeling Language User Guide. Addison-Wesley, Reading (1999)
5. Bauer, B., Muller, J.P., Odell, J.: An extension of UML by protocols for multiagent interaction. In: International Conference on MultiAgent Systems (ICMAS'00), Boston, Massachussetts, pp. 207–214 (2000)
6. Odell, J., Parunak, H.V.D., Bauer, B.: Extending UML for Agents. In: Wagner, G., Lesperance, Y., Yu, E. (eds.) Proceedings of the Agent-Oriented Information Systems Workshop at the 17th National Conference on Artificial Intelligence, Austin, Texas. ICue Publishing (2000)
7. Huget, M.P.: Extending agent UML protocol diagrams. In: Giunchiglia, F., Odell, J.J., Weiss, G. (eds.) AOSE 2002. LNCS, vol. 2585, pp. 150–161. Springer, Heidelberg (2003)

8. Huget, M.P.: Agent UML class diagrams revisited. Technical Report, Department of Computer Science, University of Liverpool, p. 1–13 (2002)
9. Ferber, J.: Les systèmes Multi-Agents: vers une intelligence collective, Inter edn., Paris, France (1995)
10. Omicini, A.: Soda: Societies and infrastructures in the analysis and design of agent-based systems. In: Ciancarini, P., Wooldridge, M.J. (eds.) AOSE 2000. LNCS, vol. 1957, pp. 185–193. Springer, Heidelberg (2001)
11. Message,
    http://www.eurescom.de/public/projects/P900-series/p907/
12. Message, Metamodel,
    http://www.eurescom.de/~public-webspace/
    P900-series/P907/MetaModel/index.Htm
13. Clavel, M., Duran, F., Eker, S., Lincoln, P., Marti-Oliet, N., Meseguer, J., Talcott, C.: Maude Manual (version 2.2). In: SRI International, Menlo Park, CA 94025, USA (2005)
14. Olveczky, P.C.: Real-Time Maude 2.3 Manual. Department of Informatics, University of Oslo (2007)
15. Heinze, C., Papasimeon, M., Goss, S.: Specifying Agent behaviour with use Case (2000)
16. Papasimeon, M., Heinze, C.: Specifying Requirement in Multi-agent System with use Cases (2000)
17. Bauer, B., Odell, J.: UML 2.0 and Agents: How to Build Agent-based Systems with the New UML Standard (2005)
18. Shen, W., Norrie, D.-H.: Agent-Based Systems for Intelligent Manufacturing: A State-of-the-Art Survey. Knowledge and Information Systems 1, 129–156 (1999)

Do You Get It? User-Evaluated Explainable BDI Agents

Joost Broekens[1], Maaike Harbers[2], Koen Hindriks[1],
Karel van den Bosch[3], Catholijn Jonker[1], and John-Jules Meyer[2]

[1] Delft University of Technology
[2] Utrecht University
[3] TNO Institute of Defence, Security and Safety, The Netherlands

Abstract. In this paper we focus on explaining to humans the behavior of autonomous agents, i.e., explainable agents. Explainable agents are useful for many reasons including scenario-based training (e.g. disaster training), tutor and pedagogical systems, agent development and debugging, gaming, and interactive storytelling. As the aim is to generate for humans plausible and insightful explanations, user evaluation of different explanations is essential. In this paper we test the hypothesis that different explanation types are needed to explain different types of actions. We present three different, generically applicable, algorithms that automatically generate different types of explanations for actions of BDI-based agents. Quantitative analysis of a user experiment (n=30), in which users rated the usefulness and naturalness of each explanation type for different agent actions, supports our hypothesis. In addition, we present feedback from the users about how they would explain the actions themselves. Finally, we hypothesize guidelines relevant for the development of explainable BDI agents.

1 Introduction

Explaining to users how AI systems come to their conclusions is an area of research with a history in expert systems and planning (see e.g., [1][2]). In this paper we focus on explaining to humans the behavior of autonomous agents. Explainable agents that use natural language for their explanations are useful in many domains. In scenario-based training (e.g. disaster or military training) the agents in the training should be able to explain the rationale for their actions so that students can understand why the training unfolds as it does [3]. In tutor and pedagogical systems, natural dialog between the user and system has been shown to increase the training effect of such systems [4]. Debugging tools for BDI agent programs might benefit from a natural way of interaction involving asking why agents perform certain actions instead of looking at execution traces and internal mental states [5]. In gaming and interactive storytelling [6][7], having automatic mechanisms to generate explanations of agent actions (the "story") could enhance the flexibility and appeal of the storyline.

Humans understand and explain (vocalize) their own and others' behavior in terms of *folk psychology*, that is, in terms of its underlying mental states like beliefs, desires and intentions [8]. To automatically generate similar explanations of agent behavior, it is convenient to have explicit representations of agent beliefs, goals and plans. This can be accomplished by using a BDI-based (belief desire intention) agent programming

J. Dix and C. Witteveen (Eds.): MATES 2010, LNAI 6251, pp. 28–39, 2010.

approach. Behavior in BDI agents is motivated by goals (desires), and selected based on whether or not an agent believes a particular behavior will satisfy a goal or subgoal. Behavior is then committed to (an action or sequence of actions is planned) transforming it into an intention. The outcome of a BDI agent's reasoning, i.e., its actions, can then be explained by the goals and beliefs that were responsible for it. Our approach to generating explanations is based on using the already available (relations between) mental constructs in the agent program that generates the agent behavior. It was found, that humans usually provide action explanations that only contain one or two mental concepts [9]. Thus, in particular when agents are complex, providing as explanation the complete trace of beliefs and goals underlying an action is undesirable. Instead, an explanation based on a selection of beliefs and goals underlying the action is needed.

Our hypothesis is that different actions require different *types of explanations*, i.e., an interaction effect exists between type of explanation and action on the perceived quality of an explanation. We present a study in which users evaluate three algorithms that each automatically generate a different type of explanation for 10 different agent actions. For each action and explanation type subjects rated usefulness and naturalness.

In Section 3 we distinguish different action types, and we present three generically applicable algorithms for automatically generating different explanation types for BDI agent actions. In Section 5 we present a quantitative analysis of a user evaluation experiment (n=30) to assess the usefulness and naturalness of the generated explanation types for different agent actions. We also present feedback from the users about how they would explain the actions themselves. Finally, in the discussion we hypothesize guidelines for the kind of information that should be modeled in the BDI agent if meaningful explanations are to be generated. First we discuss related work in the next section.

2 Related Work

In the introduction we have mentioned several application domains of explainable agents. Most of the related work is in virtual training systems. We now briefly review explainable agent approaches in this domain.

Debrief is the first system that explains agent behavior [10]. Debrief is implemented as part of a fighter pilot simulation and allows trainees to ask an explanation about any of the artificial fighter pilot's actions. To generate an answer, Debrief modifies the recalled situation repeatedly and systematically, and observes the effects on the agent's decisions. Based on the observations, Debrief explains which factors must have been responsible for the agent's decisions.

Another account of explainable agents is the XAI (eXplainable Artificial Intelligence) explanation component [11]. The XAI system has been incorporated into a simulation-based training for commanding a light infantry company. After a training session, trainees can select a time and an agent, and ask questions about the agent's state, e.g. its location or health.

A second version of the XAI system was developed to overcome the shortcomings of the first. It is claimed that the new XAI system supports domain independency, modularity and the ability to explain the motivations behind agents' actions. The system is described in [12] and [3], where it is applied to a tactical military simulator, and a virtual trainer for soft skills such as leadership, teamwork, negotiation and cultural awareness, respectively. For the generation of explanations, the system depends on information that is made available by the simulation.

Both Debrief and the first XAI system lack the ability to provide explanations involving the motivations behind an agent's actions. The XAI system only provides information about an agent's physical state, and not about its mental. Debrief does provide explanations in terms of an agent's beliefs, but never gives explanations including its underlying goals and intentions. The second XAI system can provide explanations in terms of an agent's goals, but only if those are represented as such in the simulation, which is often not the case [13]. If the agent's goals are not represented in the simulation, a hand-built XAI representation of the behaviors has to be made. Consequently, changes in the agent specification must also be reflected in the explanation component.

3   Explainable Agent Model

In this section we describe an explainable agent model that can provide different types of explanations about agent behavior. The basic principle of the model is that the mental concepts responsible for an agent's action are also used to explain that action. Because not all mental concepts underlying an action are needed to explain that action, we also present three different explanation algorithms that select a mental concept that is most appropriate to generate an explanation.

As mentioned in the introduction, BDI-based agent programming languages allow for the explicit representation of an agent's mental state, and actions are the result of a deliberation process on the agent's mental concepts. In our study, we have used the BDI language GOAL [14]. A GOAL agent program consists of six different sections, including the agent's knowledge, beliefs, goals, action rules, action specifications and percept rules. Together, the knowledge, beliefs and goals of an agent make up its mental state. Although GOAL distinguishes itself from other BDI-based languages in the exact way agents are specified and executed, we would like to stress that the explanation approach presented in this paper can also be applied to other BDI-based agents.

To explain agent behavior by the underlying mental concepts, we need two things. First, the agent's past goals and beliefs must be accessible when the explanation is constructed. Second, when there is a request to explain an action, the proper goals and beliefs explaining that action must be selected. We have implemented an explanation module that satisfies these two requirements.

3.1   Tree-Based Behavior Log

The explanation module includes a mechanism to construct a behavior "log", to which an agent's goals and beliefs are updated. The explanation module can be connected to any GOAL agent, and during run-time of the agent, the explanation module examines and logs the execution of the agent program.

The behavior "log" in the explanation module is a tree structure that is constructed while the agent reasons and performs actions based on its agent program (so formally it is not a log, as in a timed list of actions). It is made such that it automatically

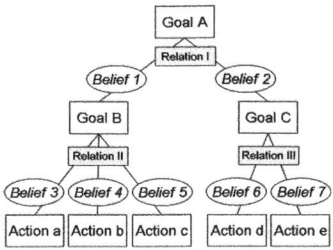

Fig. 1. Example behavior "log" (goal tree) of a BDI agent

construct a goal tree based on the actual behavior of the agent, see e.g. Figure 2 representing a particular execution of the agent program as used in the experiment (please also see our notes at the end of Section 3.2). The algorithm (in text) is as follows: The agent's initial goal becomes the top node of the tree (Goal A in Figure 1). If the program decides to adopt a goal in order to achieve another goal, this is represented as a subgoal (Goal B and C). The adoption conditions of a goal, i.e., beliefs that determine whether the agent program should adopt a subgoal, are represented along the branches of the tree (Belief 1-7). The agent's actions form the leaves of the tree (Action a-e). This algorithm automatically constructs a tree structure that is different depending on the actual behavior and choices of the agent.

In addition to this tree, one has to supply the behavior log with goal-relation information. Currently we add this manually, but this information could be explicitly represented, or extracted from the agent program. Goals can have three different relations to their subgoals (relation I-III): *all*, *one* and *seq*. A goal with an *all* relation to its subgoals/actions means that all subgoals/actions must be fulfilled in arbitrary order to achieve the goal, relation *one* means that exactly one of the subgoals/actions must be fulfilled to achieve the goal, and relation *seq* (from sequential) means that all subgoals/actions must be fulfilled in a particular fixed order. Based on these relations, we distinguish the following three types of actions.

- *All* action: relation to parent goal is of type all
- *One* action: relation to parent goal is of type one
- *Seq* action: relation to parent goal is of type seq

To summarize, we distinguish three different action types, where the action type depends on the relation to an action's parent goal and its siblings. In the next section we present three explanation algorithms that generate different types of explanations.

3.2 Explanation Algorithms

When a user requests an action explanation, an explanation algorithm is applied to the behavior log. Based on the log, the algorithm determines the goals and beliefs that are reasons for the action. Then, it selects beliefs and goals relevant for the explanation. We propose three algorithms for constructing three different types of explanation.

Algorithm I. The first explanation algorithm explains actions by the goal that motivated the selection of the action. It generates a sentence that looks like "Because I want to <goal>". We expect that this algorithm delivers useful explanations for actions of the type *all*, meaning that the action and all its sibling actions have to be executed in order to achieve their parent goal. For example, if relation II in Figure 1 would be of the type *all*, we expect that action b is best explained by goal B.

Algorithm II. The second algorithm explains an action by its enabling condition, i.e. the belief because of which it was executed. It generates a sentence that looks like "Because I believe that <belief condition>". We expect that these explanations are useful in particular for actions of the type *one*, meaning that only one of a goal's children actions needs to be executed to achieve it. In Figure 1 for example, if relation III would be of the type *one*, we expect that belief 6 provides the explanation for action d. Namely, belief 6 determined that action d was chosen to achieve goal C and not action e.

Algorithm III. In the third algorithm, an action is explained by the first action or task that must follow after the action. Thus, if an action is part of a sequence of actions that must be executed in a particular order to achieve a goal, the action can be explained by the next action in the sequence. It generates a sentence that looks like "Because I want to <next goal>". We expect that this algorithm will deliver most useful explanations for actions of the type *seq*. For instance, if relation II is of the type *seq*, action b is explained by action c according to this algorithm. In other words, action b enables the execution of action c. If an action is not part of such a sequence, the algorithm considers the parent goal of the action, and checks whether this goal is part of a sequence of goals. In Figure 1, if relation II is not of the type *seq*, relation I is considered and if that is a *seq* relation, goal C is given as the explanation for action b. If the top goal is reached without finding a relation of the type *seq*, the top goal is provided as an explanation.

Note that the execution of GOAL agents that are designed according to a hierarchical goal model will result into a goal tree, i.e. there is one main goal and each goal has a limited number of subgoals or actions. As the explanation module automatically constructs a goal-condition-subgoal structure based on the execution trace of the agent, other agent programs may result into less regular tree-shaped graphs, e.g. one main goal with many subgoals, several separated trees when multiple independent initial goals are present, or several partly connected trees when multiple dependent initial goals are present. In principle, the explanation algorithms can be applied to all kinds of goal graphs to generate explanations, but we expect that the explanation algorithms will in general deliver more useful explanations when applied to a proper tree. The assumption of a hierarchical goal model is plausible, as it is based on existing knowledge elicitation methods. Namely, hierarchical task analysis (HTA), which is a well-accepted cognitive task analysis technique [15].

Also note that explanations could be asked for during runtime, as the goal tree is build up continuously. Although in this paper we assume the agent has executed its complete program, as long as the tree contains enough information for the explanation algorithm to generate an explanation, it does not need to be complete.

Fig. 2. Cooking agent behavior log. Grey boxes denote the 11 actions used in the experiment.

4 Experimental Setup

To evaluate how users perceive the different explanation types for different actions, we have to test these in an application domain. We have chosen for a cooking agent that bakes pancakes and explains its actions. The reason for choosing a domain like this is that for average users to evaluate whether an explanation is useful and natural, the user must be familiar with the domain. He/she has to judge the explanation. This excludes more sophisticated domains such as disaster or negotiation training, as users are typically less familiar with these. Picking a domain limits the generalizability of our results, and we will come back to this issue in the discussion.

The cooking agent (Figure 2) was programmed in GOAL, and executed. To evaluate the effect of the different explanation types for the three action types, the agent program was constructed such that it included actions of all types. Action 2, 3, 4 and 5 are of type *all* (actions that all need to be executed), action 1, 6 and 10 are of type *one* (mutually exclusive actions), and action 7, 8, 9 and 11 are of type *seq* (actions that all need to be executed in a particular order). For all three explanation types, a list of explanations for all actions was generated. Post analysis excluded action 11 from the statistical result analysis as this action was misplaced in the tree (see Results section).

To investigate our hypothesis, we followed a between subject 10x3 design (10 actions, 3 algorithms) with dependent variables usefulness, naturalness. Subjects were randomly assigned to the different conditions with exactly 10 subjects per condition (n=30, 12 female, age(avg=32, stdev=9), cooking skills (5-point Likert scale, avg 3.6), average education level between Bachelor and Master, subjects were a balanced mix of family, friends, colleagues and students of the first two authors). All subjects scored all actions for a particular condition, resulting in 10 measurements per action per condition. The first two authors each administered 15 tests, no effect of experimenter bias was found during analysis of the data.

The procedure for gathering feedback from the subjects was organized as follows. Subjects were told to read the instructions (stating that the study was about developing smart agents for virtual training purposes), after which they received the first feedback form. On this form subjects wrote down their own explanations for the 11 actions listed on the form (see also the gray boxes in Figure 2), as if they were the cook explaining how to bake pancakes to a student. This feedback was aimed at extracting the "ideal" explanations as perceived by the user, and to help subjects get into the right context. We do not evaluate this qualitative data in this paper. When finished, subjects received the second form. This form asked for 5-point likert feedback on the naturalness of each action's automatically generated explanation (1=not natural, 5=very natural). Subjects took the role of observer when judging the naturalness of the explanation. Naturalness was explained as follows: "With a natural explanation we mean an explanation that sounds normal and is understandable, an explanation that you or other people could give". When finished, a similar form was presented for 5-point likert feedback about the usefulness of the explanations. Subjects were asked to imagine they were the student learning to cook while judging the usefulness. Useful was explained as follows: "Indicate how useful the explanations would be for you in learning how to make pancakes". Finally, subjects were presented with the goal tree (the graphical representation of the behavior log as shown in 2). We asked users to indicate all elements in the tree they deemed useful for giving an explanation of each of the 11 actions, by putting the action number next to the element. Subjects were asked to imagine they were the cook while numbering elements. This feedback was aimed at extracting information about what could be a good and feasible version of an explanation algorithm, given our way of automatically generating tree-based behavior logs.

5   Results

To test our main hypothesis, i.e., different actions require different types of explanations, we performed a 10x3 2-way MANOVA with explanation type (3 conditions) and action (10 conditions) as independent variables, and usefulness and naturalness as dependent variables. The MANOVA test is used to identify if signifiant differences in means of dependent variables are introduced by variation in independent (experimental) variables. Values of independent variables define groups, in our case 3x10=30 groups. Analysis showed a main effect of algorithm type ($F(4, 538) = 3.973, p < 0.01$), a main effect of action ($F(18, 538) = 1.917, p < 0.05$), and an interaction effect between action and algorithm ($F(36, 538) = 2.638, p < 0.001$). Post hoc testing (Tukey) for the influence of action alone on naturalness and usefulness revealed no significant differences between the actions on both measures. This indicates that the actions are equal with respect to explainability, meaning that no action is easier to explain than another. The same post hoc testing for the influence of algorithm type revealed only a significant effect on the perceived usefulness. Algorithm I (parent goal as explanation) performed significantly better ($p < 0.01$) than the other two algorithms ($Mean(I) = 3.1, Mean(II) = 2.5, Mean(III) = 2.5$). This indicates that there is a significant influence of explanation type on the perceived usefulness of the explanation, and that explaining an action with its parent goal (Algorithm I) is the best default method. However, the interaction effect indicating that different actions need different explanations (supporting our main hypothesis), is more important, as we will see next.

In Figure 3 an overview is given of the average naturalness and usefulness of the actions per algorithm type. In Figure 4 an overview is given of the number of times subjects indicated a particular element in the tree-based user feedback.

As can be seen, actions 1, 2, 6 and 9 score high on both measures when the parent goal is given as explanation (Algorithm I), while actions actions 3, 4, and 5 score high on both measures when the next action or goal is given as explanation ("I want to mix the ingredients", Algorithm III), and actions 7 and 10 score high when the enabling condition (belief) is given as explanation (algorithm II). Action 8 does not score well on either of the algorithms. Action 11 is explained well by Algorithm III (next goal/action), but this is a side effect of two factors. First, action 11 was misplaced, it should have been under "I want to eat pancakes", as also indicated by the tree-based user feedback. Second, Algorithm III defaults to the top level goal when no next steps are available in the sequence, which in our case happened to be the most logical option for explanation. We exclude action 11 from our analysis.

Actions 2, 3, 4 and 5 are actions of the type *all*; they are all needed in arbitrary order to achieve the parent goal. For 3, 4 and 5, the parent goal is not very descriptive, when the action has already been read (I put X in the bowl - because I want to put all ingredients in the bowl). As can be seen in Figure 4 subjects included in their own choice of elements the goal numbered 13 ("I want to make pancake mix"), indicating that subjects indeed need a more descriptive goal. Action 2 is well explained by its parent goal, as indicated by the naturalness and usefulness feedback as well as the tree-based feedback.

Actions 1, 6 and 10 are actions of the type *one*. Action 1 and 6 score high on using the parent goal as explanation, but in addition to that they seem to require extra information for an adequate explanation. In Figure 3 we can see that for action 1 and 6 subjects use the goal two levels up in the hierarchy. Action 10 is well explained by Algorithm II (enabling condition). This is reflected in the tree-based feedback, as for action 6 and 10 subjects use the enabling conditions for the action and for the parent goal. Action 6 thus has a rather complex explanation structure using two goals and two conditions.

As indicated by the tree-based feedback, enabling conditions in combination with the parent goal are also used for action 7, 8, and 9; all three actions are actions in a sequence, type *seq*. However, action 8 and 9 use only the enabling condition for the action itself, while action 7 uses both the enabling condition for the action itself as well as the enabling condition for the action's parent goal. We will interpret these results in more detail in the discussion.

Finally, we have conducted correlations between the subject demographics and usefulness and naturalness. We found four significant correlations. Two of the correlations were positive: the one between usefulness and naturalness ($p < 0.001, r = 0.491$), and the one between cooking skill and usefulness ($p < 0.001, r = 0.145$). The first correlation is as expected: natural explanations are more useful and vice versa. The second is somewhat counterintuitive: more experienced cooks judge the explanations slightly more useful. This could be due to the fact that a better cook is better able to understand

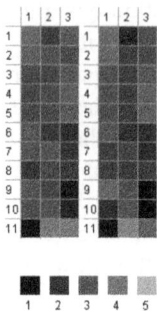

Fig. 3. Average naturalness (left) and usefulness (right) of actions (1-11) per condition (1-3)

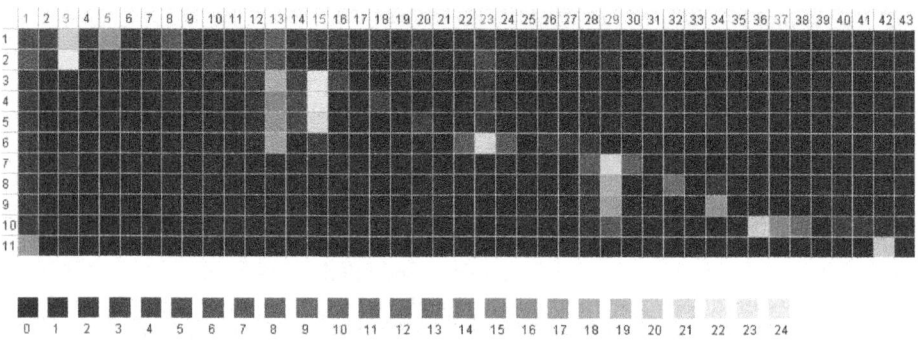

Fig. 4. Distribution of tree elements used to generate explanations for different actions (1-11) as given by the subjects. Elements number from 1 to 43 and refer to numbers in Figure 2.

the explanation in the first place, but as the correlation coefficient is rather small, we do not pay further attention to this in this paper. Furthermore, we found two negative correlations: between action number and naturalness ($p < 0.001, r - 0.200$), and between action number and usefulness ($p < 0.01, r = -0.178$). As actions were always scored from top to bottom, and this corresponds to the action number, this might indicate two different things: for the later actions it is more difficult to automatically generate explanations, or, subjects got tired of scoring explanations. This issue needs future experiments.

6   Discussion

We first discuss the results in more detail. Then we summarize the discussion by hypothesizing guidelines for the development of explainable BDI agents that generate explanations based on their behavior and mental processes. We end the discussion with several limitations of our study, such as the choice of domain and the choice of particular actions, subgoals and the linkage between them in the goal tree.

Our results indicate two things. First, the results support our main hypothesis: different actions need different explanation types, as indicated by the 2-way ANOVA showing significant interaction between action and type of explanation. Second, our expectations on how action types and explanation algorithms are related are too simplistic. We expected that *all* actions (AND relation with siblings) would be explained best by the action's parent goal, that *seq* actions (AND and sequence relation with siblings) would be explained best by the next action/goal in the sequence, and *one* actions (XOR relation with siblings) would be best explained by their enabling condition. Looking at the tree-based feedback, most of the actions seem to need at least one additional element for explanation, in addition to their parent goal. The kind of additional information seems to depend on the action's role in the process and the action's type (seq, all, or one).

First consider the actions of type *all*: action 2, 3, 4 and 5. Of all actions, only action 2 is explained well by only one element, its parent goal. Action 3, 4 and 5 are well explained by the next action in the sequence (Figure 3), but when subjects produce their own tree-based feedback (Figure 4), they choose for a combination of the parent goal and the parent's parent goal. We currently can not explain this inconsistency, but it does indicate that neither the enabling condition nor the parent goal are descriptive enough in this particular case.

Now consider actions 1, 6 and 10 which are of type *one*. The way this type of action is modeled in the tree is such that the parent goal presents a choice, while the enabling condition of the action's parent explains why the choice has to be made. For this action type, the parent goal is not descriptive enough to provide a satisfying explanation. Instead, both the enabling condition of the action and the enabling condition of the parent goal are needed (Figure 4).

Finally, consider the actions 7, 8, 9, and 10 which are part of the same sequence (note that 7, 8 and 9 are of type *seq*, but 10 is of type *one*). According to the tree-based feedback (Figure 4), these actions should be explained by their parent goal and their enabling condition, contrary to our expectation that such actions would need the next action/goal in the sequence. In addition, action 7 and 10 also need the enabling condition of their parent's goal in their explanations. A possible explanation for this difference is that action 8 and 9 are in the middle of a sequence. Their parent goal explains what is to be done, and the enabling condition explains where we are in the process. Action 10 does need its parent goal and its enabling condition because it is an action of type *one*. The enabling condition of its parent goal needs to be given because it is also, though implicitly, part of the sequence involving action 7 to 10. Action 7 can be explained in the same way. It is the first action of a next phase in the process (baking). Phase in this case is defined as either preparation for baking, or baking. The parent goal of action 7 is about that next phase, but it does not explain why we ended up in this phase. This is what the parent goals' enabling condition is about, hence, action 7 needs again two enabling conditions (it's own and that of its parent goal).

According to studies in psychology, humans explain intentional behavior using reasons while they explain unintentional behavior using causes [16]. Furthermore, when behavior was made possible by opportunity, skill or by removal of an obstacle, people tend to use a description of enabling factors for explaining the behavior (e.g., why does a person start driving when waiting for a traffic light? Because the light turns green). Obviously, all of our agent behavior is intentional, but for a human, actions of the type *one* (OR, XOR) could well be considered driven by opportunity in our case (having ingredients at home or not, having a mixer or not). It is therefore in line with [16] that these actions need their enabling condition for explanation. Also the actions in sequence 7-10 need an enabling condition. When performing an action sequence, the whole sequence is intentional, but the actions within the sequence are controlled by external factors or the logic of the process. These can thus be considered non-intentional, and it is therefore again in line with [16] that also these actions need their enabling condition.

6.1 Guidelines

We now sum up this discussion and present several guidelines relevant for the development of explainable BDI agents. The guidelines are hypotheses, and should be tested in further research. First, as the parent goal of an action seems essential in its explanation, explanation methods should first attempt to use this. This also suggests that explainable-agent programmers should make these parent goals as meaningful as possible in light of an explanation. Second, actions that start a new phase in a process need additional explanation in the form of the enabling conditions for the action and the parent goal. Third, care should be taken when explaining XOR choices (*one* action type) using a common parent goal as "abstract action", because such a parent goal is often non descriptive. This means that either the explanation method must take this into account (e.g., by using agent-program meta information), or such choices should be modeled differently. Fourth, sequenced actions need to be "chained" using their enabling condition, so that the user can position the action in the sequence.

6.2 Limitations and Future Work

We have chosen a domain that is well-known to the subjects because we wanted all subjects to be able to judge the naturalness and usefulness of the explanations. Our current aim was not to investigate if these explanations actually result in, e.g., a better training session. In future work we plan to perform similar experiments with subjects that are not familiar with the domain (e.g., a disaster training) to test whether generated explanations increase the understanding of these subjects.

Furthermore, the particular agent program used to represent beliefs, goals and resulting action selection, produces a particular hierarchical goal structure. Although we expect similar structures are ubiquitous in programs, more research is needed on relaxing these structural constraints.

A similar issue is the particular instantiation of our BDI program. Our results might be limited to our specific goal tree. However, we have taken care to construct the goal hierarchy such that it contains duplication of action types at different places. Therefore, we feel that similar results for action explanation at two different places indicates that the result is generic for that action type.

7 Conclusion

In this paper we have presented a study involving user evaluations of explanations about agent behavior. We distinguished three action types and three algorithms automatically generating different explanation types. We investigated which explanation types are preferred for which actions. Our hypothesis that different actions require different types of explanations, as generated by different explanation algorithms, was supported by the results. We found that an action should always be explained by its parent goal, and depending on the action type, particular additional information is needed. We have abstracted this and other findings into four guidelines relevant for the development of explainable BDI agents and explanation algorithms.

Acknowledgements

This research has been supported by the GATE project, funded by the Netherlands Organization for Scientific Research (NWO) and the Netherlands ICT Research and Innovation Authority (ICT Regie), as well as STW (NWO) VICI-project 08075.

References

1. Cortellessa, G., Cesta, A.: Evaluating mixed-initiative systems: An experimental approach. In: ICAPS'06, pp. 172–181 (2006)
2. Gilbert, N.: Explanation and dialogue. The Knowledge Engineering Review 4(03), 235–247 (1989) 10.1017/S026988890000504X
3. Core, M., Traum, T., Lane, H., Swartout, W., Gratch, J., Van Lent, M.: Teaching negotiation skills through practice and reflection with virtual humans. Simulation 82(11), 685–701 (2006)
4. Graesser, A.C., Chipman, P., Haynes, B.C., Olney, A.: Autotutor: an intelligent tutoring system with mixed-initiative dialogue. IEEE Transactions on Education 48(4), 612–618 (2005)
5. Broekens, J., DeGroot, D.: Formalizing cognitive appraisal: from theory to computation. In: Trapple, R. (ed.) Cybernetics and Systems 2006, Vienna, Austrian, Society for Cybernetics Studies, pp. 595–600 (2006)
6. Cavazza, M., Charles, F., Mead, S.J.: Character-based interactive storytelling. IEEE Intelligent Systems 17(4), 17–24 (2002)
7. Theune, M., Faas, S., Heylen, D.K.J., Nijholt, A.: The virtual qstoryteller: Story creation by intelligent agents. In: TIDSE 2003: Technologies for Interactive Digital Storytelling and Entertainment, Darmstadt, pp. 204–215. Fraunhofer IRB Verlag (2003)
8. Keil, F.: Explanation and understanding. Annual Reviews Psychology 57, 227–254 (2006)
9. Harbers, M., Van den Bosch, K., Meyer, J.: A study into preferred explanations of virtual agent behavior. In: Ruttkay, Z., Kipp, M., Nijholt, A., Vilhjálmsson, H. (eds.) IVA 2009. LNCS, vol. 5773, pp. 132–145. Springer, Heidelberg (2009)
10. Johnson, W.: Agents that learn to explain themselves. In: Proc. of the 12th Nat. Conf. on Artificial Intelligence, pp. 1257–1263 (1994)
11. Van Lent, M., Fisher, W., Mancuso, M.: An explainable artificial intelligence system for small-unit tactical behavior. In: Proc. of IAAA 2004. AAAI Press, Menlo Park (2004)
12. Gomboc, D., Solomon, S., Core, M.G., Lane, H.C., van Lent, M.: Design recommendations to support automated explanation and tutoring. In: Proc. of BRIMS 2005, Universal City, CA (2005)
13. Core, M., Lane, H., Van Lent, M., Gomboc, D., Solomon, S., Rosenberg, M.: Building explainable artificial intelligence systems. In: AAAI (2006)
14. Hindriks, K.: Programming Rational Agents in GOAL. In: Multi-Agent Programming: Languages, Tools and Applications, pp. 119–157. Springer, Heidelberg (2009)
15. Schraagen, J., Chipman, S., Shalin, V. (eds.): Cognitive Task Analysis. Lawrence Erlbaum Associates, Mahway (2000)
16. Malle, B.: How people explain behavior: A new theoretical framework. Personality and Social Psychology Review 3(1), 23–48 (1999)

Reputation in Multi Agent Systems and the Incentives to Provide Feedback

Miriam Heitz, Stefan König, and Torsten Eymann

University of Bayreuth
Chair of Information Systems Management
95440 Bayreuth, Germany
miriam.heitz@gmail.com
http://www.bwl7.uni-bayreuth.de

Abstract. The emergence of the Internet leads to a vast increase in the number of interactions between parties that are completely alien to each other. In general, such transactions are likely to be subject to fraud and cheating. If such systems use rational software agents to negotiate and execute transactions, mechanisms that lead to favorable outcomes for all parties instead of giving rise to defective behavior are necessary to make the system work: trust and reputation mechanisms. This paper analyzes different incentive mechanisms helping these trust and reputation mechanisms in eliciting users to report own experiences honestly.

Keywords: Reputation, Incentives.

1 Introduction

Think of e-commerce systems in which completely rational agents automatically search for providers and negotiate terms of trade after detecting a need. Since these agents are set up to maximize the profit of the party they are acting for, they will cheat on their trading partners and refrain from paying for services that have already been delivered, if the rules of the game are not designed in such a way that cheating reduces their expected future gains from trade.

Reputation mechanisms can play a major role in making reliable promises between rational and anonymous actors possible. Such systems transform once-off interactions between agents in repeated interactions, and hence make cooperation a rational strategy.

Reputation mechanisms promise to signal whether a partner is trustworthy or not. They can facilitate "to promote cooperative and honest behavior among self-interested economic agents" [1, p. 210]. The mechanisms need feedback from the agents engaged in trade. Unfortunately, it is not in the best interest of a rational agent to report feedback, since that would provide a competitive advantage to the other agents. Suppose, for example, that a trading partner cheated on an agent. Why should this agent report the cheating? If it competes with the agents that would benefit from the report, it would provide them with valuable information that gives them a competitive advantage. If, on the other

J. Dix and C. Witteveen (Eds.): MATES 2010, LNAI 6251, pp. 40–51, 2010.

hand, the interaction went well, and the agent gave positive feedback, that would increase the reputation of the trading partner and therefore diminish its own. In an unregulated environment it is not rational for agents to report feedback either way.

In consequence, a trust establishing mechanism has to be implemented with two features: first, it has to encourage rational agents to give honest feedback. Second, it has to serve as a tool to communicate hidden characteristics of and feedback about the transaction partner's behavior. We assume that only the buyers (trustors) rate the behavior of the providers (trustees), because of advanced payment. This is done for reasons of simplicity and could also be the other way around, within the same system (see e.g. [2] for a detailed discussion on that).

This paper will discuss and analyze several trust and reputation mechanisms that exhibit these characteristics. It does not intend to give a exhaustive survey of trust and reputation models. Therefore we refer for example to [3–8]

This paper is organized as follows: chapter 2 will exemplify four incentive setting reputation mechanisms for multi agent environments. Chapter 3 will compare the introduced mechanisms and stress the advantages of each. Finally, chapter 4 concludes with an overview of the reputation mechanisms and the incentives that are necessary to make it rational to report feedback truthfully.

2   Implementing Incentive Setting Reputation Mechanisms in Multi Agent Systems

Reputation mechanisms have to fulfill two main functions. They have to elicit feedback from rational agents which will not submit feedback without incentives and secondly, they have to be able to detect untrustworthy and further trustworthy feedback. In the following we introduce four approaches that attempt to solve these two problems.

2.1   Liu and Issarny: An Incentive Compatible Reputation Mechanism for Ubiquitous Computing Environments

Liu and Issarny [9] introduce a reputation mechanism which has the following objectives: It needs to be able to distinguish between trustworthy and untrustworthy agents and also between honest and dishonest recommenders. Additionally, it should achieve to enforce honest recommendations. If untrustworthy feedback is given, it penalizes the dishonest behavior and punishes any exploitation of the system. Therefore only honest recommendations are taken into account. Old reputation values need to be discounted over the past because they become irrelevant when behavior of the target changes. Hence, more weight is given to recent experiences. The authors assume the beta distribution of reputation for modeling reputation. It expresses the probability for having an event T the next time. There are two possible outcomes T and $-T$, with r and s being the observed numbers of T and $-T$ respectively. The advantages of beta reputation include the simple estimation of the trustworthiness of an entity by calculating $\frac{\alpha}{\alpha+\beta}$, with $\alpha = r + 1$ and $\beta = s + 1$ these are assumed to be two independent events. Only newcomers hold a value of 0. The aggregation of observation is due to dynamic adjustment by addition and accumulation of more experiences. The time fading factor ρ stresses recent experiences compared to older ones:

$$\alpha' = 1 + (\alpha - 1) \times \rho^{\Delta T} \tag{1}$$

$$\beta' = 1 + (\beta - 1) \times \rho^{\Delta T} \tag{2}$$

There are two roles, the trusting entity (trustor) a and a trusted entity (trustee) o. In the following, the trustee will always be the provider and the trustor always the consumer. Hence, $Rep_a(o)$ is o's reputation from a's point of view. The authors differentiate between three different kinds of reputation. The Service reputation ($SRep$) combines direct experiences one agent has with experiences of another agent. Therefore, it is updated after each new experience. Overall reputation ($ORep$) describes direct experiences an agent had from transactions if they are significant enough to derive a trust decision. This is the case, if the accumulation ($s_p + s_n - 2$) exceeds a certain threshold, whereas s_p represents positive and s_n negative experiences. Otherwise the trustor asks other entities for recommendations. Then the combination of own direct experiences and recommendations from others makes up the $ORep$ of the trustee. An example will clarify this: entity a asks entity r for recommendations about o. Then r gives $Rec_r(o) = (r_p, r_n)$. a checks if the recommendation is trustworthy in two steps: (1) Is r honest? If $\frac{r_p}{r_p+r_n}$ is high enough, r is considered honest. (2) The $RRep$ is evaluated with ($r_p + r_n - 2$) to ensure it relies on sufficient evidence. If those two criteria are met by the recommendation of r, the recommendation is taken into account and weighted according to the formula: $w_r = E(Beta(r_p, r_n)) = \frac{r_p}{r_p+r_n}$. This is done for each recommendation. The complete $ORep$ is then calculated from the sum of all those:

$$ORep = \delta \times SRep + (1 - \delta) \times \frac{\sum_{r \in R}(Rec_r(o) \times w_r)}{\sum_{r \in R}(w_r)} \tag{3}$$

δ represents the weight given to each recommendation. It is usually greater than 0.5 due to the fact that own direct experiences are more valuable than recommendations from other entities.

Recommendation reputation ($RRep$) evalutes the usefulness of a recommendation from another agent. It is exclusively made up of direct experiences using recommendations. It has the form (c_p, c_n) and is equal to the $SRep$ for honest recommenders. The beta reputation provides now a simple calculation to check whether an agent is an active recommender: $r_p + r_n - 2$. The value is expected to be high for active recommenders. To check whether an agent is providing honest recommendations the value of $f(p|r_p, r_n)$ is expected to be high, too.

The higher the first value (r_p), the more positive values were observed. The higher the sum, the higher is the number of recommendations the agent has given. The two values δ_h and δ_a are the thresholds for trustworthiness (honesty) and activeness in providing recommendations respectively. Therefore a provider would be considered active if $r_p + r_n - 2 \geq \delta_a$, and honest if $\frac{r_p}{r_p + r_n} \geq \delta_h$. This leads to five distinct states of a recommender: active truthteller, inactive truthteller, active liar, inactive liar and newcomer. The stages change due to behavior, activity and inactivity. $RRep$ decays if an agent does not provide recommendations and moves it from an active liar or truthteller to the inactive counterpart or even a newcomer. The distinction between five groups of recommenders is crucial for the reputation propagation because the groups are treated differently in granting access to reputation information. Hence, these five states set incentives to share honest recommendations with other agents.

If an agent o then asks agent a for recommendations, agent a first evaluates the state of the agent o and if it has a significant number of direct experiences. If it does and agent o is an honest recommender it sends back the recommendation immediately. In the case that agent o is considered inactive, it sends back the recommendation with probability of diff $= \delta_a - (r_p + r_n - 2)$. The distinction between inactive liars and truthteller is made by the fact that inactive recommenders do not necessarily withhold their recommendations. "The less active an entity is, the less possible that it receives helpful recommendations from others" [9, p. 304]. Therefore all rational entities will try to appear as active truthtellers.

2.2   Jøsang and Ismail: The Beta Reputation System

Jøsang et al.[10] use a different family of continuous probability distribution, the gamma distribution. The following function is used to categorize agents:

$$f(p|\alpha, \beta) = \frac{\Gamma(\alpha + \beta)}{\Gamma(\alpha) + \Gamma(\beta)} p^{\alpha-1}(1 - p)^{\beta-1} \tag{4}$$

where $0 \leq p \leq 1$ and $\alpha, \beta < 0$. The expectation value within the restrictions $p \neq 0$ if $\alpha < 1$ and $p \neq 1$ if $\beta > 0$ is similar to Liu et al.. There are two possible outcomes, here called x and $\bar{x}$, which are corresponding to T and $-T$ in Liu et al.'s beta reputation. The observed number of x is called r and of $\bar{x}$ is s, both of them need to be greater or equal to zero ($r, s \geq 0$). The probability density function of observing outcome x in the future can be expressed as a function of past observations by setting: $\alpha = r + 1$ and $\beta = s + 1$ where $r, s \geq 0$. With the beta function the authors are trying to visualize that the relative frequency of outcome x in the future is somewhat uncertain and that the most likely value corresponds to $E(p)$. Hence, the reputation function predicts the expected relative frequency with which x will happen in the future. r_T^X and s_T^X represent the positive and negative feedback tuple about target T provided by entity X. Those tuples are called reputation parameters. The probability expectation value of reputation function is accordingly

$$E(\varphi|p(r_T^X, s_T^X)) = \frac{r_T^X + 1}{r_T^X + s_T^X + 2} \tag{5}$$

This again is similar to Liu et al. where it is defined as $E(p) = \frac{\alpha}{(\alpha + \beta)}$.

The accumulation of feedback is similar to Liu et al., too. When feedback from entity X (r_T^X, s_T^X) and entity Y (r_T^Y, s_T^Y) about target T is received, the r-parameters and the s-parameters are added up as follows: $r_T^{X,Y} = r_T^X + r_T^Y$ and $s_T^{X,Y} = s_T^X + s_T^Y$. This leads to the updated reputation function $E(\varphi|p(r_T^{X,Y}, s_T^{X,Y}))$. Jøsang et al. add that the independence between the ratings must be assumed so that no feedback can count twice. The authors present two different kinds of discounting. Beliefs are discounted, because "feedback from highly reputed agents should carry more weight than feedback from agents with low reputation rating" [10, p. 6]. Therefore, they introduce w_T^A which reflects the opinion of A about target T. The opinion consists of belief, disbelief and uncertainty.

In addition to belief discounting the authors introduce reputation discounting in order to discount "feedback as a function of the reputation of the agent who provided the feedback" [10, p. 6].The authors take into account that a recommendation must not necessarily be true and consider the opinion the agent has about the target and the recommender. $\varphi(p|r_T^{X:Y}, s_T^{X:Y})$ is the reputation function of T given a recommendation from Y, which is discounted by agent X. This means that the given function is T's discounted reputation function by X through Y:

$$r_T^{X:Y} = \frac{2r_Y^X r_T^Y}{(s_Y^X + 2)(r_T^Y + s_T^Y + 2) + 2r_Y^X} \tag{6}$$

$$s_T^{X:Y} = \frac{2r_Y^X s_T^Y}{(s_Y^X + 2)(r_T^Y + s_T^Y + 2) + 2r_Y^X} \tag{7}$$

Similar to Liu et al. [9] Jøsang et al. introduce a forgetting factor which discounts old feedback in order to adapt to behavior changes of the ratee.

2.3   Buchegger and Boudec: A Robust System for P2P and Mobile Ad-hoc Networks

Buchegger and Boudec [11] create a reputation system which detects misbehavior, but does not set any direct incentives to submit reputation. The only incentives set are used to enforce correct feedback and to maintain a good personal reputation. Like the other introduced reputation mechanisms so far, it uses Bayesian estimation to detect false reports.

The reputation of a given agent (which the authors call node) is the collection of ratings about this agent. This information is kept and maintained by others instead of being stored in a centralized institution. Hence, the reputation system is fully distributed. Reputation values appear in three different kinds. First of all the reputation rating $(R_{i,j})$ which indicates the opinion of agent i about agent j's behavior in the system. The trust rating $(S_{i,j})$ expresses agent i's opinion about how honest agent j is. These two ratings and additionally the first hand information $(F_{i,j})$ from agent i on agent j make up the reputation of agent j maintained by agent i. The three kinds of reputation values are represented in tuples so that e.g. $F_{i,j}$ has the parameters (α, β) of the beta distribution by agent i in its Bayesian view of agent j's behavior, initially set to (1,1). When agent i makes a first hand experience with agent j it updates $F_{i,j}$ and $R_{i,j}$. From time to time the first hand ratings are published and participants can include them in their reputation ratings about other agents. In order to integrate the published rating, agent i has to estimate if the other agent. is trustworthy. If agent k is considered trustworthy or the submitted $F_{k,j}$ is close to $R_{i,j}$, the first hand information $F_{k,j}$ is accepted and used to slightly modify $R_{i,j}$. If it does not satisfy one of these criteria, $R_{i,j}$ is not updated. In every case the trust rating $T_{i,k}$ is updated. The trust rating slightly improves if $F_{k,j}$ is close to $R_{i,j}$ or slightly worsens if not. Then it helps to maintain an opinion about the honesty of a agent. During the publication process only $F_{i,j}$ is submitted; $T_{i,j}$ and $R_{i,j}$ are never disseminated. Trust ratings help the agents to estimate how honest another agent is. They are updated whenever a report about an agent is published.

This process works as follows: Agent i believes that every other agent provides false reports with a certain probability. Let the probability of agent k providing false reports be ϕ. In order to estimate the expectation of the distribution of ϕ agent i uses the prior $Beta(\gamma, \delta)$. The trust rating $T_{i,j}$ is therefore equal to (γ, δ). This is set initially to $(1,1)$. In order to test a rating a deviation test is used to estimate if agent k is already considered trustworthy or not. If the deviation test succeeds $s = 1$, $s = 0$ otherwise. After the test the trust rating is updated with a discount factor v: $\gamma := v\gamma + s$ and $\delta := v\delta + (1 - s)$. Similar to the first hand observations the reputation ratings have the form $R_{i,j}$ which has the parameters (α', β'), initially set to $(1,1)$. $R_{i,j}$ is always updated when a first hand observation is made ($F_{i,j}$ is updated) and when $R_{k,j}$ from another agent is published and accepted. The update of $R_{i,j}$ due to a new $F_{i,j}$ functions just like updating $F_{i,j}$ so that $\alpha' := u\alpha' + s$ and $\beta' := u\beta' + (1 - s)$. An inactivity update, in order to enable time fading just removes the last part of the two equations: $\alpha' := u\alpha'$ and $\beta := u\beta'$. If agent i receives a first hand observation $F_{k,j}$ from agent k about agent j, agent i tries to find out if this information is correct by taking trust and compatibility into account. Agent i will then check if agent k reaches the threshold for honest recommendations (defined below). If it does, it will include $F_{k,j}$ in $R_{i,j}$ as follows. $F_{k,j}$ is modified by a factor w which is a small positive constant that allows agent i to give the feedback from agent k a different weight than its own reputation ratings. $F_{k,j}$ is then added to $R_{i,j}$: $R_{i,j} := R_{i,j} + wF_{k,j}$. If agent k is considered untrustworthy, it will apply a deviation test. $E(Beta(\alpha, \beta))$ is defined as the expectation of the distribution $Beta(\alpha, \beta)$. What they do then is to compare the expectations of the distribution of the tuples from $F_{k,j}$ and $R_{i,j}$.

If the deviation test is positive, agent i will not consider the first hand information $F_{k,j}$ because it is incompatible. Otherwise $F_{k,j}$ is used to update $R_{i,j}$ as if $F_{k,j}$ would have been considered trustworthy. For the decision making process all the information from first hand experiences is taken into account which means that all $R_{i,j}$ and $T_{i,j}$ are updated. To make a final decision, the beta distribution is used again. This is similar to the method used for the reputation rating. The first estimation is done for $R_{i,j} = (\alpha', \beta')$. They consider $E(Beta(\alpha', \beta'))$ for

θ so that normal behavior would satisfy: $E(Beta(\alpha', \beta')) < r$. Misbehaving would be indicated when $E(Beta(\alpha', \beta')) \geq r$. The same is done for $T_{i,j} = (\gamma, \delta)$. It is considered trustworthy for: $E(Beta(\gamma, \delta)) < t$. In the case of $E(Beta(\gamma, \delta)) \geq t$ agent i would consider agent j as untrustworthy.

2.4   Jurca and Faltings: Towards Incentive Compatible Reputation Management

The reputation mechanism represented by Jurca and Faltings [12] introduces a mechanism to detect false feedback and additionally a framework of incentives which makes it rational to report truthfully for rational agents. They do this by introducing a side payment scheme which is maintained by broker agents. Those are called R-Agents and they are the only ones who can trade with reputation values. The following assumptions are made by Jurca et al.:

1. Payments are only conducted by R-Agents. No side payments occur between any normal agents.
2. All agents behave rationally.
3. There are n agents in the system with a_i for $i = 1...N$.

In this mechanism agents can acquire information on another agent at the cost of F from an R-Agent. After a transaction between two agents, other than R-Agents, the agents can sell reputation information for C. Suitable values for F and C will be estimated below. Agents are only allowed to sell reputation to an R-Agent about an agent that they have purchased information about before. The agents buy systematically reputation information before interacting with another agent in Jurca et al.'s scenario.

In contrast to the reputation mechanisms introduced so far, Jurca et al. use a single real number representation of the reputation information r_i. It can have the value 0 for defecting and 1 for cooperative behavior. Reputation can be calculated by $r_i = \frac{\sum_{j=1}^{k} report_j}{N}$. So that the reputation value is computed as the average of all the reports about that specific agent. The $report_j$, $j = 1...k$ represents all the reports on that agent a_i.

In order to make the mechanism incentive compatible, the following features of the model are assumed by the authors:

1. Agents which report truthfully at all times should not lose any money as a result of an interaction with another agent: $E[F] \leq E[C|\text{truthful report}]$
2. Agents which do not report truthfully should gradually lose their money as a result of an interaction with another agent: $E[F] \geq E[C|\text{false report}]$

R-Agents will pay only for reports which match the next report about the concerned agent. This is done because — as we will see below — it is optimal for a rational agent to report truthfully because it will be paid at least in 50% of the cases. This was calculated by considerating of the probabilities of different behavior schemes:

- agent a_i cooperates in two consecutive rounds: p_i^2
- agent a_i defects in two consecutive rounds: $(1 - p_i)^2$

- agent a_i cooperates then defects: $p_i(1 - p_i)$
- agent a_i defects then cooperates: $p_i(1 - p_i)$

This means that the probability of acting in the same way in two consecutive rounds is: $(1 - p_i)^2 + p_i^2 \iff 1 - 2p_i + 2p_i^2$ which is bound by $[0.5,1]$. The probability for a change in behavior in two consecutive rounds is: $2p_i(1 - p_i)$ which is bound by $[0,0.5]$. Then Jurca et al. assume that other agents report the truth and that a_i will behave in the same way in the next round. Hence, it is rational for the agent to report truthfully because it is paid with a probability of not less than 0.5. Those assumptions are slightly different from the ones made by Buchegger et al. [11], because they introduce a function that estimates a time span in which the agent believes that the transaction partner acts the same way over multiple rounds. The assumption that the behavior is the same in consecutive rounds is needed for the calculation of the payoff by Jurca et al.. Hence, their mechanism is more static. In later works they have eliminated this assumption and created a more flexible mechanism (see [13–15]).

Agents purchase information about a prospective interaction partner but can only sell information if they did interact with that agent. Business only takes place if both agents agree. Hence, the agent can expect a payoff after analyzing three possible situations:

case 1. When the reputation of a_i that the agent purchased from an R-Agent is too low, it will not interact with that agent and can therefore not sell any information. The payoff is 0.

case 2. When business has taken place and it submits a report to a R-Agent but it is considered false because the other agent has changed its behavior in the next round. The payoff is 0.

case 3. When business is conducted and the other agent behaves accordingly in the next round, the payoff equals C.

The expected payoff can be computed as: $E[\text{payoff}] = 0 \cdot Pr(\text{case } 1) + 0 \cdot Pr(\text{case } 2) + C \cdot Pr(\text{case } 3)$

As stated above agents only interact with other agents if they expect a profit. This means that the probability that an agent will trust and interact with another agent q is equal to the probability of a positive outcome Out: $q = Prob(Out > 0)$. $Out = \frac{1}{2}[(1 - p_i) \cdot f(\frac{I}{2}) + p_i \cdot f(I)] - \frac{I}{2}$ is the business payoff function when I units have been invested. In this function $Out > 0$ is equal to $p_i > \theta$ if a monotone increasing function is assumed. θ is a constant that the authors use which depends only on the business payoff function. The constant is used to define q which equals the probability that p_i is greater than θ: $q = Pr(p_i > \theta)$. In order to estimate the payoff now, we need the probability that the agents interact with another. The probabilities for cases 1 and 2 are given by Jurca et al. but are not considered here to make it simpler because the payoff would be 0 in those two cases (for explanation see above). The payoff can be estimated with

$$Pr(\text{case } 3) = q^2(1 - 2p_j + 2p_j^2) \tag{8}$$

So that the average value of the payoff and therefore the price is

$$E[\text{payoff}] = C \cdot \frac{\sum Nj = 1q^2(1 - 2p + 2p_j^2)}{N} = F \qquad (9)$$

With this function we can compute the average payoff for the seller and the price for the buyer (F) with the help of the payments made to acquire the reputation (C).

3   An Analysis of Incentives in Reputation Models

The four introduced reputation mechanism tried to encourage participants to submit ratings by different methods. This section will compare these incentives and focus on the differences between them.

In 2.1 we discussed *Liu and Issarny's* approach to work with three different reputation values *ORep*, *RRep* and *SRep* in order to estimate the trustworthiness of an agent. We have seen that the agents rate their partners due to the reputation values and divide them into the groups (called states of the recommender) active truthteller, inactive truthteller, active liar, inactive liar and newcomer. This represents incentives because if an agent sends a request for information (second hand recommendation) it is given an answer according to his state. Therefore, all rational agents will try to become a truthteller which is active in order to receive the most answers to their requests.

Jøsang and Ismail in 2.2 is introduced in this paper, because it is fairly easy to implement but still rests on a sound statistical basis. Additionally, the authors present three different discounting methods (reputation discounting, belief discounting and forgetting) that give a detailed approach how to rate feedback from other agents. Similar to Liu et al. [9], Jøsang et al. introduce a forgetting factor which discounts old feedback in order to adapt to behavior changes of the ratee. In order to estimate the trustworthiness of feedback from an agent the three factors belief, disbelief and uncertainty are taken into account and are weighted with the opinion the agent has about the feedback provider and the target agent. Jøsang et al. add that their model does not provide objectivity because honesty cannot be enforced with this reputation mechanism which is also true for Liu et al. but is treated differently because Liu et al. make use of *RRep* to enforce honesty in rational agents. The incentives set by Jøsang et al. are similar to Liu et al. [9] because they both establish a *meta-rating* reflecting an indication how truthful the agent reports. Liu et al. call it recommendation reputation (*RRep*) and Jøsang et al. call it belief. The mechanism does not set any further incentives than that and has to be modified further to be fully satisfying for a MAS with rational agents.

We have shown in 2.3 that *Buchegger and Boudec* also introduce a reputation rating and a trust rating that estimates how truthful another agent reports. This *meta rating* allows different treatment if the other agent asks for feedback or when their feedback is incorporated for decision purposes. Liu et al. go a step further than Buchegger et al. at this point, because they do not automatically publish recommendations, but evaluate the other agent and send back a recommendation only with a certain probability, according to the state of the asking agent. In Buchegger's approach, recommendations are published automatically and all agents have access. Their incentives are not as clear cut as with the other authors but a close examination shows that Buchegger uses a very precise estimation on how honest the provider of information is and can therefore detect false reports very quickly and refrain from conducting business with the concerning agent. That makes the stored recommendations (direct and indirect) more valuable and therefore sets an incentive to behave properly.

Finally in 2.4, we show *Jurca and Faltings* achieve to incorporate both: elicitation of honest feedback and setting incentives to provide feedback by payments. The authors introduce R-Agents which are broker agents. They serve as a mediator who collect feedback and sell it to other agents. After the transaction with the agent which the other agent had bought feedback about, it can sell that information to the R-Agent again. Additionally, the submitted reports are checked if they are honest or not and only paid for if they appear honest.

Table 1. Summary of Reputation Mechanisms

	Liu and Issarny [9]	Jøsang and Ismail [10]	Buchegger and Boudec [11]	Jurca and Faltings [12]
Ratings	Three different kinds: RRep, SRep and ORep	Reputation rating r_t^x (from X about T)	Two kinds: Reputation rating $R_{i,j}$ and Trust rating $T_{i,j}$ (from i about j)	Reputation rating
Elicitation of honest feedback	Judging feedback upon trust rating of the provider and estimating the probability of such behavior with the beta reputation.	Considering the opinion about the provider of information in order to discount the feedback accordingly.	Deviation test checks if the feedback is considered honest.	R-Agents check the behavior of the concerning agent in the following round.
Incentives	Rating the agents and establishing five states of recommenders; information is shared according to those with different probabilities favoring active, honest recommenders → incentives through meta-reputation.	No clear incentives.	Incentives through meta reputation ratings but not fully implemented (as done by Liu and Issarny).	Payments if report is considered honest.

The table 1 summarizes the main characteristics of each of the reputation mechanisms. Summarizing, we can state that three main types of incentives could be identified: (1) The honest evaluator gets more information than the dishonest evaluator, (2) the influence of each rating bases on the evaluator's behavior before or (3) the evaluator is paid for accurate evaluations.

4   Conclusion and Future Work

Each of the four approaches that were presented here stresses a very important aspect which should be considered in a "perfect" reputation mechanism. From Liu and Issarny we have to take into account the three ratings. From Jøsang and Ismail we would incorporate the three different kinds of discounting feedback in order to rate feedback precisely according to the trustworthiness of the recommender and our opinion about the target agent. Buchegger and Boudec would contribute a factor that allows an estimation of how stable a target agent's behavior is. This is important for discounting of feedback and taking behavior changes into account.

Finally, Jurca and Faltings provide the incentive setting payment mechanism that rewards submission of honest feedback. By combining the strengths of all the approaches, one could design a reputation mechanism that elicits feedback successfully and eliminates untrustworthy behavior through a very precise detection of it.

Further work has been carried out by many involved researchers. Especially the work of Jurca and Faltings has been improved by going beyond the ideas considered in this paper leading to more sophisticated incentive frameworks [13–17].

The problems, which still arise in reputation mechanisms are manifold and cannot be solved by the reputation mechanism alone. Future work should take the following aspects into account:

Since detection of false feedback is not always accurate, it should be considered whether liars should be punished or not. However, the system might sometimes punish even truthful agents e.g. if a trustor experienced a defection but the trustee has never defect before and does not defect in the consecutive round. The system will identify the truthful feedback most likely as untrustworthy and punish the "liar". Hence, the system would discourage giving feedback because there is a small probability that even truthful reporting is punished. This case is especially relevant if the reporting agent is not payed but rated with a trust rating as in sections 2.1 and 2.3. Another problem in such reputation mechanisms is connected to the identity of the participants. In an anonymous system we can never be sure that a participant with a very bad reputation, who exploited the system by defecting, starts over by re-entering the system with a "fresh identity". A further problem that cannot be addressed by the reputation mechanism itself but must be solved by other institutions is collusion. Agents could try to achieve a better reputation value by making minimal transactions and rate each other positively in order to establish a high reputation they can exploit in the following interactions. One could imagine to weigh the feedback according to the amount of money transferred within the transaction. Still, collusion can take place and has to be inhibited by independent institutions.

This work itself should be extended to a reputation incentive framework in future. Such a framework could help reputation system designers to identify incentives in dependence of the system's context. In order to substantiate this framework, the incentive mechanisms have to be applied in different (simulated) environments.

References

1. Dellarocas, C.: Reputation mechanisms. In: Handbook on Economics and Information Systems (2006)
2. König, S., Hudert, S., Eymann, T., Paolucci, M.: Towards reputation enhanced electronic negotiations for service oriented computing. In: Proceedings of the CEC/EEE 2008, Washington, DC, pp. 285–292 (2008)
3. Artz, D., Gil, Y.: A survey of trust in computer science and the semantic web. Web Semant. 5(2), 58–71 (2007)
4. Balke, T., König, S., Eymann, T.: A survey on reputation systems for artifcial societies. University of Bayreuth, Bayreuther Arbeitspapiere zur Wirtschaftsinformatik 46 (October 2009)
5. Josang, A., Ismail, R., Boyd, C.: A survey of trust and reputation systems for online service provision. Decision Support Systems 43(2), 618–644 (2007)
6. Marti, S., Garcia-Molina, H.: Taxonomy of trust: categorizing p2p reputation systems. Computer Networks 50(4), 472–484 (2006)
7. Resnick, P., Kuwabara, K., Zeckhauser, R., Friedman, E.: Reputation systems. ACM Commun. 43(12), 45–48 (2000)
8. Sabater, J., Sierra, C.: Review on computational trust and reputation models. Artif. Intell. Rev. 24(1), 33–60 (2005)
9. Liu, J., Issarny, V.: An incentive compatible reputation mechanism for ubiquitous computing environments. International Journal of Information Security 6(5), 297–311 (2006)
10. Josang, A., Ismail, R.: The beta reputation system. In: Proceedings of the 15th Bled Electronic Commerce Conference (2002)
11. Buchegger, S., Boudec, J.L.: A robust reputation system for P2P and mobile ad-hoc networks. In: Proceedings of the Second Workshop on the Economics of Peer-to-Peer Systems (2004)
12. Jurca, R., Faltings, B.: An incentive compatible reputation mechanism. In: Proceedings of the IEEE Conference on E-Commerce, pp. 285–292 (2003)
13. Jurca, R.: Obtaining reliable feedback for sanctioning reputation mechanisms. Journal of Artificial Intelligence Research (JAIR) 29, 391–419 (2007)
14. Jurca, R.: Truthful reputation mechanisms for online systems. PhD, Ecole Polytechnique Federale de Lausanne (2007)
15. Jurca, R., Faltings, B.: Incentives for expressing opinions in online polls. In: Procedings of the 9th ACM Conference on Electronic Commerce, pp. 119–128. ACM, Chicago (2008)
16. Jurca, R., Faltings, B.: Minimum payments that reward honest reputation feedback. In: Proceedings of the 7th ACM Conference on Electronic Commerce, pp. 190–199. ACM, New York (2006)
17. Jurca, R., Faltings, B.: Robust Incentive-Compatible, Feedback Payments, pp. 204–218 (2007)

Normative Deliberation in Graded BDI Agents

Natalia Criado, Estefania Argente, and Vicent Botti

Departamento de Sistemas Informáticos y Computación
Universidad Politécnica de Valencia
Camino de Vera s/n. 46022 Valencia (Spain)
{ncriado,eargente,vbotti}@dsic.upv.es

Abstract. Norms have been employed as a coordination mechanism for Open MAS, but to become effective, they must be internalized by agents; i.e. these agents must be able to accept norms while maintaining their autonomy. Nevertheless, traditional BDI agent architectures only represent beliefs, intentions and desires. In this paper, the multi-context BDI agent architecture has been extended with a recognition context and a normative context in order to allow agents to acquire norms from their environment and consider norms in their decisions.

1 Introduction

Open Multi-agent Systems (MAS) are characterised by a high uncertainty and limited trust in their performance [1], since they are formed by heterogeneous and autonomous agents which are situated in a dynamic environment. For these reasons, Open MAS require mechanisms which guide agent behaviours and control the system performance. *Normative multi-agent systems* (NMAS) have been proposed as a solution to these needs [2]. Norms, to become effective as a coordination mechanism, must be recognised as norms by agents. In addition, agents must be able to accept norms while maintaining their autonomy [3].

This work has been motivated by the fact that proposals on agent architectures which support normative reasoning ([4,5]) do not consider norms as dynamic objects which may be acquired and recognised by agents. On the contrary, these proposals consider norms as static constraints that are hard-wired on agent architectures. Thus, agents obey blindly norms since they are not autonomous for making a decision about norm compliance.

Therefore, there is a need to develop normative autonomous agents capable of reasoning about norms; i.e. recognising norms, evaluating the effect of norms and their consequences and taking a decision about norm compliance [6]. These reasoning capabilities require pragmatic decision making procedures rather than obeying fixed theories or rules. Traditionally, this complex issue has been addressed by adapting cognitive theories to the MAS field [7]. For this reason, in this paper we propose an extension of the BDI agent architecture, in particular the multi-context graded BDI architecture [8], with recognition and normative reasoning capabilities in order to allow agents to consider norms in their decision making process. The fact that mental attitudes of agents are graded will

J. Dix and C. Witteveen (Eds.): MATES 2010, LNAI 6251, pp. 52–63, 2010.

not only make the model semantics richer, but it will also help agents to make better decisions. In this sense, it allows them to reason in uncertain and dynamic environments which are controlled by norms.

Along this paper a running example scenario of the management of water in a basin, named m-Water [9], is employed. The m-Water problem addresses scenarios where there are conflicts over different basin waters, in many cases, caused by potential or actual water scarcity. This problem is approached by building an Open MAS that is designed as a regulated environment (i.e. a NMAS) where autonomous agents are the water users in a closed basin. In particular, our case study is formed by an *irrigator* which belongs to an *irrigation community*. This community represents an organization which acts on behalf of its members by defending their rights and interests. However, each community can impose some norms or restrictions to its members. This case study illustrates how a concrete *irrigator* agent makes a decision between his own motivations and the norms imposed by his *irrigation community*.

This paper is structured as follows: first the background of the multi-context BDI proposal is summarised. Section 3 explains our conceptual model of norms. Next, the proposed BDI architecture is described in Section 4. This proposal has also been evaluated experimentally in Section 5. Finally, this work is concluded with a discussion of related works.

2   Background: Multi-context BDI

A multi-context system [10] is defined as a set of interconnected units $\langle \{u_i\}_{i \in I}, \Delta \rangle$. Each unit $u_i \in \{u_i\}_{i \in I}$ is a tuple $\langle L_i, A_i, \Delta_i \rangle$, where L_i, A_i and Δ_i are the language, axioms and inference rules defining the logic of each unit, respectively. Δ is the set of bridge rules between the units; i.e. inference rules whose premises and conclusions belong to different contexts; e.g. $u_1 : \phi, u_2 : \psi \Rightarrow u_3 : \theta$.

A general BDI agent is defined as a multi-context agent architecture in [8]. It is mainly formed by (Figure 1 grey units): *mental* units to characterize beliefs, intentions and desires; and *functional* units for planning and communication.

2.1   BDI Contexts

In particular, the BDI architecture presented in [8] brings support to graded mental propositions. The main idea beyond this work is to employ a weight to represent the certainty or desirability degree of a mental proposition. Next, mental contexts are described:

- *Belief Context (BC)*. It is formed by propositions belonging to the BC-Logic [8]; i.e. logic propositions such as $(B\gamma, \delta) : \delta \in [0, 1]$; where $B\gamma$ represents a belief about proposition γ of an agent, $\gamma \in \mathcal{L}_{\mathcal{DL}}$ is a dynamic logic [11] proposition and δ represents the certainty degree associated to this belief.
- *Desire Context (DC)*. It is formed by propositions belonging to the DC-Logic [8]; i.e. logic propositions such as $(D^*\gamma, \delta) : \delta \in [0, 1]$; where $D \gamma$ represents a desire about proposition $\gamma \in \mathcal{L}_{\mathcal{DL}}$ of an agent; δ represents the desirability

degree; $* \in \{+, -\}$ represents positive desires and negative desires, respectively. Thus, degrees of positive or negative desires allow setting different levels of preference or rejection.
– *Intention Context (IC).* It is formed by propositions belonging to the IC-Logic [8]; i.e. logic propositions such as $(I\gamma, \delta) : \delta \in [0, 1]$; where $I\gamma$ represents an intention about proposition $\gamma \in \mathcal{L}_{\mathcal{DL}}$ of an agent and δ is the certainty degree assigned to this intention.

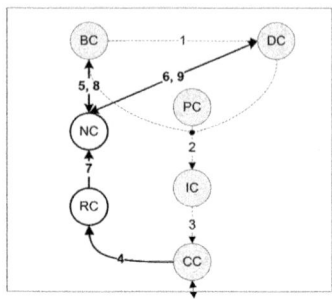

Fig. 1. Multi-Context BDI Architecture is formed by the grey contexts and dash lines (bridge rules). The normative extensions are the white contexts and bold bridge rules.

Functional units have been also defined [8]: the *Planner Context* (PC) allows agents to decide the intended set of actions, according to their desires; and the *Communication Context* (CC) communicates agents with their environment.

In the m-Water scenario, the *irrigator* agent represents a farmer who wants to pick up high quality vegetables. Thus, he has two different irrigation possibilities: to irrigate all of his cultivation daily or to irrigate only a half of his cultivation. Logically, he believes that it is more probable to obtain a good crop if all his land is irrigated:
$((B[fullIrrigation]highQuality, 0.75)$ and $(B[halfIrrigation]highQuality, 0.5)$.
In addition, the irrigator agent beliefs that there is a rather possibility of drought according to the meteorological conditions, i.e. $(B\ drought, 0.6)$. He also wants to obtain high quality vegetables from his plantation: $(D^{+}highQuality, 1)$; and he does not desire to be fined: $(D^{-}payFine, 0.8)$. Finally, he has two different cultivation plans: one which contains the full irrigation action, i.e. $plan(fullIrrigation)$; and another which performs the action corresponding to the irrigation of a half of his cultivation, i.e. $plan(halfIrrigation)$.

2.2 Bridge Rules

Several bridge rules have been defined in the existing literature in order to determine different types of BDI agents. Next, only those bridge rules which have an impact on the normative reasoning process are described.

Deriving Concrete Desires. This bridge rule allows abstract or generic desires to be concreted into more realistic ones according to the agent beliefs (Figure 1 Rule 1):

$$DC : (D^*\varphi, \delta_\varphi), BD : (B[\alpha]\varphi, \delta_\phi) \Rightarrow DC : (D^*[\alpha]\varphi, f_D(\delta_\varphi, \delta_\phi)) \tag{1}$$

More concretely, generic agent desires $(D^*\varphi, \delta_\varphi)$ derive more realistic desires $(D^*[\alpha]\varphi, f_D(\delta_\varphi, \delta_\phi))$; taking into account the existence of actions that allow them to be reached $(B[\alpha]\varphi, \delta_\phi)$. Thus, the preference degree of the concrete desire relies on the original desirability (δ_φ) and the possibility of achieving it by means of action α (δ_ϕ). This is calculated by f_D function; if we define it as the product of these two values we obtain the expected satisfaction or disgust value.

In the case of the *irrigator* agent, he refines his abstract desires into more realistic ones according to his beliefs:

$$DC : (D^+ highQuality, 1), BC : (B [fullIrrigation]highQuality, 0.75) \Rightarrow$$
$$DC : (D^+ [fullIrrigation]highQuality, 0.75)$$

$$DC : (D^+ highQuality, 1), BC : (B [halfIrrigation]highQuality, 0.5) \Rightarrow$$
$$DC : (D^+ [halfIrrigation]highQuality, 0.5)$$

Deriving Agent Intentions From Positive Desires. The set of preferred formulas which are reachable by some existing plan will derive the intended formulas of the agent (Figure 1 Rule 2):

$$DC : (D^+[\alpha]\varphi, \delta), DC : (D^+\alpha, \delta_\alpha^+), DC : (D^-\alpha, \delta_\alpha^-), PC : plan(\Omega), \alpha \in \Omega,$$

$$DC : (D^-[\alpha]\psi_1, \delta_{\psi_1}), ..., DC : (D^-[\alpha]\psi_n\delta_{\psi_n}), (\delta + \delta_\alpha^+) \geq (\sum_{k=1}^{n} \delta_{\psi_k + \delta_\alpha^-}) \tag{2}$$

$$\Rightarrow (IC : (I[\alpha]\varphi, f_I(\delta + \delta_\alpha^+, \sum_{k=1}^{n} \delta_{\psi_k} + \delta_\alpha^-))$$

In particular, those positive desires $(D^+[\alpha]\varphi, \delta)$ which can be achieved by an action α belonging to a plan $(plan(\Omega))$ will generate a new intention $(I[\alpha]\varphi, f_I(\delta + \delta_\alpha^+, \sum_{k=1}^{n} \delta_{\psi_k} + \delta_\alpha^-))$ if the desirability degree of both the action and the state $(\delta + \delta_\alpha^+)$ is greater than the sum of the negative effects of the action $(\sum_{k=1}^{n} \delta_{\psi_k} + \delta_\alpha^-)$. Finally, f_I is a function that combines both positive and negative effects of an action; in this case it is defined as: $f_I(\delta^+, \delta^-) = min(max(0, \delta^+ - \delta^-), 1)$

In the m-Water scenario, the derived specific desires allow the *irrigator* agent to determine which actions will be intended according to the existing plans:

$$DC : (D^+ [fullIrrigation]highQuality, 0.75), PC : plan(fullIrrigation), 0.75 > 0 \Rightarrow$$
$$IC : (I[fullIrrigation]highQuality, 0.75)$$

$$DC : (D^+ [halfIrrigation]highQuality, 0.5), PC : plan(halfIrrigation), 0.5 > 0 \Rightarrow$$
$$IC : (I[halfIrrigation]highQuality, 0.5)$$

Deriving Actions From Intentions. Finally, that intention which has the maximum degree $(I[\alpha]\varphi, \delta_{max})$ will define the next action to be performed by the agent $(act(\alpha))$ (Figure 1 Rule 3):

$$IC : (I[\alpha]\varphi, \delta_{max}) \Rightarrow CC : act(\alpha) \tag{3}$$

In the m-Water scenario, the *irrigator* agent will perform the most intended action: $IC : (I[fullIrrigation]highQuality, 0.75) \Rightarrow CC : (act(fullIrrigation))$

3   Normative Model Proposal

In this section we propose a model of norms for NMAS. This model classifies norms into two categories: *Constitutive* and *Deontic* norms. *Constitutive* norms allow giving an abstract meaning to facts, environmental elements, etc. *Deontic* norms define a deontic control over an action or a state of affairs. They also allow defining the enforcing mechanisms in terms of punishments and rewards carried out by representative agents of the NMAS. Thus, *deontic norms* define a practical connection between a regulation and its consequences.

Definition 1 (Normative Context). *The set of norms (N) of a NMAS is defined as:* $N = N_{Constitutive} \cup N_{Deontic}$

Definition 2 (Constitutive Norm). *A constitutive norm* $n_c \in N_{Constitutive}$ *is defined as* $n_c = \langle A, E, \alpha \rightarrow \gamma \rangle$ *where:*

- *A, E are wff that determine the norm validity period, i.e. they define the activation and expiration conditions, respectively;*
- $\alpha \rightarrow \gamma$ *is the norm condition where* α *represents a concept or set of basic concepts and* γ *represents the new abstract concept defined by the norm;*

Definition 3 (Deontic Norm). *A deontic norm* $n_d \in N_{Deontic}$ *is defined as* $n_d = \langle D, A, E, C, S, R \rangle$ *where:*

- $D \in \{Obligation, Prohibition\}$;
- *A, E are wff that determine the norm validity period;*
- *C is a logic formula that represents the normative goal or action that must be carried out in case of obligations, or that must be avoided in case of prohibition norms.*
- *S, R are expressions which describe the actions (sanctions S and rewards R) that will be carried out in case of norm violation or fulfillment, respectively. They are enforcement mechanisms employed for persuading agents to fulfill norms.*

This model uses a closed world assumption where everything is considered as permitted by default. Therefore, permissions are not considered in this paper, since they can be defined as normative operators that invalidate the activation of an obligation or prohibition.

In the m-Water scenario, the *irrigator* agent is affected by norms as a consequence of being a member of an irrigator community. In this example the community forbids agents to irrigate all their cultivation if a drought state has been declared in this area, so any agent which violates this norm will be sanctioned by paying a fine. Thus, the following deontic norm is defined:

$$\langle Prohibition, drought, -, fullIrrigation, payFine, - \rangle$$

Next section illustrates our Normative BDI architecture. It enables the definition of agents with capabilities for acquiring norms belonging to the proposed normative model and mechanisms for considering norms in their reasoning processes.

4   Normative BDI Architecture

Taking as a reference the graded BDI agent architecture (see Section 2), our proposal consists in extending it by adding new units and bridge rules in order to allow agents to make decisions with norms.

The work described in [12] analyses the psychological architecture subserving norms, among other contributions. This architecture is formed by two closely linked innate mechanisms: one responsible for norm acquisition, which is responsible for identifying norm implicating behaviour and inferring the content of that norm; and the other in charge of norm implementation, which maintains a database of norms and generates motivations to comply with those norms. Thus, the norm acceptance problem deals with: norm recognition and norm decision [3]. In this sense, norms are not previously implemented on agents' minds, but agents are able to acquire new norms and deliberate about norm compliance autonomously. This fact allows agent societies to generate and acquire new norms in response to changes in the dynamic environment. Accordingly, our proposal consists in extending the general BDI multi-context agent architecture by adding two functional contexts (Figure 1, white units): the *Recognition Context* (RC), which is responsible for the norm identification process; and the *Normative Context* (NC), which allows agents to consider norms in their decision making processes. In this sense, norms affect agents in two manners: i) firstly, when a norm is recognised and accepted then it is considered in order to define new plans; and ii) when accepted norms are active then their instances are employed for selecting the most suitable plan that complies with norms. This paper tackles with this last effect of norms.

4.1   Recognition Context (RC)

Basically, the norm decision process starts when the RC derives a new norm through analysing its environment. The RC context receives the environmental facts, both observed and communicated, and identifies the set of norms which control the agent environment. As argued in [5], the inherent dynamical and uncertain features of open systems makes mandatory for agents to be capable of recognising norms autonomously. The definition of this module is beyond the scope of this paper. Thus, for this paper it will be considered as a *black box* which receives cues for detecting norms as input and generates norms as output.

This context is formed by expressions which are defined as $(RC\ \alpha, \delta)$; where α is a first order formula which represents a norm belonging to our normative model (described in the previous section). On the other hand, $\delta \in [0, 1]$ is the certainty degree ascribed to the recognised norm. These recognised abstract norms are translated into a set of inference rules included into the NC.

In the m-Water scenario, once the *irrigator* becomes a member of the community, he is informed by a representative about norms which affect him. Thus, the agent assigns the maximum certainty degree to the norm recognition:

$$(RC\ \langle Prohibition, drought, -, fullIrrigation, payFine, -\rangle, 1)$$

4.2   Normative Context (NC)

In our approach norms are not static constraints implemented on agents. On the contrary, agents are able to acquire and accept norms dynamically in an autonomous way. Thus, performance of the NC is: i) mental contexts inject formulas inside the NC; ii) the NC carries out an inference process in order to reason about norms considering the current mental state; and iii) BDI units are modified according to the new mental propositions derived from norms.

The NC is formed by expressions like $\lceil \gamma \rceil$; where γ is a first-order logic formula, an inference rule, which relates mental attitudes of an agent. The expression $\lceil \gamma \rceil$ means that γ is embedded in the normative context as a term; i.e. modal logic expressions are modelled as first order theories. γ corresponds to a translated norm from the RC.

NC logic consists of the axiom schema K, closure under implication, together with the consistency axiom. Therefore, contradictory norms are allowed; i.e. it is possible to define $\lceil \gamma \rceil \wedge \lceil \neg \gamma \rceil$. This fact is interesting for our work since agents are usually controlled by conflicting norms addressed at the different roles played by the agent or there may be a conflict among agent goals and norms. However, contradictory predicates such as $\lceil \gamma \rceil \wedge \neg \lceil \gamma \rceil$ are not allowed, i.e. expressions that claim that certain norm exists and not exists are not allowed.

4.3   Normative Bridge Rules

Updating the RC Rule. Agent observations and communications which it perceives from its environment $(input(\beta))$ are included into the RC as a new term or theory $(\lceil input(\beta) \rceil)$ (see Figure 1 Rule 4):

$$CC : input(\beta) \Rightarrow RC : \lceil input(\beta) \rceil \tag{4}$$

Updating the NC Rules. Both agent desires and beliefs (γ) are included into the normative context as first order formulas $\lceil \gamma \rceil$ in order to determine when a norm is active (Figure 1 Rules 5 and 6):

$$BC : \gamma \Rightarrow NC : \lceil \gamma \rceil \tag{5}$$

$$DC : \gamma \Rightarrow NC : \lceil \gamma \rceil \tag{6}$$

Norm Transformation Rule. Inside the recognition unit new norms are acquired. Those abstract recognised norms $(RC\ \alpha, \delta_\alpha)$ are transformed into an inference rule $(\varphi \to \psi)$ (see Figure 1 Rule 7). The definition of this inference rule depends on the concrete type of norm which is being translated. Next, bridge rules for translating each type of norm are described:

– *Constitutive Norm Transformation Rule:*

$$RC : (RC \langle count - as, A, E, \alpha \to \gamma \rangle, \delta_{nr}) \Rightarrow$$
$$NC : \lceil (B\ A, \delta_A) \wedge (B \neg E, \delta_E) \wedge (\Phi\ \alpha, \delta_\alpha) \to (\Phi\ \gamma, f(\delta_\alpha, f_{activation}(\delta_A, \delta_E, \delta_{nr}))) \rceil$$

where $\Phi \in \{B, D^+, D^-\}$

If an agent considers that the norm is currently active $((B\ A, \delta_A) \wedge (B\neg E, \delta_E))$ and the basic fact α, affected by the constitutive norm, is an agent belief or desire $(\Phi\alpha, \delta_\alpha)$ then a new belief or desire will be inferred corresponding to the new abstract fact, i.e. $(\Phi\gamma, f(\delta_\alpha, f_{activation}(\delta_A, \delta_E, \delta_{nr})))$ where $f_{activation}$ is a function that combines the belief degrees related to the norm conditions $(\delta_A$ and $\delta_E)$ and the certainty degree of the norm (δ_{nr}). The certainty degree, which is related to the norm activation, together with the certainty or desirability degree assigned to the basic fact (δ_α) are employed by the function f in order to assign a degree to the new mental proposition γ. The concrete definition of both $f_{activation}$ and f functions is problem dependent and beyond the scope of this paper.

– *Deontic Norm Transformation Rule*: a characteristic feature of norm internalization is that norms become part of the goals of the agent. In this sense, the process of norm internalization has been defined in [7] as a dynamic relation between the norms and desires. Accordingly, the bridge rule for transforming deontic norms is defined as follows:

$$RC : (RC\ \langle D, A, E, C, S, R\rangle, \delta_{nr}) \Rightarrow$$
$$NC : \lceil (B\ A, \delta_A) \wedge (B\neg E, \delta_E) \wedge (D^*C, \delta_C) \wedge (D^-S, \delta_S) \wedge (D^+R, \delta_R) \rightarrow$$
$$(D^*C, f(f_{compliance}(\delta_C, \delta_S, \delta_R), f_{activation}(\delta_A, \delta_E, \delta_{nr}))) \rceil$$

Basically, a deontic norm is translated by this bridge rule into an inference rule which adds a new desire (D^*C) if the norm is active according to the current state. $* \in \{+, -\}$ is the sign ascribed to the new desire inferred from the norm. In case of obligation norms a positive desire of achieving the norm condition is inferred. On the contrary, a prohibition is transformed into an inference rule which asserts a negative desire if the norm is active. The degree of the new desire is defined as $f(f_{compliance}(\delta_C, \delta_S, \delta_R), f_{activation}(\delta_A, \delta_E, \delta_{nr}))$ where f is a function that combines the certainty degrees assigned to norm activation $(f_{activation})$ and the desirability of norm compliance assigned to the norm compliance function $(f_{compliance})$. In this case, $f_{compliance}$ takes as input parameters the desirability of the norm condition (δ_C) and the degrees assigned by the agent to the sanction (D^-S, δ_S) and reward (D^+R, δ_R). This function can implement different strategies for norm compliance, such as *egoism*, *fearful* and so on. However, in [13] the definition of different strategies for norm compliance is illustrated.

In the m-Water case-study, once the norm has been recognised by the RC it is transformed into an inference rule inside the NC (Bridge Rule 7):

$$RC : (RC\ \langle Prohibition, drought, -, fullIrrigation, payFine, -\rangle, 1) \Rightarrow$$
$$NC : \lceil (B\ drought, 0.6) \wedge (D^- payFine, 0.8) \rightarrow (D^- fullIrrigation, 0.48) \rceil$$

On the one hand, the norm activation function takes as input the certainty value assigned to the occurrence of the norm activation condition (0.6) and the confidence value assigned to the norm recognition (1). In this example, $f_{activation}$ has been implemented as the product of its not null parameters:

$$f_{activation}(\delta_A, \delta_E, \delta_{nr}) = \delta_A \times \delta_E \times \delta_{nr} = 0.6$$

On the other hand, the $f_{compliance}$ function only considers the undesirability of the sanction (0.8) since there is not any desire related to the norm condition and no reward has been defined by the norm. $f_{compliance}$ has been also defined here as the product of its not null parameters:

$$f_{compliance}(\delta_C, \delta_S, \delta_R) = \delta_C \times \delta_S \times \delta_R = 0.8$$

Finally, these two values are combined by f function which has been implemented as the product of both values. Thus, inside the NC a new desire derived from the prohibition norm is inferred:

$$NC : \lceil (D^- fullIrrigation, 0.48) \rceil$$

Updating Mental Context Rules. After performing the inference process for creating new beliefs ($\lceil (B\ \gamma, \delta) \rceil$) and desires ($\lceil (D^*\ \gamma, \delta) \rceil$) derived from norm application, the normative context must update mental contexts (Figure 1 Rules 8 and 9):

$$NC : \lceil (B\ \gamma, \delta) \rceil, \delta > \delta_{thres} \Rightarrow B : (B\ \gamma, \delta) \tag{7}$$

$$NC : \lceil (D^*\ \gamma, \delta) \rceil, \delta > \delta_{thres} \Rightarrow D : (D^* \gamma, \delta) \tag{8}$$

In order to avoid the propagation of insignificant terms, only those new terms whose degree exceeds δ_{thres} will be transformed into mental objects. The definition of this threshold is also problem dependent.

In the m-Water scenario, the inferred normative desire is inserted into the DC (Bridge Rule 9), being $\delta_{threshold} = 0.4$:

$$NC : \lceil (D^- fullIrrigation, 0.48) \rceil \wedge 0.48 > \delta_{thres} \Rightarrow DC : (D^- fullIrrigation, 0.48)$$

Normative Decision Making. In our case-study, the IC is updated through Bridge Rule 2 creating a new intention whose intentionality has been reduced (0.75 − 0.48) since the action has a negative desire:

$$DC : (D^+ [fullIrrigation]highQuality, 0.75), DC : (D^- fullIrrigation, 0.48),$$
$$PC : plan(fullIrrigation), 0.75 > 0.48 \Rightarrow IC : (I[fullIrrigation]highQuality, 0.27)$$

Finally, the intention update implies the modification of the agent behaviour. More concretely, the agent has two different intentions: $((I[halfIrrigation]highQuality, 0.6)$ and $(I[fullIrrigation]highQuality, 0.27))$. According to Bridge Rule 3, the most intended action will be carried out. Thus, the agent fulfils the norms imposed by its community and changes its irrigation policy. As a result, he has to irrigate half of his land so as to avoid being fined.

To provide an evaluation of this proposal, the next section details a set of experimentations which have been carried out.

5   Case Study Execution

In order to provide an evaluation of the proposal a set of simulations of the case-study have been carried out. These simulations consist of a scenario formed by a set of *irrigator* agents (A) which are in a drought situation. More concretely, each agent needs a fixed Daily Need of Water $(DNW : A \to \mathbb{N})$ along its Cultivation Period $(CP : A \to \mathbb{N})$. The total amount of Available Water (AW), the water needs and cultivation periods are assigned to agents randomly in each simulation. In each iteration (i.e. each day), agents should decide their irrigation policy; i.e. they must choose to irrigate all their cultivation or a half of it, according to the amount of water available in the community.

For each simulation, the average satisfaction of the irrigator agents has been measured with respect to the seriousness of the drought. Individual Daily Satisfaction of an agent $(IDS : A \times \mathbb{N} \to [-1,1])$ is calculated as the relationship among the amount of water employed for Irrigating $(I : A \times \mathbb{N} \to \mathbb{N})$ this day and the required amount of water. However, the situations in which there is not water for irrigating are penalised by assigning a value of -1 to individual satisfaction. The seriousness (Se) of the drought is calculated as one minus the quotient among the available amount of water and the total amount of water which is required. Finally, the average satisfaction (S) of agents belonging to the irrigation community depends on the individual satisfactions of agents, their cultivation periods and the total amount of available water.

$$IDS(a,d) = \begin{cases} undefined & \text{if } d > CP(a) \\ -1 & \text{if } I(a,d) = 0 \\ \frac{I(a,d)}{DNW(a)} & \text{otherwise} \end{cases} \qquad Se = 1 - \frac{AW}{\sum_{a \in A} DNW(a) \times CP(a)}$$

$$S = \frac{\sum_{a \in A} \frac{\sum_{d=1}^{CP(a)} IDS(a,d)}{CP(a)}}{AW}$$

In each experimentation, *irrigator communities* are formed by agents which belong to only one of these three categories: i) classic BDI agents, which are *non-normative* and they always irrigate all their cultivation if there is enough water; ii) *normative* agents, which always irrigate a half of their plantation since there is a drought situation; and iii) *graded normative* agents which consider how restrictive the situation is; i.e. they decide to irrigate a half of their cultivation if there is a serious drought (the amount of required water is more than twice the available amount).

Figure 2 shows the results obtained in the experimentations, comparing the seriousness of the drought situation (Se) and the average satisfaction (S) of agents belonging to the irrigation community. In communities formed by non-normative agents there is not an equal employment of resources (i.e. they try to irrigate all their land if there is enough water), so the satisfaction level decreases linearly as the seriousness increases. In addition, in those societies formed by normative agents which do not represent the drought state as a graded proposition there is an underutilization of resources when the situation is not very critical. They obey norms automatically and, as a consequence, they do never irrigate all their cultivation even if there is enough water. Finally, societies formed by graded normative agents obtain better satisfaction results in general, since agents are able to apply restriction policies only when the situation is highly critical. In light drought situations, in which there is a 20% of water shortage, an egoist

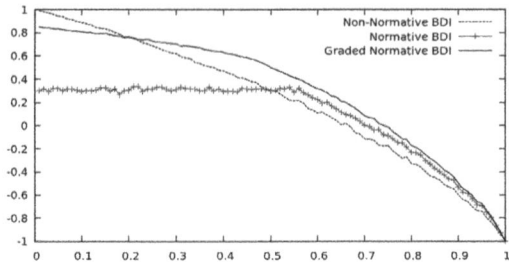

Fig. 2. Average agent satisfaction S (vertical axis) with respect to the seriousness of the drought situation Se (horizontal axis)

employment of resources (i.e. the non-normative agent behaviour) can achieve a better level of satisfaction for the whole society. However, when the water shortage exceeds the 20% societies formed by graded BDI agents achieve better satisfaction levels.

6   Discussion

Regarding recent works on normative reasoning, the BOID architecture [4] represents obligations as mental attributes and analyses the relationship and influence of such obligations on agent believes, desires and intentions. This approach is very similar to the work proposed here. However, our approach overlaps the main drawbacks of the BOID proposal in different ways: i) our normative model does not only consider obligation norms but it gives support to constitutive and deontic norms; ii) it employs graded BDI logics for representing mental attitudes, which allows agents to face with uncertain and conflicting mental states; and iii) it considers norms as dynamic entities that agents should acquire from their environment. In relation with this last feature, the EMIL proposal [5], which has developed a framework for autonomous norm recognition, might be employed for complementing the RC component of our normative BDI architecture. Thus, agents would be able to acquire new norms by observing the behaviour of other agents which are situated in their environments. The main advantage of our proposal with respect to EMIL is that our agent architecture allows agents to decide based on their own motivations and interests whether to comply the norms or not. On the contrary, EMIL agents obey all recognised norms automatically by deriving new normative goals.

In this paper, the multi-context BDI agent architecture is extended with a recognition and a normative context in order to allow agents to acquire new norms from their environment and consider them in their decision making process. The fact that mental attitudes of agents are quantified allows them to reason in open environments which are controlled by norms. In this sense, graded modalities allow agents to represent uncertain knowledge about the current state of the world. Moreover, graded intentions and desires enable agents to make decisions according to their satisfaction criterion. This is specially interesting when designing normative agents whose behaviour can be affected by conflicting norms. Thus, the desirability degrees of desires and intentions allow agents to decide between norm violation or fulfilment according to their priorities. As future work we plan to work on carrying out an experimental analysis of different norm compliance strategies. Finally, we will continue by analysing the effect of norms on the definition of feasible plans for the achievement of the agent's goals.

Acknowledgments

This work was partially supported by the Spanish government under grants CONSOLIDER-INGENIO 2010 CSD2007-00022, TIN2009-13839-C03-01 and TIN2008-04446 and by the FPU grant AP-2007-01256 awarded to N. Criado.

References

1. Artikis, A., Pitt, J.: A formal model of open agent societies. In: AGENTS, pp. 192–193. ACM, New York (2001)
2. Boella, G., Torre, L., Verhagen, H.: Introduction to the special issue on normative multiagent systems. Auton. Agents Multi-Agent Syst. 17(1), 1–10 (2008)
3. Conte, R., Castelfranchi, C., Dignum, F.: Autonomous norm acceptance. In: Rao, A.S., Singh, M.P., Müller, J.P. (eds.) ATAL 1998. LNCS (LNAI), vol. 1555, pp. 99–112. Springer, Heidelberg (1999)
4. Broersen, J., Dastani, M., Hulstijn, J., Huang, Z., van der Torre, L.: The boid architecture - conflicts between beliefs, obligations, intentions and desires. In: AAMAS, pp. 9–16. ACM Press, New York (2001)
5. Andrighetto, G., Campenní, M., Cecconi, F., Conte, R.: How agents find out norms: A simulation based model of norm innovation. In: NORMAS, pp. 16–30 (2008)
6. Castelfranchi, C.: Prescribed mental attitudes in goal-adoption and norm-adoption. Artif. Intell. Law 7(1), 37–50 (1999)
7. Conte, R., Andrighetto, G., Campennì, M.: On norm internalization. a position paper. In: EUMAS, pp. 1–13 (2010)
8. Casali, A., Godo, L., Sierra, C.: A logical framework to represent and reason about graded preferences and intentions. In: K.R. (ed.) KR, pp. 27–37. AAAI Press, Menlo Park (2008)
9. Botti, V., Garrido, A., Giret, A., Noriega, P.: Managing water demand as a regulated open mas. In: COIN, pp. 1–10 (2009)
10. Giunchiglia, F., Serafini, L.: Multilanguage hierarchical logics, or: How we can do without modal logics. Artificial Intelligence 65(1), 29–70 (1994)
11. Meyer, J.: Dynamic logic for reasoning about actions and agents. In: Logic-Based Artificial Intelligence, pp. 281–311. Kluwer Academic Publishers, Dordrecht (2000)
12. Sripada, C., Stich, S.: A framework for the psychology of norms. The Innate Mind: Culture and Cognition, 280–301 (2006)
13. Criado, N., Argente, E., Botti, V.: Rational Strategies for Autonomous Norm Adoption. In: COIN, pp. 9–16 (2010)

Inducing Desirable Behaviour through an Incentives Infrastructure*

Roberto Centeno, Holger Billhardt, and Sascha Ossowski

Centre for Intelligent Information Technologies (CETINIA)
University Rey Juan Carlos - Spain
{roberto.centeno,holger.billhardt,sascha.ossowski}@urjc.es

Abstract. In open multiagent systems, where agents may join/leave the system at runtime, participants can be heterogeneous, self-interested and may have been built with different architectures and languages. Therefore, in such a type of systems, we cannot assure that agents populating them will behave according to the objectives of the system. To address this problem, organisational abstractions, such as roles and norms, have been proposed as a promising solution. Norms are often coupled with penalties and rewards to deter agents from violating the rules of the system. But, what happens if a current population of agents does not care about these penalties/rewards. To deal with this problem, we propose an incentives infrastructure that allows to estimate agents' preferences, and can modify the consequences of actions in a way that agents have incentives to act in a certain manner. Employing this infrastructure, a desirable behaviour can be induced in the agents to fulfil the preferences of the system.

1 Introduction

A particular type of MultiAgent Systems (MAS from now on) are Open MAS. These systems are usually designed from a global perspective and with a general purpose in mind. However, at design time, the agents that will populate the system might be unknown, heterogeneous, self-interested and the number of them may vary dynamically, due to they can join/leave the system at runtime.

With this in mind, designers cannot assume agents will behave according to the preferences of the system. In order to address this problem, organisational structures have been proposed as a promising solution. In these approaches, authors use organisational abstractions such as roles, norms, etc. [1–3] so as to regulate the activity of the participants. Therefore, the normative systems emerge as a key concept for regulating MAS [1–3]. However, norms, from the point of view of agents, are just information that tell them what actions they are (not) allowed to perform in the system. Thus, in order to be effective, norms should be coupled with detection mechanisms – to detect when they are not obeyed – and with penalties/rewards – to be applied when they are violated. In most cases, systems, as well as the norms and their penalties/rewards, are designed before knowing the agents that will populate them. In this sense, the question arises what

---
* The present work has been partially funded by the Spanish Ministry of Education and Science under projects TIN2006-14630-C03-02 (FPI grants program) and "Agreement Technologies" (CONSOLIDER CSD2007-0022, INGENIO 2010).

J. Dix and C. Witteveen (Eds.): MATES 2010, LNAI 6251, pp. 64–75, 2010.

happens if a current population of agents is not sensitive to these penalties/rewards. Then, norms can not be effectively enforced.

To deal with this problem, *hard norms* can be defined, which agents are not able to violate because the system relies on mechanisms to avoid such violations. For instance, in Electronic Institutions [1], by means of their infrastructure (Ameli [4]), agents are only able to perform actions which are acceptable in the current state. Nevertheless, in some domains the use of this kind of norms is not feasible due to their complexity and size, it could be impossible to take into account all possible exceptions. Therefore, it is often easier and more efficient to define norms based on penalties/rewards, instead of using hard norms. However, as we said before, these penalties/rewards should be effective for the current population of the system.

Addressing this situation, we propose an incentive mechanism, following the work presented by Centeno et al. in [5], that allows to estimate agents' preferences, and can modify the consequences of actions in a way that agents have incentives to act in a certain manner. Employing this infrastructure, a desirable behaviour can be induced in agents to fulfil the preferences of the system.

The rest of the paper is organised as follows, Section 2 provides a formalisation of the model and describes the problem we address. In Section 3 an incentives infrastructure is presented by describing its components. Section 4 shows the experimental results; finally Section 5 puts forward some related work and presents conclusions and some lines of future work.

2 The Model

In our work we assume that agents are rational utility maximizers. Following the work presented by Centeno et al. in [5], a *rational agent* is modelled as a tuple $\langle S, \mathcal{O}, g, per, \mathcal{U}, t, s_0 \rangle$; where S is the set of internal states of the agent; $\mathcal{O}$ is the observation space; $g : \mathcal{O} \times S \rightarrow S$ is the agent's state transition function; $per : \mathcal{X} \rightarrow \mathcal{O}$ is the perception function; $\mathcal{U} : S \rightarrow \mathbb{R}$ is the utility function that assigns a value to each possible internal state; and t the agent's decision function such that $t : S \rightarrow \mathcal{A}$ follows the principle of maximising the expected utility (MEU). That is, $t(s) = argmax_{a \in \mathcal{A}} eu(a, s) = argmax_{a \in \mathcal{A}} \sum_{s' \in S} \mathcal{U}(s') \cdot \overline{P_s}(s'|s, a)$, where $eu(a, s)$ is the expected utility of performing the action a in the state s; $\mathcal{U}(s')$ is the utility of the state s' estimated by the agent; and $\overline{P_s}(s'|s, a)$ is the agents' estimate, at state s, of the probability that state s' will occur when executing action a in state s. The utility function of an agent is defined over the possible internal states, so, it is *local* to the agent and, thus, has to be defined with respect to what the agent observes from its environment. Therefore, the utility function is a means to solve the decision problem, from the agents own perspective, rather than as a measure of its performance in solving some given task as seen from the outside.

Agents are embedded in a MAS that specifies the environment in which they perform. We model a MAS as a tuple $\langle Ag, \mathcal{A}, \mathcal{X}, \Phi, \varphi, \mathcal{U}, x_0 \rangle$; where Ag is a set of agents, $|Ag|$ denotes the number of agents; $\mathcal{A}$ is a possibly infinite action space that includes all possible actions that can be performed in the system; $\mathcal{X}$ is the environmental state space; $\Phi : \mathcal{X} \times \mathcal{A}^{|Ag|} \times \mathcal{X} \rightarrow [0..1]$ is the MAS transition probability distribution, describing how the environment evolves as a result of agents' actions; $\varphi : \mathcal{Ag} \times \mathcal{X} \times \mathcal{A} \rightarrow \{0, 1\}$ is the agents' capability function describing the actions agents are able to perform in a given state of the environment (*physical* restrictions); $\mathcal{U} : \mathcal{X} \rightarrow \mathbb{R}$ is the global utility function of the system that assigns a value to each environmental state; and, finally, $x_0 \in \mathcal{X}$ stands for the initial state.

MAS are usually designed with a general purpose in mind – the global objective of the system. In this model, such an objective is represented by means of a set of preferences which are captured through the utility function $\mathcal{U}$. From the point of view of the designer, the problem consists of how to optimize the global utility of the system assuming that agents will try to optimize their own individual utilities. In [5] propose to introduce organisational mechanisms in the system, with the aim of influencing the behaviour of agents. In particular, we focus on *incentive mechanisms* that change the consequences agents' actions may have. The rationale behind this approach is that changing the consequences of actions may produce variations in the expected utility of agents, what, in fact, can be seen as the introduction of penalties or rewards. Accordingly, incentive mechanisms are formalised as a function $\Upsilon_{inc} : \mathcal{X}' \rightarrow [\mathcal{X} \times \mathcal{A}^{|\mathcal{Ag}|} \times \mathcal{X} \rightarrow [0..1]]$ that changes the consequences of actions (i.e., the transition probability distribution Φ), taking into account the partial view the mechanism has about the environment ($\mathcal{X}'$).

Based on this model, we make the following assumptions:

Assumption 1. *The action space in the system is finite.*

Assumption 2. *Agents are utility maximisers. The utility functions of both, the global system and the agents, capture the utility at a long term, for instance by Bellman's Principle of Optimality [6]. That is, agents are able to calculate how good/bad is an action and they always choose the action that maximises their utility in the next state.*

Assumption 3. *The environment of a system can be discretized by a finite set of attributes: $\mathcal{X} = \{X_1, X_2, \ldots, X_n\}$. An environmental state $x_i \in \mathcal{X}$ can be modelled as a set of tuples $x_{i,j} = \langle attribute, value \rangle$ that assigns a value to each attribute.*

Assumption 4. *As consequence of assumption 3, the utility of an environmental state is the output of a multi-attribute utility function [7].*

Assumption 5. *The attributes are additively independent. That is, the utility function of the system can be expressed as: $u(x_i) = \sum_{j=1}^{n} w_j \cdot u_{i,j}$ where $u_{i,j}$ is the utility of the attribute $x_{i,j}$ and w_j is the weight of attribute X_j in the global utility function.*

Assumption 6. *All the participants in the system share the same ontology. This means that from the system level and from the perspective of the agents attributes refer to the same concepts. For example, the car agent a_i owns would be denoted in the same way from the agents and from the system as $car\_agent_{a_i}$.*

Following the model and taking into account assumption 3, changes in the MAS transition probability distribution (Φ) can be produced by changes in the probabilities of transiting to environmental states in which some of the attributes have been modified. Also, the agents' perception functions *per* become functions that given an environmental state – a set of attributes –, creates an observation consisting of a subset of that attributes. Similarly, an incentive mechanism Υ_{inc} modifies the system transition probability distribution taking into account the partial view the mechanism has about the system: the subset of attributes the mechanism is able to perceive.

2.1   The Problem

As we have said previously, an incentive mechanism is defined as a function Υ_{inc} that given a partial view of the system – a subset of attributes –, modifies the consequences of actions – the system transition probability distribution. So, the problem of designing an incentive mechanism boils down to address the following issues:

1. Deciding when the incentive mechanism should change the consequences of an action. In the model, this means which values of its the partial view of the world $\mathcal{X}'$ will fire the mechanism.
2. Selecting the action(s) whose consequences should be modified by the mechanism, that is, which actions in $\mathcal{A}$ should be incentivized/punished.
3. Deciding which agent(s) will be affected by the incentive.
4. Deciding the modification the mechanism should perform in order to influence the behaviour of an agent. In our model this corresponds to the environmental states that may be reached as consequences of actions in the transition probability distribution Φ.

Summarising, the problem of designing an incentive mechanism requires to learn which attributes should be modified, so as to make the consequences of a particular action more or less attractive for an agent. This includes the estimation of agents' preferences, as well as, to decide how the consequences of an action should be changed in order to incentivize it.

3   Incentives Infrastructure

The objective of an incentive mechanism is to induce agents to perform an action(s), that maximises the utility of the system, by modifying the consequences of such actions. Since agents are autonomous and independent entities, we cannot assume the system will know agents' preferences. Thus, the objective of the incentive mechanism is twofold: *i)* discovering agents' preferences; and *ii)* selecting the appropriate incentive to induce agents to behave in a certain manner. With this objective in mind, we propose an incentives infrastructure able to deal with those issues.

Similar to the use of governor agents in Electronic Institutions [4], we propose an infrastructure where interactions between external agents and the system are mediated by institutional agents called *incentivators*. Each external agent has assigned an incentivator and all actions selected by the agents will be performed in the system through their incentivators. Incentivator agents are in charge of both, discovering the preferences of their associated external agent, and modifying the consequences of certain actions with the aim to promote desired behaviour. Figure 1 shows the proposed architecture of both the infrastructure and an incentivator.

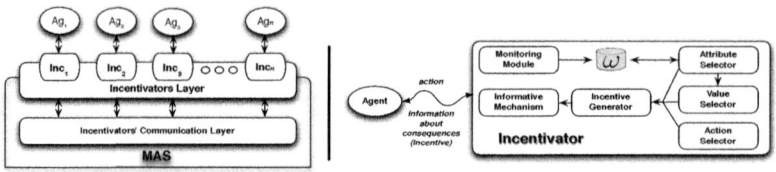

Fig. 1. Incentives Infrastructure and Incentivators architecture

An incentivator is responsible for an external agent by using the following modules:

- *Action Selector*: this module has the objective of selecting the action that, if it would be performed by the agent in the current state, would be the best action for the system (e.g., regarding the systems global utility function).
- *Attribute and Value Selector*: these modules are in charge of determining the next incentive. That is, they decide which attribute will be modified and the new value of this attribute, as consequence of a particular action.
- *Incentive Generator*: this module receives a modification of an attribute from the attribute and value selector modules and a candidate action for modifying its consequences in the current environmental state. Taking into account this information it should decide if the proposed modification, applied as a consequence of the selected action, is still beneficial[1] for the system.
- *Monitoring Module*: it observes the actual activity of the agent and tends to model the agent's preferences.
- *Informative Mechanism*: the incentivator provides information to the agent about the potential consequences of its actions (e.g. the incentives associated to an action).

3.1   Discovering Agent's Preferences

An incentivator has to know or at least has to estimate an agent's preferences in order to be able to incentivize certain actions. Here we assume that agents may have different and a priori unknown preferences.

A possible approach for identifying agents' preferences is either to ask agents a set of questions or to give them a questionnaire asking directly about their preferences. Taking into account the answers given, their utility functions are estimated [8]. However, this approach might be difficult to apply in an open multiagent system where agents are autonomous and the system is not able to impose any actions.

We propose a mechanism that learns an agent's preferences from monitoring its behaviour in response to given incentives.

An incentivator is endowed with a structure where an agent's preferences are estimated. More formally, we define a preferences vector as: $\omega_{ag_i} = [\omega_1, \ldots, \omega_n]$, where:

- n is the number of attributes in the system, such that it corresponds with the attributes that compounds an environmental state;

---

[1] With beneficial we mean that the system improves its utility with regard to the current state.

– ω_j is the weight agent ag_i has estimated on the utility of attribute X_j; we assume $\sum_{j=1}^{n} \omega_j = 1$;

– ω_{ag_i} is the estimated preferences vector for agent ag_i.

For instance a vector $\omega_{ag_1} = [0.1, 0.2, 0.7]$ means that the environmental state is composed of three attributes and that agent ag_1 is interested 0.1 in the attribute X_1, 0.2 in the attribute X_2 and 0.7 in the X_3.

The task of the incentivator is to estimate the preferences vector of its assigned external agent. In order to do that, we use Q-learning with immediate rewards and ϵ-greedy action selection [9]. In the scope of this learning method, the action space Z_i of the incentivator for agent ag_i is composed of the attributes it can modify as consequence of its action. More formally: $Z_i \subseteq \{X_1, \ldots, X_n\}$, where X_j are the attributes that compose an environmental state.

The idea behind this approach is that the incentivator estimates the preferences of an agent by modifying an attribute as consequence of an action and observing if the agent is induced to perform such an action. Thus, when an incentivator takes the action z_j, that means to modify the attribute X_j, during the learning process, it receives a reward that rates that action, and it updates its action-value function estimation as follows:

$$\mathcal{Q}_{t+1}(z_j) = \mathcal{Q}_t(z_j) + \alpha \cdot [\mathcal{R}_t(z_j) - \mathcal{Q}_t(z_j)] \qquad (1)$$

where α is the learning rate and $\mathcal{R}_t(z_j)$ is the reward. As reward the incentivator focuses on how the agent reacts to the modification proposed. It rates the action positively when the agent performs the action the incentivator wanted to, and negatively in other case:

$$\mathcal{R}_t(z_j) = \begin{cases} +1 \text{ if agent performed the action} \\ -1 \text{ i.o.c.} \end{cases} \qquad (2)$$

In order to discover new attributes in which the agent could be interested in, incentivators select a random attribute modification with small probability ϵ, and exploit the attribute with a the highest Q-value, the attribute in which the agent is most interested in (*greedy* action), with probability $(1 - \epsilon)$.

The next step in the learning process is to learn the most appropriate value of a selected attribute, in order to incentivize the agent. This task is carried out by the *Value Selector Module*. Similarly to the attribute selection process, this task is developed by using Q-learning with immediate rewards and ϵ-greedy action selection. In this case, the action space Y_i of the value selector module is composed of the different values the attribute proposed by the attribute selector may take. Formally, $Y_i = \{value_j \in [value_{X_i}^{min}, value_{X_i}^{max}]\}$, where $value_j$ stands for the set of different values the attribute X_i may take. The update and reward functions are the same as before (formulas 1 and 2). So, observing how the agent reacts to the new consequences the incentivator is able to estimate the attributes and their appropriate values that affect the utility of an agent. Obviously, the incentivator can only modify those attributes it is capable and has enough permission to change.

Summarising, as a result of the tasks carried out by those modules, a modification of an attribute of the environmental state is proposed. Formally, $x_{i,j}^* = \langle attribute, value \rangle$, where *attribute* is selected by the attribute selector, and *value* by the value selector. The next step is to select the action to incentivize.

3.2 Selecting the Action to Incentivize

At the same time that an incentivator is selecting the next incentive, it has to select the action to incentivize. This task is carried out by the *Action Selector*. This module follows an intuitive approach, trying to induce the action that gives the highest utility for the system. The incentivator, on behalf of the system, wants the agent to perform the action that would lead to the state with the best utility from a system perspective.

Therefore, what the incentivator has to do is to estimate the result of each possible action the agent is able to perform, and calculate the utility of the system in each resulting state. The simulation of the result of an action is domain-dependent, so it depends on the particular system we are dealing with. Note that in the current work we focus on how to induce a desirable behaviour in an agent. For this reason, when the incentivator estimates the result of an action performed by its agent, it will not take into account possible conflicts among other actions performed by other agents in the same state.

The domain-dependent algorithm executed by the action selector module returns a list of actions ranked by an estimation over the utility the system would get in case the agent performs each possible action. Formally, it is represented by $\triangledown_{x_j}^{ag_i} = \langle a_1, \ldots, a_n \rangle$ such that $eu(\overline{x_j, ag_i, a_1}) \geq \ldots \geq eu(\overline{x_j, ag_i, a_n})$, where:

- $\triangledown_{x_j}^{ag_i}$ stands for the list of actions agent ag_i is able to perform in the environmental state x_j, sorted by the expected utility of the system;
- $eu(\overline{x_j, ag_i, a_k})$ is the expected utility of the system in the state reached as consequence of the action a_k, performed by the agent ag_i, in the state x_j.

As soon as this list is calculated, and the incentive $(x_{i,j}^*)$ is proposed, both parameters are introduced in the incentive generator in order to decide whether this combination is still beneficial for the system.

3.3 Testing the Proposed Incentive

When a new incentive is proposed it could be necessary to assure that such an incentive is not damaging the objective of the system. That is, the changes in the environment proposed as an incentive could produce undesirable states for the global system. To evaluate whether or not the new consequences of the action are still the best option (not only for the agent but also for the system) is the task of the *Incentive Generator Module*. The result of this process may be the rejection of the proposed incentive $(x_{i,j}^*)$ if the result would be even worse for the system than if the agent performs the worst action (from the point of view of the system).

The decision is taken by the algorithm 1. Summarizing, it focuses on finding an action to incentivize, such that if the agent performs this action, and the proposed incentives are applied in the resulting state, the expected utility of the system is greater or equal than if the agent performs the same action (without the changes in the environment). Another case when the action should be incentivized, is when the expected utility of the system with the new consequences is greater or equal than if the agent performs the following best action, with regard to the utility of the system. The possible solutions of the algorithm are either the best action to incentivize by using the incentive proposed, or no action that means that is better not to give the incentive proposed to the agent.

Algorithm 1. deciding if the proposed incentive is given or not

---

Input: $\nabla_{x_j}^{ag_i}, x_{i,k}^*$
Output: $a_s \in \nabla_{x_j}^{ag_i}$ such that a_s is the best action to incentivize

1 **for** $s = 1$ *to* n **do**
2     $a_s \leftarrow \nabla_{x_j}^{ag_i}[s]$;
3     $a_{s+1} \leftarrow \nabla_{x_j}^{ag_i}[s+1]$;
4   **if** $(eu(\overrightarrow{(x_j x_{i,k}^*), ag_i, a_s}) \geq eu(\overrightarrow{x_j, ag_i, a_s}))\vee$
       $(eu(\overrightarrow{(x_j x_{i,k}^*)ag_i, a_s}) \geq eu(\overrightarrow{x_j, ag_i, a_{s+1}}))$ **then**
5   **return** a_s;
6   **end if**
7 **end for**
8 **return** $a_s \leftarrow \emptyset$;

3.4 Monitoring and Informing the Agent

As we said in previous sections, in order to discover the agent's preferences the incentivator observes the reaction of the agent regarding a proposed incentive for a given action. In particular, the incentivator monitories the action the agent actually performs and evaluates if this action is the same as the action selected by the incentivator. It then uses this information to provide the required feedback for the Q-learning algorithms presented before. It could be possible that an agent actually performed an action because its own interests (and not because of the incentives). However, the incentivator does not have any way to distinguish such a situation. We assume that the exploration/exploitation process in the Q-learning algorithms will detect such cases and converges to an estimation of the agent's correct preferences. In order to enable agents to reason about incentives, the incentivator informs the agents about the consequences of their actions (the incentives that may apply). Before an agent selects its new action to perform, it can query the informative mechanism about the incentives that apply to which action.

4 Experimental Results

To evaluate the incentives infrastructure proposed in this work we have designed and implemented a small "toy" example. The system is composed of a grid NxN, where each column is filled with a different colour: red, black or blue (see figure 2). Rational agents are situated in such a grid, being able to move around it, moving a position up, down, left or right. That is, the action space of the system is: $\mathcal{A} = \{moveUp,$ $moveDown, moveLeft, moveRight, skip\}$. An agent's position changes when it performs one of these action (except for skip). Furthermore, each agent has assigned an amount of money that is reduced by one unit when it changes its position. On the other hand, the system has also an amount of money that is increased by the money that agents spend on moving around the grid. An environmental state is composed of the following attributes: $\mathcal{X} = \{agent_1 Position, \dots, agent_1 Money, \dots, gridSize,$ $squaresColours_1, \dots, systemMoney\}$ where their possible values are *i)* the position, in terms of coordinates, of each agent; *ii)* the current money each agent owns; *iii)* the size of the grid (the parameter N); iv) the current colour of each square (red, black or blue); and iv) the amount of money owned by the system. The environment is designed in a deterministic way, i. e. two o more agents can be in the same position.

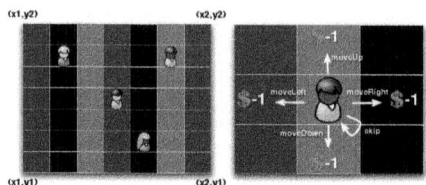

Fig. 2. Grid representation and action space of an agent

The objective of the system is that agents are in the central position, as well as, to get as much money as possible. These preferences are expressed by means of the following utility function: $\mathcal{U}(x_j) = \mathcal{U}_{systemMoney}(x_j) \cdot w_0 + \sum_{k=1}^{|Ag|} \mathcal{U}_{agent_k Position}(x_j) \cdot w_k$ where the utility over the position of each agent is measured as how far they are from the central position – by using the Manhattan distance –; and the money of the system is measured such that the more money the system gets the more utility it obtains. On the other hand, the objective of the agents is threefold, to reach a corner, to stay in a particular colour and to save as much money as possible. It is expressed by the general utility function: $\mathcal{U}_{a_k}(x_j) = \mathcal{U}_{agent_k Position}(x_j) \cdot w_1 + \mathcal{U}_{squaresColours_{agent_k Position}}(x_j) \cdot w_2 + \mathcal{U}_{agent_k Money}(x_j) \cdot w_3$, where the utility of their position is measured as how far they are from the corner they want to reach; the utility of the colour is 1 when they are on a square with the preferred colour (0 in other case); and the utility of the money is measured like in the case of the system.

In order to evaluate and compare our approach, we design a normative system to regulate the system described before. Such a system defines a global norm that is known by all participants and says that *"it is prohibited to go beyond a established area from the central point of the grid"*. This norm is coupled with penalties that reduce the agents' money when they violate the norm. We assume perfect (100%) detection of norm violations and fines are applied automatically. Thus, the system fulfils its original objectives: agents should stay as close as possible to the central position, and on the other hand, the system gets money if agents violate the norm. In comparison to the normative approach, we endowed the same system with the incentives infrastructure and where incentivators have enough permissions to modify the attributes $squaresColours_j$ (changing the colour of a particular square to black, red or blue) and $agent_k Money$ (increasing/decreasing the money of agents). When an incentivator gives/takes money to/from an agent, this money is taken/given from/to the system.

We have set up the system with the parameters specified in the table 1, carrying out two different experiments. In experiment 1, the weights of the parameters of the utility functions of both agents and system are selected randomly. When the system is regulated by the normative system, the allowed area is established to 10 squares from the central point and a fine of 50 units of money is applied when agents violate it.

Table 1.

	Exp1	**Exp2**
Grid/Agents/Steps	$200/30/100$	$200/30/100$
$\mathcal{U}_{Ag}$	$Random(w_1, w_2, w_3)$	$w_1, w_2 = 0.45\ w_3 = 0.1$
$\mathcal{U}_{MAS}$	$Random(w_0, w_k)$	$Random(w_0, w_k)$
Norm Limit/Penalty	$10/-50$	$10/-50$
$agent_i Money_0/agent_i Money^*$	$Random(1.000)/\pm 5\%$	$Random(1.000)/\pm 5\%$
$agent_i Position_0$/corner to reach	$(100, 100)/Random(4)$	$(100, 100)/Random(4)$

Figures 3(a) and 3(b) plot the utility of both the system and the agents in experiment 1. The blue line represents the case when the system is regulated by the norm while the red line represents the results when using the incentives infrastructure. Both the system and agents get better results, with regard to their utility in the case in which the system is regulated by the incentive infrastructure. In case of agents' utility we can observe clearly, how their utility increases in both situations, however when the normative system is working and the system is in the time-step 10, agents' utility decrease constantly. It happens due to some agents at this time are in the limit of going out of the established area (10 squares from the central point) and they decide to go beyond it violating the norm; and the system penalizes them decreasing their money. After that, their utility starts rising up again due to they are closer to the corner they want to reach. Regarding the system's utility, we can observe that in both situations the utility starts in the maximum possible. This is because the agents' initial position is in the central point of the grid. As agents are moving around the grid, the system looses utility, but this loss is lower when the incentive infrastructure is working. This is because incentivators are able to incentivize their agents to stay closer to the central position.

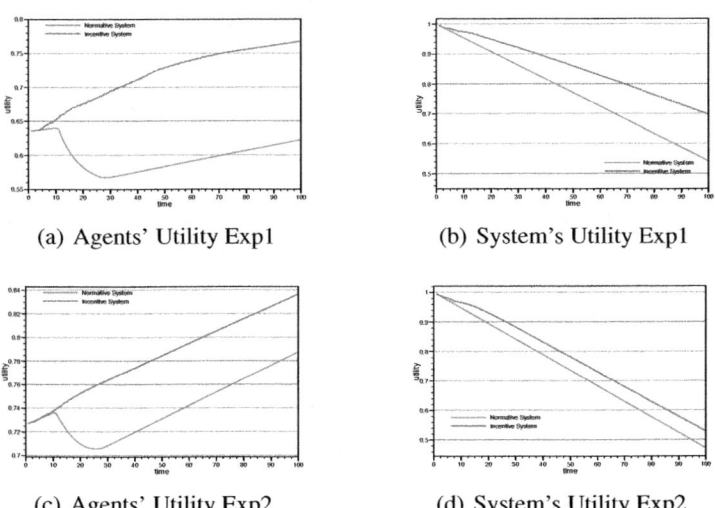

(a) Agents' Utility Exp1   (b) System's Utility Exp1

(c) Agents' Utility Exp2   (d) System's Utility Exp2

Fig. 3.

Figures 3(c) and 3(d) plot the results obtained after executing the system with the parameters defined in experiment 2. In this case, the system is populated with agents that do not care so much about the money (parameter $w_3 = 0.1$ in agents' utility function). The system's utility is quite similar with both mechanisms, norms and incentives, even so, the system looses less utility when it is regulated by the incentives infrastructure. Comparing the two experiments, we can conclude that the approach presented in this work, based on an incentives infrastructure works better to regulate a system when it is populated by agents unknown at a design time. Besides, not just the system performs better (regarding its utility); also the agents obtain more utility because the incentives infrastructure is able to discover their preferences and applies personalised incentives/penalties.

5   Conclusion

In this paper we have presented an incentives model and infrastructure that is able to *i)* discover the agents' preferences that might be based on different attributes of the environment; and *ii)* provide the suitable incentive by modifying the consequences of a particular action, such that desirable behaviours are induced. The incentives infrastructure is designed by using institutional agents called *incentivators*. Each incentivator is in charge of one external agent. In particular, it tries to discover the preferences of its agent, decides which would be the most desired action regarding the systems objectives, and incentivizes its agent to do that desired action. Incentivators use reinforcement learning techniques (Q-learning with immediate rewards and ϵ-greedy action selection) to learn the best incentivation policy for the agents they are in charge of.

The concept of *norm* appears as a main piece where there is no control over agents in order to regulate their activities. Norms define control policies to establish and reinforce agents to accomplish the objective of the system. So, the main objective is to restrict the agents' action space such that they behave how the system wants them to behave. Some approaches, like [1], focus on defining the set of allowed actions in each possible state of the system, such that agents are just allowed to perform valid actions. However, there exist domains (e.g. traffic, e-commerce, etc.) where due to their complexity and size, it is very difficult to define all possible valid actions for each state. For this reason, other approaches, like [2], propose to couple norms with penalties/rewards which gives agents the possibility to violate a norm. These penalties/rewards are usually designed off-line, where participants of the system are still unknown. Therefore, designers have to assume two main assumptions: *i)* agents, that will populate the system, are interested in a particular attribute (e.g. the money); and *ii)* the grade that a modification in this attribute affects agents such that they are deterred to perform certain actions. In order to avoid these assumptions, other approaches, like [10, 11], are emerged to induce desirable behaviours to agents participating in a system. One difference between these approaches and the one presented in this paper, is that the authors in [10, 11] focus on how to discover an appropriate reward to teach a particular policy to an agent. In our work, we consider incentives as something that could be positive or negative, that is, it is a modification in the consequences of an action. In fact, the valuation of such modifications depend on the agents. Some agents may consider as a positive modification what others consider to be negative. Another difference is that in [10, 11] the authors assume that all agents might be incentivized by adding a reward; that is only one possible attribute is considered. In comparison, we try to discover which attributes affect each individual agent in order to provide a personalised incentive.

In this work, we have only considered scenarios where the actions performed by agents do not influence the actions or the utility of other agents at the same time. However, this is a simplifying assumption. In our future work, we want to deal with cases where agents do influence each other. In particular, we will use multiagent learning techniques, to coordinate incentivators in order to be able to induce a desired joint action of the agents in the system. That is why the infrastructure architecture allows incentivators to communicate each others. Furthermore, we would like to apply the approach in a real world domain, e.g. peer-to-peer applications.

References

1. Esteva, M., Rodriguez, J., Sierra, C., Garcia, P., Arcos, J.: On the formal specification of electronic institutions. In: Sierra, C., Dignum, F.P.M. (eds.) AgentLink 2000. LNCS (LNAI), vol. 1991, pp. 126–147. Springer, Heidelberg (2001)
2. Dignum, V., Vazquez-Salceda, J., Dignum, F.: OMNI: Introducing social structure, norms and ontologies into agent organizations. In: Bordini, R.H., Dastani, M.M., Dix, J., El Fallah Seghrouchni, A. (eds.) PROMAS 2004. LNCS (LNAI), vol. 3346, pp. 181–198. Springer, Heidelberg (2005)
3. DeLoach, S., Oyenan, W., Matson, E.: A capabilities-based theory of artificial organizations. J. Autonomous Agents and Multiagent Systems 16, 13–56 (2008)
4. Esteva, M., Rosell, B., Rodríguez-Aguilar, J., Arcos, J.: AMELI: An agent-based middleware for electronic institutions. In: Proc. of AAMAS, vol. 1, pp. 236–243 (2004)
5. Centeno, R., Billhardt, H., Hermoso, R., Ossowski, S.: Organising mas: A formal model based on organisational mechanisms. In: Proc. of SAC, pp. 740–746 (2009)
6. Bellman, R.: Dynamic Programming. Princeton University Press, Princeton (1957)
7. Keeney, R., Raiffa, H.: Decisions with Multiple Objectives: Preferences and Value Tradeoffs. Cambridge University Press, Cambridge (1993)
8. Boutilier, C., Patrascu, R., Poupart, P., Schuurmans, D.: Regret-based utility elicitation in constraint-based decision problems. In: Proc. of IJCAI, pp. 929–934 (2005)
9. Watkins, C.: Learning from Delayed Rewards. PhD thesis, King's College, Cambridge, UK (1989)
10. Zhang, H., Parkes, D.: Value-based policy teaching with active indirect elicitation. In: Proc. of AAAI, pp. 208–214. AAAI Press, Menlo Park (2008)
11. Dufton, L., Larson, K.: Multiagent policy teaching. In: Proc. of AAMAS 2009 (2009)

SONAR/OREDI: A Tool for Creation and Deployment of Organisation Models

Endri Deliu and Michael Köhler-Bußmeier

University of Hamburg, Vogt-Kölln-Straße 30, 22527 Hamburg, Germany
koehler@informatik.uni-hamburg.de

Abstract. The need for handling the increasing complexity in software systems has allowed the introduction and establishment of an organisational paradigm as an alternative in software modelling and development. Especially within the multi-agent systems community, organisational concepts are enjoying increasing popularity for efficiently structuring multi-agent behaviour. Organisational specifications and their implementation as multi-agent systems lack however a streamlined transition between each other. In this paper we address this problem by introducing a software tool capable of creating and editing organisation models as well as deploying such models as multi-agent systems. The tool is built on SONAR, a formal organisational specification based on Petri nets. By unifying in one tool the organisational specification and deployment process quick reaction cycles to incremental changes of system design become possible.

1 Introduction

Important influxes from sociology and organisation theory have begun delineating what may dissolve the trade-off between agent autonomy and multi-agent system reliability and predictability. Between the system and the agents composing it, other levels of control have been introduced which are mainly derived from sociological concepts. The concept of organisation is used as an umbrella term for groups of agents and their dependencies, interaction channels or relationships (cf. [1] for an survey or organisational approaches to agent systems). As a result, an organisational perspective on multi-agent systems has gradually emerged which focuses on organisational concepts such as groups, communities, organisations, etc., in contrast to the former focus of multi-agent systems on the agent's state and its relationship to the agent's behaviour (cf. [2]).

Modelling agent organisations requires a modelling language that is able to express most (possibly all) of the notions that the concept of organisation encompasses in an intuitive and easily understandable way. Petri nets are well suited for use in modelling systems and simultaneously offer a complete formal frame. In this context, a framework for the development of concurrent and distributed software systems has been built as a multi-agent system basing on reference nets [3], a high level Petri net formalism. Our multi-agent architecture MULAN (**mul**ti-**a**gent **n**ets) [4,5] provides the framework's reference architecture used for

J. Dix and C. Witteveen (Eds.): MATES 2010, LNAI 6251, pp. 76–87, 2010.
© Springer-Verlag Berlin Heidelberg 2010

the the multi-agent system. MULAN is built on Java and reference nets and can be executed in RENEW [3], a Petri net editor and simulator.

In this work, OREDI (**or**ganisation **edi**tor), a Petri net based tool will be presented. It enables editing organisation models as well as deploying such models as multi-agent systems, e.g. as MULAN systems. OREDI is built on top of RE-NEW and relies on SONAR (self **o**rganising **n**et **a**rchitecture **r**eference), a formal organisational specification for electronic institutions based on Petri nets. Section 2 will shortly introduce the main concepts of SONAR which are supported by OREDI. In Section 3, the deployment of SONAR organisation models into agent organisations with OREDI is presented.

2   SONAR: A Formal Model of Organisations

In the following we give a short introduction into our modelling formalism, called SONAR. A detailed discussion of the formalism can be found in [6], its theoretical properties are studied in [7]. A SONAR-model encompasses:

1. A set of interaction models (called *distributed workflow nets*, short: DWF nets) based on a data ontology and a role model;
2. An organisational model that defines a network of organisational sub-units (usually called *positions*) and their resources together within a net model, that describes the team-based delegation of tasks;
3. A stratification model that assigns a hierarchy level n to all components;
4. A set of transformation rules together with a model metric;
5. A refinement/abstraction operation to build nested SONAR-models.

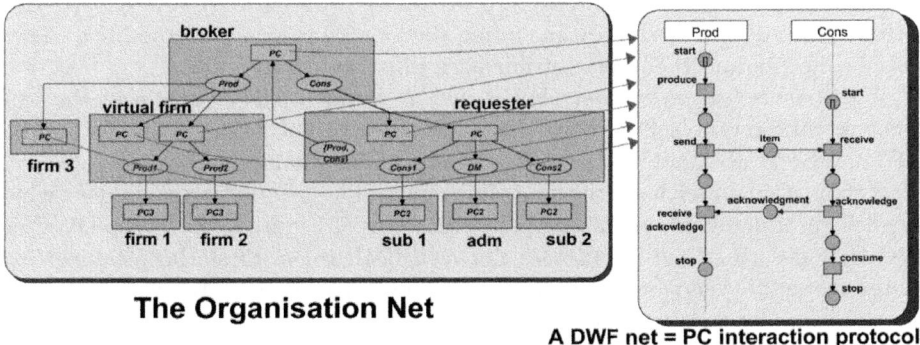

Fig. 1. A SONAR-Model

Figure 1 illustrates the basic relationships between the SONAR interaction model, the role/delegation model and the position network. The example describes the relationship between some positions (drawn as grey boxes: *broker, virtual firm, requester*, etc.) in terms of their respective roles (*Producer, Consumer* etc.) and associated delegation links. In this scenario, we have a requester and two suppliers of some product. Coupling between them is provided by a bro-ker.[1] From a more fine-grained perspective, the requester and one of the suppliers consist of delegation networks themselves. For example, in the case of the *virtual firm* supplier, we can identify a management level and two subcontractors. The two subcontractors may be legally independent firms that integrate their core competencies in order to form a virtual enterprise (e.g. separating fabrication of product parts from their assembly). The coupling between the firms constitut-ing the virtual enterprise is apt to be tighter and more persistent than between requester and supplier at the next higher system level, which provides more of a market-based and on-the-spot connection.[2]

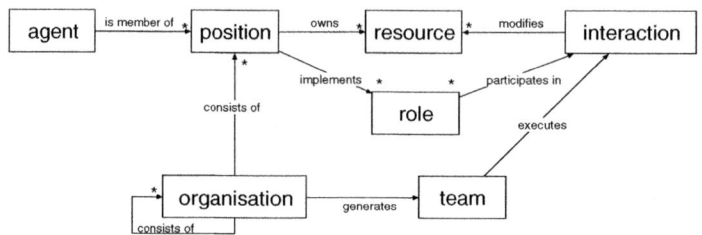

Fig. 2. Basic SONAR Concepts and their Relationships

In general an *organisation* consists of (sub)organisations and atomic organisa-tions, called positions. *Positions* are staffed by agents. Staffed agents have access to *resources* owned by the position and they implement the *roles* assigned to the position. Agents interact in *teams* in which they play roles. Interaction proto-cols describe the possible interaction processes between roles. As a byproduct of their interaction resources, including data or knowledge are modified. These basic concepts and their relationships are illustrated in Figure 2.

A *distributed workflow net* (DWF net) is a multi-party version of the well-known workflow nets [8] where the parties are called *roles*. Roles are used in DWF nets to abstract from concrete agents. For example, the two roles *Pro-ducer* and *Consumer* have the same form of trading interaction no matter which agent is producing or consuming. The right side of Figure 1 shows the DWF net *PC* that describes the interaction between both roles: First the producer exe-cutes the activity *produce*, then *sends* the produced *item* to the consumer, who *receives* it. The consumer sends an *acknowledge* to the producer before he *con-sumes* the item.[3] Technically speaking roles are some kind of type for an agent

---

[1] Note that for this simplified model brokerage is an easy job, since there are exactly two producers and one consumer. In general, we have several instances for both groups with a broad variety of quality parameters making brokerage a real problem.

[2] This coupling is usually expressed using the refinement/abstraction operator of SONAR, but is omitted here for simplicity reasons.

[3] To simplify the presentation we have omitted all data-related aspects in our discus-sion of distributed workflow nets. In SONAR each DWF net uses data object based on the model's ontology. Cf. [9,10] for details.

describing its behaviour. Note that agents staffed to positions usually implement several roles.

An organisation net is a Petri net $N = (P, T, F)$ where each task is modelled by a place p and each task implementation (delegation/execution) is modelled by a transition t. Each place p is labelled by a role $R(p)$ and each transition t with a DWF net $D(t)$. Each place and each transition is assigned to the position O it belongs to. This is illustrated by surrounding boxes in Figure 1.

In general a delegation t comes along with a behaviour refinement. In our example, the position *requester* implements the role *Cons* by generating subtasks for the roles *Cons 1*, *DM*, and *Cons 2*. These subtasks are handled by the positions *sub 1*, *adm*, and *sub 2* that implement their respective roles according to the DWF PC_2 (not shown here) which decomposes the behaviour of role *Cons* into the composition of *Cons 1*, *DM*, and *Cons 2*. In well formed organisations it is guaranteed that the service generated from the refined DWF PC_2 and the roles *Cons 1*, *DM*, and *Cons 2* has the same communication behaviour as the service generated from the original DWF PC and the role *Cons*.

Team formation can be expressed in a very elegant way: If one marks one initial place of an organisation net *Org* with a token, each firing process of the Petri net models a possible delegation process. More precisely, the *token game* is identical to the team formation process (cf. Theorem 4.2 in [7]). Team formation generates a *team net* and a *team DWF*.

As another aspect, SONAR-models are equipped with transformation rules. Transformation rules describe which modifications of the given model are allowed. They are specified as graph rewrite rules [11]. The minimal requirement for rules in SONARÂ is that they must preserve the correctness of the given organisational model.

3   Deploying SONAR Organisations

OREDI contains an editing tool for SONAR formal organisations. It is built as a set of RENEW plugins. OREDI users can create SONAR formal organisations without being directly aware of their underlying constraints. The process of creating formal organisations involves two steps. The first step being the creation of DWF nets and some additional models, that represent refinement relationships between roles. The second step is the creation of organisation nets and the assignment of DWF nets and roles to transitions and places, respectively. The completion of both steps leads users to organisational models. Each step is handled in separate editors. Thus, an editor for modelling DWF nets is used first. Then the results of the first step are loaded in a second editor where the organisation is modelled.

At the end of the modelling process, OREDI supports the deployment of the modelled organisation as an agent organisation consisting of Organisation Agents, Organisation Position Agents (OPA), and Organisation Member Agents (OMA) we describe in the following section.

3.1   Agent Organisations as OPA/OMA Networks

Now that we have obtained a picture of what constitutes a formal organisation according to our approach, we can elaborate on the activities of a multi-agent systems behaving according to a SONAR-model. The basic idea is quite straight-forward: With each position of the SONAR-model we associate one dedicated agent, called the *organisational position agent* (OPA).

Figure 3 illustrates our specific philosophy concerning MAS organisations utilising the middleware approach. In SONAR, we describe a formal organisation in terms of interrelated *organisational positions*.

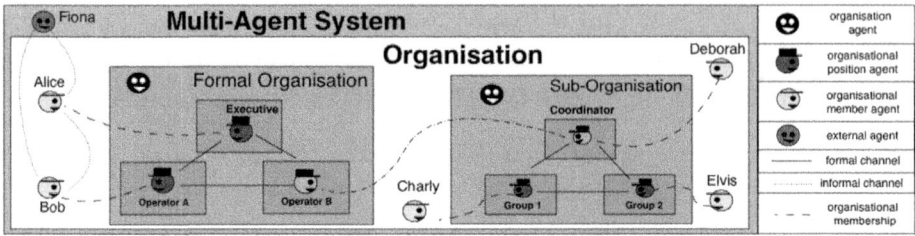

Fig. 3. An Organisation as an OPA/OMA Network

An OPA network embodies a formal organisation. An OPA represents an organisational *artifact* and not a *member/employee* of the organisation. However, each OPA represents a conceptual connection point for an *organisational member agent* (OMA). An organisation is not complete without OMAs. It depends on domain agents that actually carry out organisational tasks, make decisions where required and thus implement/occupy the formal positions. Note that an OMA can be an artificial as well as a human agent. An OPA both enables and constrains organisational behaviour of its associated OMA. Only via an OPA an OMA can effect the organisation and only in a way that is in conformance with the OPA's specification. In addition, the OPA network as a whole relieves its associated OMAs of a considerable amount of organisational overhead by automating coordination and administration. To put it differently, an OPA offers its OMA a "behaviour corridor" for organisational membership. OMAs might of course only be partially involved in an organisation and have relationships to multiple other agents than their OPA (even to agents completely external to the organisation). From the perspective of the organisation, all other ties than the OPA-OMA link are considered as informal connections.

To conclude, an OPA embodies two conceptual interfaces, the first one between micro and macro level (one OPA versus a network of OPAs) and the second one between formal and informal aspects of an organisation (OPA versus OMA). We can make additional use of this twofold interface. Whenever we have a system of systems setting with multiple scopes or domains of authority (e.g. virtual organisations strategic alliances, organisational fields), we can let an OPA of a given (sub-)organisation act as a member towards another OPA of another organisation. This basically combines the middleware perspective with a holonic perspective (cf. [15]) and is not as easily to be conceptualised in the context of other middleware approaches that take a less distributed/modular perspective. In this paper the aspect of holonic systems is not discussed any further – cf. [16] for an in depth discussion.

All OPAs share a common structure which we call the *generic OPA (GOPA)*. An OPA O is an instance of this GOPA that is parametrised by that part of the organisational model that describes O, i.e. its inner structure (subtask and delegation/execution activities) and all the surrounding OPAs. The architecture of the GOPA is discussed in [17].

3.2 Deploying SONAR Organisations as OPA/OMA Networks

OREDI supports the deployment of SONAR formal organisations as OPA/OMA networks. The formal organisation net is exported in a XML format. The XML file generated from the organisation net is parsed and the deployment process begins. The generation of the XML file and its subsequent parsing was conceived to provide a platform and application independent solution to deploy SONAR organisations. As such, the generated XML file contains all formal information of the SONAR-model and can be used for deployment in any multi-agent platform. Here, we opted for an implementation of the deployment steps in our MULAN-architecture [4,5] as it supports building multi-agent systems with reference nets. This allowed using Petri nets both as a modelling as well as a programming technology thus easing and streamlining the gap between modelling and development. So, MULAN is our first choice, but of course any agent oriented languages would have done too.

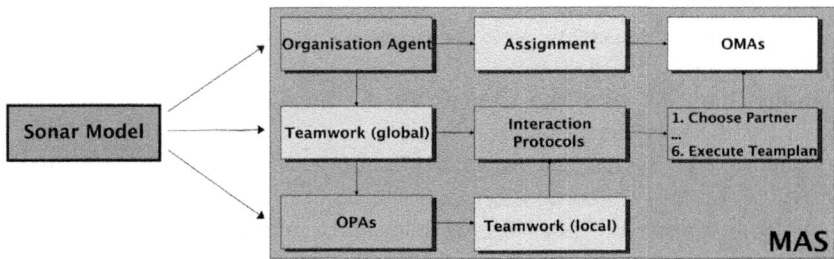

Fig. 4. Deployment of SONAR-Models

Deploying a SONAR organisation as OPA/OMA networks involves

1. the generation of an organisation agent, serving as a platform for the OPAs,
2. the generation all the OPAs, and
3. the assignment of OMAs to OPAs.

After these phases team processes such as team formation, team plan formation, and team plan execution can follow as specified in [6]. The whole compilation is sketched in Figure 4. In this work, only the generation of the organisation agent and the OPAs and the assignment of OMAs is handled. For a discussion of the teamwork cf. [18,17].

Organisational positions of the organisation net are deployed as OPAs.[4] The generated OPAs know the identity of their neighbour OPAs and communicate with them through a set of encrypted messages. The assignment of OMAs to OPAs is made in a market based fashion with OPAs making open position announcements and interested OMAs competing for the employment for the open positions. The communication between OPAs and OMAs is also encrypted.

Deployment of Organisation Agents and OPAs in Mulan. OREDI deploys formal organisation as MULAN OPAs. MULAN is a FIPA [19] compliant architecture. At first, a MULAN platform is generated where one or more agent organisations can be embedded. The position agents generated for each position in the SONAR organisation net are placed inside the created platform. Additionally, suitable MULAN protocols handle agent conversations. MULAN agents can use protocols proactively or reactively as a response to specific messages. The decision which protocol to use for a specific received message is made in the knowledge base where a mapping between message templates and protocols is consulted.

OPAs have the complete information of their corresponding positions in the SONAR organisation net specified in the XML file. This information includes the position's relative place in the organisation (knowledge about neighbour positions), the roles they are implementing/delegating and their tasks. Generating OPAs out of an organisation net specification is accomplished in agent-oriented fashion by an initial agent. The initial agent is called the *organisation agent* as it has a global view on all positions. The organisation agent is responsible for the generation of the OPAs and their initialisation with information extracted from the formal organisation net specification.

The information needed from an OPA includes which other OPAs are its neighbours. This requires the identity of the neighbours. At least in MULAN, the identity of agents and their location can only be known after the creation of these agents. This means that information about the neighbour positions has to be provided for an OPA only after, not during its creation. Thus, the information about the place of a position agent in an organisation is conveyed through a conversation with the organisation agent. During the conversation, in order to make sure that the messages come from the right parties they are signed with a cryptographic mechanism which requires that parties know their respective keys. In Figure 5, an AUML sequence diagram displays the conversation between OPAs and the organisation agent during which the organisation agent communicates to the positions all relevant information extracted from the organisation net specification. In FIPA terminology, conversations between agents are called *protocols*. MULAN *protocols* describe the behaviour of agents during

---

[4] In fact, the OPAs are *compiled* into a *complete* specification for the GOPA instance. This specification is complete in the sense that all remaining, open design aspects are gathered in the implementation of the OMAs.

conversations. The AUML diagram in Fig. 5 also serves as an overall sketch of the used MULAN protocols which can be generated automatically from the AUML diagrams. Cf. [5] for an overview of the MULAN tool family.

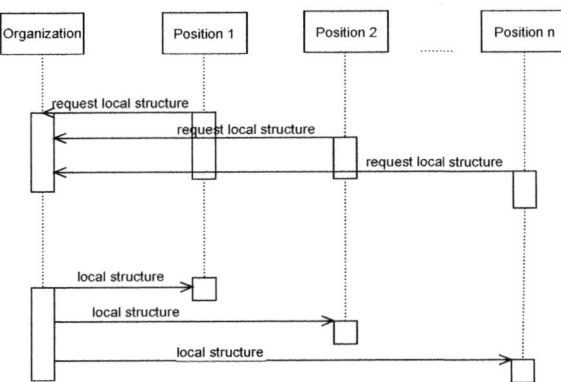

Fig. 5. The organisation agent communicating the information extracted from the respective positions to the generated OPAs

The conversation displayed in Fig. 5 is based on the assumption that the OPAs already know the identity of their organisation agent. However, the organisation agent does not know the identities of its OPAs. OPAs send a message with their identifiers to their organisation agent requesting their local structure which should include all the relevant information extracted from the respective positions in the SONAR organisation net such as the neighbours, the implementing and delegating roles, the tasks, etc. After receiving the requests for the local structure and the identifiers from all the position agents, the organisation agent proceeds and sends the respective local structure to each position agent. The conversation partners know their respective crypto keys so all the messages of the conversation are signed with the private keys of the sending parties. However, the aspect of authentication has been left out from Fig. 5 for simplicity.

Assignment of OMAs to OPAs. After the generation of the OPAs and the communication of the local structures to them, the assignment of OMAs to OPAs is started. The approach for the assignment process is leaned on [20]. As the organisation agent represents some kind of a service provider and logical platform to the OPAs and the potential OMAs, it assumes at this point the management of the assignment of OMAs to OPAs. If an OPA has an open position (either because its OMA resigned or it has been fired), the OPA sends a request to the organisation agent to start the procedure for the occupation of the open position. The organisation agent publishes a job description for the open position to a central registry component named **D**irectory **F**acilitator (DF) – see FIPA Agent Management Specification. A DF is a mandatory component of an agent platform in FIPA that provides a yellow pages directory service to

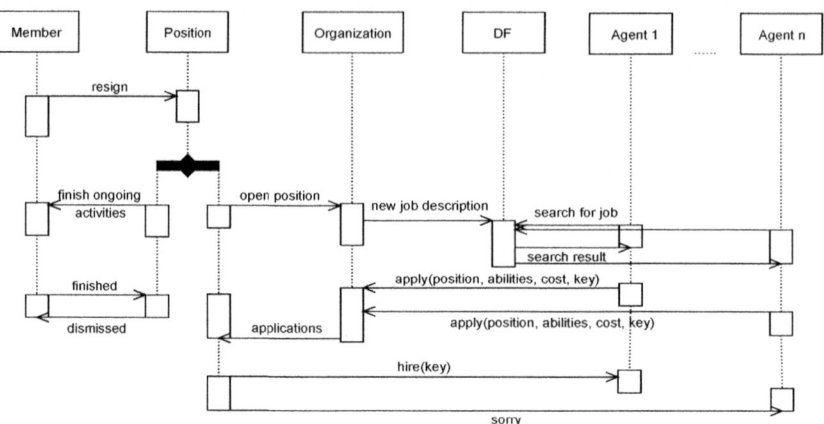

Fig. 6. The assignment of an agent as a member to a position agent

agents. Agents can advertise their services through the DF. In MULAN the DF is also an agent with which the organisation agent can communicate.

The external agents that are interested in occupying open positions in the organisation can search through the DF and apply to the organisation agent for a specific open position. The initial assignment of OPAs with OMAs is a special case where all OPAs have open positions. The diagram in Fig. 6 displays the case when the resignation of a member triggers the start of the procedure to assign a new member for the position. The organisation agent sends a description for a new job to the DF. The job description contains the identifier of the vacant OPA, the requirements that applicants have to fulfil, and a time period during which applications for the job are accepted. Agents that find that job description interesting after a search in the DF, apply to the organisation agent. Their application includes the description of the job for which they are applying, their crypto key, their personal abilities as a response to the requirements specified in the job description, and the costs for their service. The applications are received from the organisation agent.

After the application period for a vacant position expires, the organisation agent sends all received applications to the respective position agent, the OPA selects the new member and lets it know the key for the authentication during their future communication as well as the fact that it has been hired. In the case of resignation from a member, the member is dismissed only after finishing its ongoing activities on behalf of the organisation. Even if a new member may have been hired since the resignation request of the old member, the old member is dismissed only after finishing all its ongoing activities. This means that a position can have more than one member agents for limited time periods. An alternative way for an agent to get the list of open positions within an organisation is to send a message to the organisation agent itself with a request for the open positions that the organisation has.

For handling the communication for both the generation of the OPAs and the assignment of OMAs to OPAs an ontology was developed. The ontology was developed with Protégéand was employed as a domain specific shared vocabulary throughout the conversations between the agents involved in the two phases.

3.3 Related Work

Our approach lies in the research area of organisation centred design of multi-agent systems. There is a recent collection on approaches to agent systems in [1]. Among them we like to mention OPERA [21], MOISE [22], and ISLANDER [23].(Of course there are a lot of approaches on agent-oriented software engineering, like GAIA [24], but those usually do not explicitly rely in the metaphor of the organisation.) These methodologies are equipped with their middleware: OperettA [12], S-$\mathcal{M}$OISE$^+$ [13], and Amelie [14].

We provide a more detailed comparison of our SONAR-approach to MOISE and ISLANDER in [25] where we also derive conclusions concerning best fits between different approaches and application contexts. Compared to other middleware layers, we advocate complete distribution. Instead of introducing one or more middleware managers that watch over the whole organisation (cf. the manager in S-$\mathcal{M}$OISE$^+$) or at least over considerable parts (cf. institution, scene, transition managers in Amelie), we associate each position with its own *organisational position agent* (OPA).

4 Conclusion and Outlook

Oredi, the tool presented in this paper, is a Petri net based software tool for modelling Sonar organisations as well as for deploying these models to agent organisations. By providing a tool that carries out specification as well as deployment of formal organisations a close link between these two phases of system development has been provided. With Oredi users can build Sonar organisations through a combination of graphical interfaces, a set of interaction constraints and context based suggestions without being required to possess active knowledge of the formal rules underlying the models' specifications. The deployment of formal organisation models is based on the decoupling of the elements of the multi-agent system that specify the organisational structure from those that act as members of the organisation. Positions in the formal organisation are deployed as agents (OPAs) and are embedded within the organisation agent, all implemented as Mulan agents. Oredi provides the specification and implementation of the assignment of OMAs to OPAs. Provided the necessary capabilities, any agent, developed in any programming language, can be assigned to an OPA as its OMA and take over the execution of the necessary tasks.

Besides, the deployment of formal organisation nets as agent organisations can also be extended to include the team formation, team plan formation and team plan execution phases as the corresponding theoretical foundations have already been provided in [18,17,26].

In the future extensions of OREDI both the modelling and the deployment phases will be subject to further development. A special focus should be laid on the modularisation of the OREDI models – using the refinement operation of SONAR – as it can allow the distribution of the modelling process. Formal organisations can be partitioned into modules which can be developed and maintained in separate files by different parties.

This modularisation will support the holonic approach taken in SONAR where not only positions are part of an organisation, but also (sub-)organisations. Organisations can be linked to each other by delegation relationships. Linking organisations can be achieved by adding extra graphical components to OREDI that represent the link to other sub-organisations.

References

1. Dignum, V. (ed.): Handbook of Research on Multi-Agent Systems IGI Global. Information Science Reference (2009)
2. Ferber, J., Gutknecht, O., Michel, F.: From agents to organizations: An organizational view of multi-agent systems. In: Giorgini, P., Müller, J.P., Odell, J.J. (eds.) AOSE 2003. LNCS, vol. 2935, pp. 214–230. Springer, Heidelberg (2004)
3. Kummer, O., Wienberg, F., Duvigneau, M., et al.: An extensible editor and simulation engine for Petri nets: Renew. In: Cortadella, J., Reisig, W. (eds.) ICATPN 2004. LNCS, vol. 3099, pp. 484–493. Springer, Heidelberg (2004)
4. Köhler, M., Moldt, D., Rölke, H.: Modeling the behaviour of Petri net agents. In: Colom, J.-M., Koutny, M. (eds.) ICATPN 2001. LNCS, vol. 2075, pp. 224–241. Springer, Heidelberg (2001)
5. Cabac, L., Dörges, T., Rölke, H.: A monitoring toolset for Petri net-based agent-oriented software engineering. In: van Hee, K.M., Valk, R. (eds.) ATPN 2008. LNCS, vol. 5062, pp. 399–408. Springer, Heidelberg (2008)
6. Köhler-Bußmeier, M., Wester-Ebbinghaus, M., Moldt, D.: A formal model for organisational structures behind process-aware information systems. In: Jensen, K., van der Aalst, W.M.P. (eds.) Transactions on Petri Nets. LNCS, vol. 5460, pp. 98–114. Springer, Heidelberg (2009)
7. Köhler, M.: A formal model of multi-agent organisations. Fundamenta Informaticae 79, 415–430 (2007)
8. Aalst, W.v.d.: Verification of workflow nets. In: Azéma, P., Balbo, G. (eds.) ICATPN 1997. LNCS, vol. 1248, pp. 407–426. Springer, Heidelberg (1997)
9. Köhler, M., Ortmann, J.: Formal aspects for service modelling based on high-level Petri nets. In: International Conference on Intelligent Agents, Web Technologies and Internet Commerce, IAWTIC 2005 (2005)
10. Köhler, M., Moldt, D., Ortmann, J.: Dynamic service composition: A petri-net based approach. In: Conference on Enterprise Information Systems (ICEIS 2006), pp. 159–165 (2006)
11. Ehrig, H., Ehrig, K., Prange, U., Taentzer, G.: Fundamentals of algebraic graph transformation. Springer, Heidelberg (2006)
12. Okouya, D., Dignum, V.: Operetta: a prototype tool for the design, analysis and development of multi-agent organizations. In: AAMAS 2008, pp. 1677–1678 (2008)
13. Hübner, J.F., Sichman, J.S., Boissier, O.: S-Moise: A middleware for developing organised multi-agent systems. In: International Workshop on Organizations in Multi-Agent Systems (OOOP 2005), pp. 107–120 (2005)

14. Esteva, M., Rodriguez-Aguilar, J., Rosell, B., Arcos, J.: Ameli: An agent-based middleware for electronic institutions. In: AAMAS 2004, pp. 236–243 (2004)
15. Fischer, K., Schillo, M., Siekmann, J.: Holonic multiagent systems: A foundation for the organization of multiagent systems. In: Mařík, V., McFarlane, D.C., Valckenaers, P. (eds.) HoloMAS 2003. LNCS (LNAI), vol. 2744, pp. 71–80. Springer, Heidelberg (2003)
16. Wester-Ebbinghaus, M., Moldt, D.: Modelling an open and controlled system unit as a modular component of systems of systems. In: International Workshop on Organizational Modelling (OrgMod 2009), pp. 81–100 (2009)
17. Köhler-Bußmeier, M., Wester-Ebbinghaus, M.: Sonar: A multi-agent infrastructure for active application architectures and inter-organisational information systems. In: Braubach, L., van der Hoek, W., Petta, P., Pokahr, A. (eds.) MATES 2009. LNCS (LNAI), vol. 5774, pp. 248–257. Springer, Heidelberg (2009)
18. Köhler, M., Wester-Ebbinghaus, M.: Organizational models and multi-agent system deployment. In: Burkhard, H.-D., Lindemann, G., Verbrugge, R., Varga, L.Z. (eds.) CEEMAS 2007. LNCS (LNAI), vol. 4696, pp. 307–309. Springer, Heidelberg (2007)
19. FIPA: FIPA 97 Specification, Part 1 - Agent Management. Technical report, Foundation for Intelligent Physical Agents (1998), http://www.fipa.org
20. Köhler-Bußmeier, M.: SONAR: Eine sozialtheoretisch fundierte Multiagentensystemarchitektur. In: Selbstorganisation und Governance in künstlichen und sozialen Systemen. Lit Verlag, Münster (2009)
21. Dignum, V., Dignum, F., Meyer, J.J.: An agent-mediated approach to the support of knowledge sharing in organizations. Knowledge Engineering Review 19, 147–174 (2004)
22. Boissier, O., Hannoun, M., Sichman, J.S., Sayettat, C.: MOISE: An organizational model for multi-agent systems. In: 7th Ibero-American Conference on AI, pp. 156–165. Springer, Heidelberg (2000)
23. Esteva, M., de la Cruz, D., Sierra, C.: Islander: an electronic institutions editor. In: Falcone, R., Barber, S.K., Korba, L., Singh, M.P. (eds.) AAMAS 2002. LNCS (LNAI), vol. 2631, pp. 1045–1052. Springer, Heidelberg (2003)
24. Zambonelli, F., Jennings, N.R., Wooldridge, M.: Developing multiagent systems: The Gaia methodology. ACM Trans. Softw. Eng. Methodol. 12, 317–370 (2003)
25. Wester-Ebbinghaus, M., Köhler-Bußmeier, M., Moldt, D.: From multi-agent to multi-organization systems: Utilizing middleware approaches. In: Artikis, A., Picard, G., Vercouter, L. (eds.) ESAW 2008. LNCS, vol. 5485, pp. 46–65. Springer, Heidelberg (2009)
26. Köhler-Bußmeier, M., Wester-Ebbinghaus, M.: A petri net based prototype for mas organisation middleware. In: Workshop on Modelling, Object, Components, and Agents (MOCA 2009), pp. 29–44 (2009)

Enhancing the Interoperability between Multiagent Systems and Service-Oriented Architectures through a Model-Driven Approach

Christian Hahn[1,2], Sven Jacobi[2], and David Raber[1]

[1] DFKI GmbH
Stuhlsatzenhausweg 3
66123 Saarbrücken, Germany
[2] Saarstahl AG
Hofstattstrasse 106
66330 Völklingen, Germany

Abstract. Service-orientation has become the leading paradigm for modern IT system design and development as service-oriented system design has great potential for improving the efficiency and quality of the IT systems. This paper presents a model-driven approach for the generic integration of service-oriented architectures (SOA) and multi-agent systems (MAS). In fact, a model transformation from SoaML—a metamodel for SOA—to PIM4AGENTS—a platform independent metamodel for MAS—is utilized for integration. The relevance of this approach is proven by applying it to a real-world industry scenario.

1 Introduction

Service-oriented architectures (SOAs) promote services as the basic building blocks, which provide access to any type of problem solving facility regardless of its technical realization via a standardized interface [1]. This facilitates the interoperability among heterogeneous components and resources, enable the seamless integration of previously separated systems, and support the reuse and substitution of system components by decoupling the usage of IT facilities from their actual implementation [4].

Despite the various efforts on SOA technology development in industry, research, and in international standardization bodies, the provision of sophisticated development support for SOA-based landscapes remains a grand challenge. A promising approach for this is the model-driven engineering approach in accordance to OMG's Model-Driven Architecture (MDA) [9]. This approach supports the design and development of IT systems on the business-oriented computational independent model (CIM) level, the architecture-oriented platform independent model (PIM) level, and the platform specific model (PSM) level on the basis of standardized metamodels.

Although there are several recent and ongoing activities on developing MDA-based techniques for supporting the design, development, and maintenance of

J. Dix and C. Witteveen (Eds.): MATES 2010, LNAI 6251, pp. 88–99, 2010.

SOAs, there does not exist a standardized metamodel for describing services along with the relevant aspects on their provision and usage in a SOA landscape. Existing efforts are restricted to the modeling support for services, but do not provide modeling and development support for integrated systems that encompass other technologies, e.g. agent technology, in addition to services.

This paper is structured as follows: Section 2 presents related work in the area of integrating SOAs and MASs. Section 3 then discusses our model-driven approach for the integration of MASs and SOAs. Followed by Section 4, validating the approach based on a real-world scenario from the steel industry. Section 5 then discusses the general benefits of using agent-based systems in general and DSML4MAS in particular for the service execution. Finally, Section 6 concludes this paper.

2   Related Work

The similarities between agent architectures and SOAs have already been recognized (e.g. [14]). However, there is still an ongoing discussion about the relation between Web services and agents. In [2], the authors propose three relationships between agents and services: no conceptual distinction, bi-directional integration, and agents invoke Web services. However, in our view, only the last two paradigms can actually be kept, as the authors of [12] pointed out fundamental differences between both paradigms, making the first relationship indefensible.

The concepts of an agent is nowadays often used in the context of SOAs. Especially, in a business context, agents are integrated in a service-oriented environment, where the agents mainly provide and invoke services. In the following, related work in this respect is given.

In [10], the authors presented a framework called *WS2JADE* that allows integrating Web services and JADE. The integration is performed through representing a Web service by a gateway agent. This allows deploying, composing, and controlling Web services as agent service at run-time. In [11], an agent-based approach to the service composition in JACK[1] is discussed.

Apart from the wealth of literature about business process modeling, enterprise application integration and SOAs, a model-driven approach for the integration of MASs and SOAs has—to our knowledge—not yet been investigated. [3], for instance, discusses a mapping between BPMN (Business Process Modeling Notation) models to BDI agents. However, an integration of agents and Web services is no considered.

3   Model-Driven Service Integration into Multiagent Systems

This section discusses the relevant technologies necessary for the model-driven integration of SOAs and MASs.

---

[1] JACK is a commercial agent development platform that is online available at http://aosgrp.com/index.html

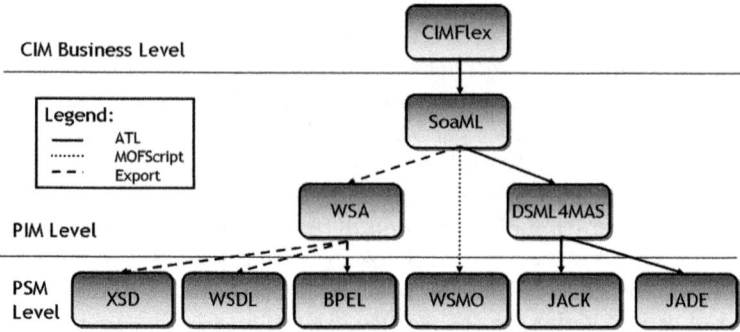

Fig. 1. An overview of the SHAPE model transformation architecture and framework

3.1 Model Transformation Architecture

Our new approach bases on the model transformation architecture (cf. Fig. 1) developed in the EU-project SHAPE[2] (Semantically-enabled Heterogeneous Service Architecture and Platforms Engineering). It illustrates the core language used within the project, their relationship to the abstraction levels CIM, PIM and PSM, as well as their relationship to other languages defined through model transformations. The model-to-model transformations are implemented in ATL[3] (Atlas Transformation Language), the model-to-text transformations are implemented using MOFScript[4].

On the highest level, business models encompass business rules, processes, services and other issues such as contracts involving humans and organizations to achieve business goals. These conform to the metamodel of CIMFlex [13]. The middle layer contains the Service-oriented Architecture Modeling Language (SoaML[5]) standardized by the OMG and extensions for semantically-enabled heterogeneous architectures like DSML4MAS or Web Service Architectures (WSA). This model transformation architecture allows the realization of one of the main goals of SHAPE namely to provide a transformation engine that maps business models to SOA models, which are then transferred to the various execution platforms, like JACK and JADE on the agent side or Web Service Modeling Ontology (WSMO) on the service side.

3.2 Service-Oriented Architecture Modeling Language

Although there are several recent and ongoing activities on developing MDA-based techniques for supporting the design, development, and maintenance of SOAs (e.g. [8]), there does not exist a standardized metamodel for describing

---

[2] http://www.shape-project.eu/
[3] http://www.sciences.univ-nantes.fr/lina/atl/
[4] http://www.eclipse.org/gmt/mofscript/
[5] http://www.omg.org/docs/ad/08-05-03.pdf

services along with the relevant aspects on their provision and usage in a service-oriented system landscape. In 2006, the OMG started standardization process for SOA by issuing a request for proposal for an UML Profile and Metamodel for Services. The main objectives of this new standard for services is (i) to enable interoperability and integration at the model level, (ii) to enable SOAs on existing platforms through the MDA initiative, and (iii) to allow for flexible platform choices. The resulting Service-Oriented Architecture Modeling Language is based on the UML 2.0 metamodel and provides minimal extensions to UML. The modeling concepts of SoaML are as follows:

Participant. The key concept of a service is a capability offered by one entity or entities to others through well-defined interfaces. Those entities are called Participants. In SoaML, capabilities are provided or required by Participants through the interaction points, i.e. the UML Ports. To express that a Participant acts as service provider, the certain UML Port is stereotyped as Service. In contrast, if the capabilities are required by the Participant, the UML Port is stereotyped as Request.

ServiceInterface. The capabilities and needs of a Service or Request port are defined by its type, which is either a ServiceInterface, or in simple cases, a UML Interface. The ServiceInterface stereotype is like an interface, but has the additional feature that it can specify a bi-directional service, where both, the provider and consumer, have responsibilities to send and receive messages. The ServiceInterface specifies the roles that will be performed by the entities involved in order to provide/request a certain service and the behaviors that specify the interaction between service provider and requester in terms of message exchange.

ServiceContract. A key part of a service is the ServiceContract that defines the choreography that interacting Participants must agree to for the service to be enacted. The ServiceContract is the full specification of a service, which includes all information, choreography and any other characteristics of the service. A Participant plays a role in the larger scope of a ServicesArchitecture and, consequently, also either plays the provider or requester role within the contained ServiceContracts. The choreography of a ServiceContract allows specifying how the roles interact from a global perspective, internal processes are omitted.

ServicesArchitecture. A ServicesArchitecture provides a top-down view on a composed service. It is a network of participant roles providing and requesting services to fulfill a purpose. It defines the requirements for the types of Participants and service realizations that fulfill those roles. The ServicesArchitecture is defined as UML Collaboration to specify the set of roles collaborating under certain conditions. In the context of SoaML, the roles are normally filled with Participants playing a certain position in this ServicesArchitecture. A role defines how entities are involved in that collaboration (how and why they collaborate) without depending on what kind of entity is involved (e.g. a person, organization or system).

ParticipantArchitecture. A ParticipantArchitecture provides a bottom-up view on a composed service. It defines the roles necessary to compose the service as well as the ServiceContracts that define in which manner the roles are interacting. To the outside, a ParticipantArchitecture provides and requires interfaces.

Agent. The concept Agent extends Participant with the ability to be active, participating components of a system. Hence, the purpose of an Agent in SoaML is to specify a classification of autonomous entities (agent instances) that can adapt to and interact with their environment, and to specify the features, constraints, and semantics that characterize those agent instances. Agent extends Participant with the ability to be active, participating components of a system. They are specialized because they have their own thread of control or lifecycle.

3.3   Domain-Specific Modeling Language for MAS

The domain-specific modeling language for MAS (DSML4MAS) includes the core features of a language like an abstract syntax, concrete syntax as well as a formal semantics. Furthermore, model transformations to the agent-programming language JACK and JADE are provided that allow the execution of the design made with DSML4MAS. A detailed discussion on DSML4MAS is given in [6].

The abstract syntax of DSML4MAS is defined by the a platform independent metamodel for MAS (PIM4AGENTS). In order to support an evolution of the PIM4AGENTS metamodel, it is structured into several views each focusing on a specific viewpoint of MASs: The *agent view* defines how to model single autonomous entities, the capabilities they have to solve tasks and the roles they play within the MAS. Moreover, the agent view defines to which resources an agent has access to and which kind of behaviors (i.e. plans) it can use to solve tasks and achieve goals. The *organization view* defines how single autonomous agents are arranged to more complex organizations that may be defined on the base of various different structures, each of them may be adequate for a certain problem solving scenario. Organizations in PIM4AGENTS can be either an autonomous acting entity like an agent (i.e. organization concept is a specialization of agent), or simple groups that are formed to take advantage of the synergies of its members. The concept of collaboration defines in which manner an organization is used in terms of binding actors of interaction protocols to domain roles of organizations. The *role view* covers the abstract representations of functional positions of autonomous entities within an organization or other social relationships. In general, a role in PIM4AGENTS can be considered as set of features defined over a collection of entities participating in a particular context. The features of a role can include (but is not limited to) activities, permissions, responsibilities, and protocols. A role offers two specializations, i.e. the domain role is use to describe the necessary functionalities needed by organizations, whereas actors illustrate the participants of interaction protocols. The *interaction view* focuses on the exchange of messages between autonomous entities or organizations from a global perspective in terms of agent interaction protocols. The *behavior view* describes how the internal behavior (i.e.

plans) of intelligent entities can be defined in terms of combining simple actions to more complex control structures or plans that are used for achieving predefined objectives or goals. The behavioral view contains basic concepts from workflow languages as well as particular tailored concepts for describing more agent-oriented processes. The *environment view* contains any kind of entity that is situated in the environment and the resources that are shared between agents, roles or organizations to meet their objectives. The core environment mainly deals with how to define objects in terms of their attributes and operations. The *multiagent view* gives an overview on the core building blocks (e.g. agents, organizations, etc.) of the MAS. Finally, the *deployment view* describes the run-time agent instances involved in the system and how these are assigned to domain roles required by an organization.

3.4 Model-Driven Integration of Service Oriented Architectures and Multiagent Systems

MASs do not exist in pure isolation, hence, mechanisms need to be explored to combine MASs with other available software engineering approaches. As SOAs and their corresponding modeling language SoaML describes IT system in a very abstract manner, they provide a nice opportunity to illustrate how to utilize agent-based computing in service-oriented environments. The technique selected for combining SOAs and MASs bases on MDA. By comparing SoaML and PIM4AGENTS, we derive a number of basic mapping rules summarized in the remainder.

Mapping rule 1 deals with the mapping between ServicesArchitecture and Organization. Both concepts nicely correspond to each other, as both refer to roles that interact in accordance to some predefined processes or protocols. However, and this is the main difference between both constructs, a ServicesArchitecture does not perform any role to the outside. Hence, the generated organization is more or less utilized as a social structure providing the space for interaction. Moreover, the organization itself does neither own any plan nor perform any role to the outside and, hence, should not be considered as an autonomous entity in the MAS, but rather as a form of grouping the necessary autonomous entities to fulfill the service.

In the same way as a ServicesArchitecture specifies the top-down view on a service, applying service choreographies to describe the interaction between its roles, a ParticipantArchitecture defines how a service is orchestrated. Since an Organization in PIM4AGENTS offers mechanisms to describe the interaction from a global as well as from a local perspective, an Organization is also the best match for a ParticipantArchitecture as defined by mapping rule 2.

In contrast to a ServicesArchitecture, a ParticipantArchitecture illustrates a concrete entity in the system described. Thus, the target Organization may perform a DomainRole, which is either required inside a ServicesArchitecture, ServiceContract, or even in other ParticipantArchitectures. As previously mentioned in Section 3.2, the main purpose of a ServiceContract is to define the roles that agreed on the contract and how these interact with each other, which is expressed through any kind of UML behavior[6]. Hence, for representing a ServiceContract in PIM4AGENTS, the right choice is a Collaboration, which defines how the DomainRoles of its Organization are bound to the particular Actors of the Organization's Interactions. This is reflected by mapping rule 3.

Apart form ServiceContracts, we also apply mapping rule 3 when transforming a UMLL Collaboration, as a Collaboration is the generalization of a ServiceContract. For generating Interactions, we only introduce Actors, but do not make any assumption about the ACLMessages that are exchanged by the Actors within an Interaction. However, as SoaML does not use the concept of ACLMessage, we only define Messages that are part of the Environment of DSML4MAS. How this is done in detail is defined by mapping rule 9.

As previously mentioned, a CollaborationUse in SoaML defines how to use a ServiceContract in terms of role bindings. Consequently, it clearly defines, which roles of a ServicesArchitecture are bound to which roles of the particular ServiceContracts. An ActorBinding in PIM4AGENTS represents a similar concept, as it defines, which DomainRole is bound to which Actor of an Interaction. As the ActorBindings are contained by Collaborations, we map the CollaborationUse as follows:

The semantics of CollaborationUse (SoaML) and Collaboration (PIM4AGENTS) nicely correspond to each other, as both are used to describe how a ServiceContract (SoaML) and Organization (PIM4AGENTS) are used for a specific purpose. Therefore, mapping rule 5 is straightforward and describes how the bindings are mapped from a CollaborationUse to a Collaboration.

For modeling service choreography and orchestration in SoaML, UML Activity Diagrams are used as they allow to model a process from the perspective of a single entity, but also offer the concept of a partition to describe how several entities interact with each other. As specified by mapping rule 6, for mapping UML Activity Diagrams, we instantiate a number of Plans in PIM4AGENTS. The actual number depends on whether the activity diagram is partitioned through the UML ActivityPartition concept (i.e. choreography) or not (i.e. orchestration). In case of the former, for each partition one Plan is generated, in case of the latter, only a single Plan is generated. Mapping rule 6 specifies which kind of information from UML Activity Diagrams is extracted to fill the body of a Plan. The concepts used within an UML Activity Diagram can mainly be transformed into corresponding Plan concepts in an one-to-one fashion.

A UML Interface defines a collection of operations and/or attributes that ideally defines a set of processes. In order to represent this in an adequate manner in PIM4AGENTS, the concept of a Capability depicts the perfect match, as both, operations as well as attributes can be included into one of its Plans.

Messages that need to be exchanged in PIM4AGENTS are derived from the UML ControlFlows (cf. mapping rule 8) that are specified across the partitions in a UML Activity Diagram.

---

[6] UML behaviors can be described in four different ways: Activity UML Diagram, Use Case UML Diagram, Interaction UML diagram, and State Machine UML diagram. However, UML Activity Diagrams are the most common used within SoaML.

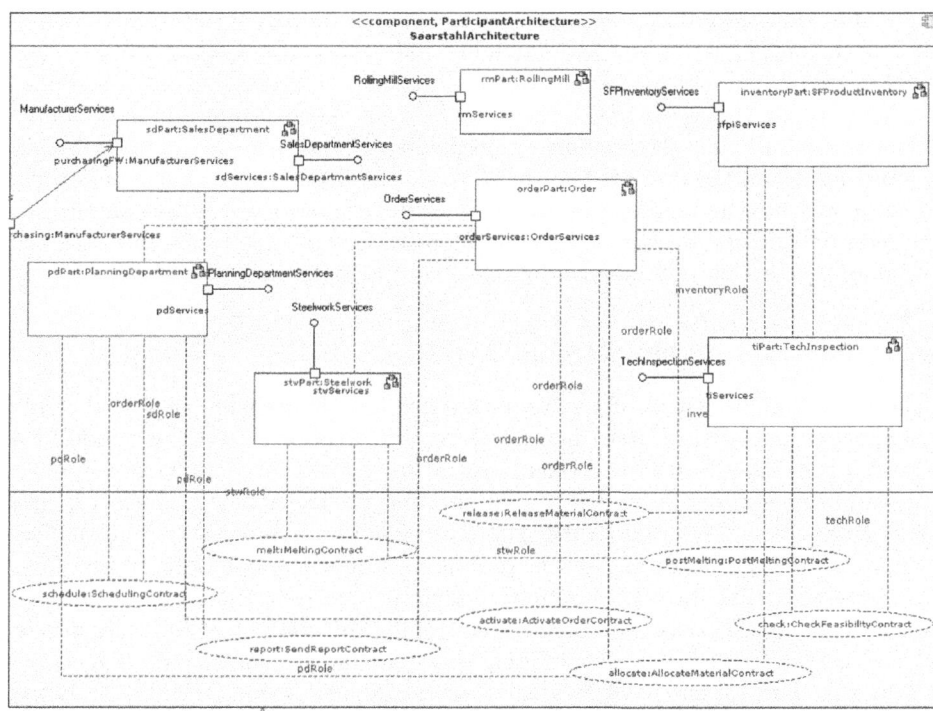

Fig. 2. Service-oriented architecture of Saarstahl AG

The mapping rules presented in this section, define a feasible transformation between SoaML and PIM4AGENTS. In the next section, we demonstrate how these transformations are applied to generate a corresponding PIM4AGENTS model. This model is further transformed to generate JADE code. For this purpose, we applied the model transformations described in [5]. This allows us to generate nearly 100% executable code with only minor manual adjustments.

4 Service-Oriented Supply Chain of the Saarstahl AG

Saarstahl AG is a German steel manufacturer with a substantial presence on the global market. The overall SOA architecture of the Saarstahl AG is as follows: All actors except the customer belong to the Saarstahl system. The customer is able to purchase products of Saarstahl by filling a purchase order form which is transfered to the sales department. The sales department then registers the order in the Saarstahl system which produces a production schedule for the order. Scheduling is done by the planning department, which validated the order's feasibility of production with the help of the technical inspection. The result is then reported to the sales department which informs the customer. If the order is feasible, the planning department activates the processing on the scheduled date. The first step of processing is to search the inventory for available material fitting the order's requirements. Available material is then assigned to the order. If there is not enough material available the planning department schedules a melting job at the steelworks. After material has been produced, the planning department validates the quality requirements. When the order quantity is completely allocated the order is transfered to the rolling mills management system. This represents the final step of the Saarstahl use case. Even if the complete architecture of Saarstahl has been modeled with SoaML, due to space restriction, we mainly focus on the Saarstahl architecture in the remainder of this section.

4.1   Saarstahl Architecture on SoaML

The ServiceArchitecture of the Saarstahl use case is depicted in Fig. 2. Every component (e.g. SalesDepartment, RollingMill, Steelwork, etc.) is modeled as Participant. Each Participant offers several services, where a service is modeled by an interface typed as ServiceCapability and instantiated by a class typed as ServiceInterface. The SaarstahlArchitecture itself encapsulates the internal services and offers an ordering service for the customers to the outside. The most important Participants of the SaarstahlArchitecture are the Order, SalesDepartment, PlanningDepartment, Steelwork, RollingMill and the ProductInventory. The interaction between the different participants is defined through service contracts. The exchange of message itself is defined through UML Activities. The PreProductionContract, for instance, is defined between the partners Sales-Department, Order and TechnicalInspector. The SaarstahlImp further includes the run-time agent instances SalesDeptImpl, RollingMillImpl, etc.

4.2   Generating the Agent-Based Design

The Pim4Agents output model, we will examine in the following, bases on the Saarstahl use case previously introduced by utilizing the model transformation from SoaML to Pim4Agents to obtain a Pim4Agents model of the use case. Due to space restrictions, we only focus on the organizational parts of the full Pim4Agents model, which is depicted in Fig. 3.

For visualization reasons, several participants and interactions are omitted. The purpose of the diagram is to give the reader an idea of how the transformation generates the corresponding MAS. In Pim4Agents, the internal architecture of SaarstahlArchitecture is specified by binding the transformed participants e.g. Order via domain roles to their responsibilities. The organizations in the diagram are created by mapping rule 2. Furthermore, the service contracts instantiated by SaarstahlArchitecture in the SOA have been transformed to interactions which are used by the SaarstahlArchitecture to coordinate its members. The diagram also shows a number of plans that are used by the organizations. These plans are generated from owned behaviors and activity partitions that are typed by roles the participant can perform.

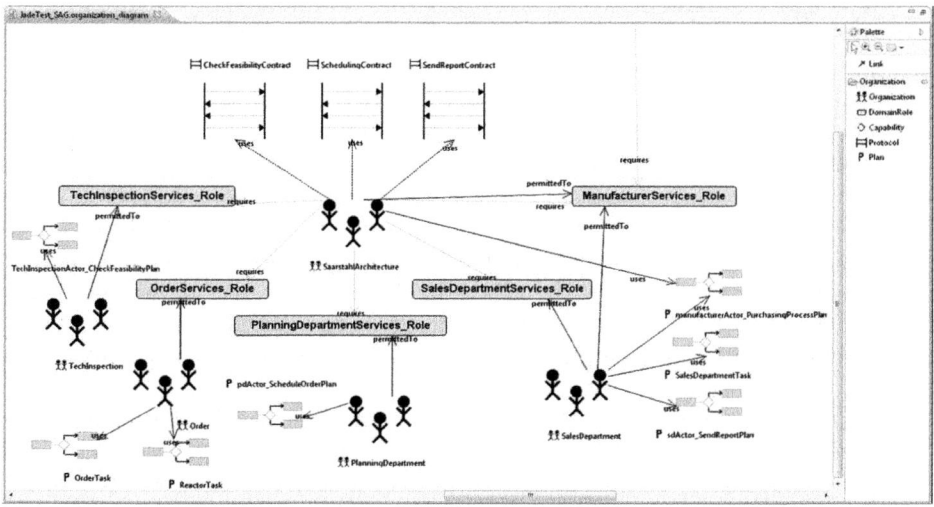

Fig. 3. Organization diagram of the Saarstahl supply chain

4.3   Relevance for Saarstahl

Saarstahl identified two major benefits by applying the presented approach. Firstly, interoperability of existing IT-solutions supporting specified problems like a short term planning for a steelwork, a detailed planning system for a rolling mill or some inventory management systems in between is improved. Secondly, there is a possibility of wrapping existing legacy systems of Saarstahl behind participants of the Saarstahl SOA. Thus, a SOA is created on top of legacy systems, the generated MASs allow the flexible orchestration of Web services. The implemented system, moreover, eases the replacement of legacy systems, as new IT-solutions can be tested in parallel to legacy systems for a period of time. Agents encapsulating a legacy system are able to forward requests to the legacy system as well as to the new systems and thus compare both results.

5   Dsml4Mas as Web Service Execution Engine

MAS are normally not considered as the standard execution architecture for SOAs. Standard Web service description formats like WSDL (Web Services Description Language) and orchestration engines like BPEL4WS (Business Process Execution Language for Web Services) might be more appropriate. However, the SHAPE model transformation architecture proofs that MASs and, in particular, DSML4MAS is an interesting option as agent systems, in general, and DSML4MAS in particular offer valuable features that are worth to investigate in the SOA context. From a research transfer point of view, the following lessons of the model-driven integration of SOAs and MASs could be learned:

– The agent paradigm is not new to SOAs, however, the presented model-driven approach between SoaML and DSML4MAS establishes one of the first proposals combining SOAs and the agent world through a generic model transformation. This allows to automatically transform the business requirements during IT design and development to a MAS that captures the business requirements, but additionally supports the execution in an intelligent manner.

– PIM4AGENTS is expressive enough to support a generic mapping from SoaML and necessary parts of UML. Most notably, the service choreography and orchestration described by SoaML can nicely be mapped to PIM4AGENTS, which allows representing service architecture from the external and internal perspective. BPEL4WS as the most known Web service orchestration engine lacks this expressivity.

– In its current version, SoaML offers only a kind of semantics expressed in natural language. Through the model transformation to DSML4MAS, the modeling constructs are grounded into analog concept of PIM4AGENTS whose semantics is clearly defined through the formal Object-Z specification given in, for instance, [7]).

6   Conclusion

This paper presented a model-driven framework to automatically transfer SOAs into MASs. The model transformation architecture bases on a mapping between SoaML and PIM4AGENTS–representing the abstract syntax of DSML4MAS. The resulting agent-based design can be generically transformed to an executable JADE implementation. The approach has been validated by modeling a real industrial use case from the steel industry. The mapping between SoaML and DSML4MAS is a necessary step in order to build interoperable agent systems on the PIM level. This is an important result towards bringing MASs into industry as any service description built upon SoaML can be automatically transformed to make use of the advantages the supported agent platforms offer.

References

1. Alonso, G., Casati, F., Kuno, H.A., Machiraju, V.: Web Services - Concepts, Architectures and Applications. In: Data-Centric Systems and Applications (2004)
2. Dickinson, I., Wooldridge, M.: Agents are not (just) Web services: Considering BDI agents and Web services. In: Proceedings of the Workshop on Service-Oriented Computing and Agent-Based Engineering, SOCABE 2005 (2005)
3. Endert, H., Hirsch, B., Küster, T., Albayrak, S.: Towards a mapping from BPMN to agents. In: Huang, J., Kowalczyk, R., Maamar, Z., Martin, D., Müller, I., Stoutenburg, S., Sycara, K. (eds.) SOCASE 2007. LNCS, vol. 4504, pp. 92–106. Springer, Heidelberg (2007)
4. Erl, T.: Service-Oriented Architecture: Concepts, Technology, and Design. Prentice Hall PTR, Upper Saddle River (2005)

5. Hahn, C., Madrigal-Mora, C., Fischer, K.: A platform-independent metamodel for multiagent systems. International Journal on Autonomous Agents and Multi-Agent Systems (JAAMAS) 18(2), 239–266 (2008)
6. Hahn, C.: A domain specific modeling language for multiagent systems. In: Padgham, L., Parkes, D.C., Müller, J., Parsons, S. (eds.) Proceedings of the 7th International Joint Conference on Autonomous Agents and Multiagent Systems (AAMAS 2008), vol. 1, pp. 233–240. IFAAMAS (2008)
7. Hahn, C., Fischer, K.: The formal semantics of the domain specific modeling language for multiagent systems. In: Luck, M., Gomez-Sanz, J.J. (eds.) AOSE 2009. LNCS, vol. 5386, pp. 145–158. Springer, Heidelberg (2009)
8. Johnston, S.: UML 2.0 profile for software services. Technical report, OMG, submitted to OMG ABSIG on SOA at 4/15 meeting in St. Louis (April 2006)
9. Kleppe, A., Warmer, J., Bast, W.: MDA Explained. The Model Driven Architecture: Practice and Promise. Addison-Wesley, Reading (2007)
10. Nguyen, X.T., Kowalczyk, R.: WS2JADE: Integrating Web Service with Jade agents. Technical Report SUTICT-TR2005.03, Information and Communication Technologies Centre for Intelligent Agents and Multi-Agent Systems (2006)
11. Padgham, L., Liu, W.: Internet collaboration and service composition as a loose form of teamwork. J. Netw. Comput. Appl. 30(3), 1116–1135 (2007)
12. Payne, T.R.: Web Services from an agent perspective. IEEE Intelligent Systems 23(2), 12–14 (2008)
13. Sadovykh, A., Hahn, C., Panfilenko, D., Shafiq, O., Limyr, A.: SOA and SHA tools developed in SHAPE project. In: Vogel, R. (ed.) Fifth European Conference on Model-Driven Architecture Foundations and Applications: Proceedings of the Tools and Consultancy Track. CTIT Proceedings Series, vol. 09-12, p. 113. University of Twente, Enschede (2009)
14. Singh, M., Huhns, M.: Service Oriented Architecture: Semantics, Processes, Agents. Wiley John & Sons, Chichester (2005)

Unifying Agent and Component Concepts
Jadex Active Components

Alexander Pokahr, Lars Braubach, and Kai Jander

Distributed Systems and Information Systems
Computer Science Department, University of Hamburg
{pokahr,braubach,jander}@informatik.uni-hamburg.de

Abstract. The construction of distributed applications is a challenging task due to inherent system properties like message passing and concurrency. Current technology trends further increase the necessity for novel software concepts that help dealing with these issues. An analysis of existing software paradigms has revealed that each of them has its specific strengths and weaknesses but none fits all the needs. On basis of this evaluation in this paper a new approach called *active components* is proposed. Active components are a consolidation of the agent paradigm, combining it with advantageous concepts of other types of software components. Active components, like agents, are autonomous with respect to their execution. Like software components, they are managed entities, which exhibit clear interfaces making their functionality explicit. The approach considerably broadens the scope of applications that can be built as heterogeneous component types, e.g. agents and workflows, can be used in the same application without interoperability problems and with a shared toolset at hand for development, runtime monitoring and debugging. The paper devises main characteristics of active components and highlights a system architecture and its implementation in the Jadex Active Component infrastructure. The usefulness of the approach is further explained with an example use case, which shows how a workflow management system can be built on top of the existing infrastructure.

1 Introduction

Building distributed applications is a demanding and complex task that naturally leads to new problems due to inherent system properties like message communication, concurrency and also non-functional challenges like scalability and fault-tolerance. In addition to these inherent properties current technology trends further increase the demand for novel software technical concepts helping to cope with these issues. Among the most prominent trends are increasing hardware concurrency and delegation of tasks to computer programs (cf. [12,16]), which will be discussed with respect to their software technical requirements.

Increased hardware concurrency results from the tendency of chip manufactors to increase processing power by creating multi-core processors with steadily more cores. This leads to the challenge on the software level of how to cope with and

J. Dix and C. Witteveen (Eds.): MATES 2010, LNAI 6251, pp. 100–112, 2010.

especially exploit this newly available degree of parallelism. Traditional rather sequential software products cannot profit much from multi-core technology except when multiple applications are run at the same time. In order to make use of the hardware resources it is necessary to provide conceptual means on the design and programming level and build massively concurrent applications that go beyond simply parallelizing for-loops. Otherwise performance gains will remain decent, because following Amdahl's law "the speedup of a program using multiple processors in parallel computing is limited by the time needed for the sequential fraction of the program".[1] Therefore, concepts for self-acting entities are required for embracing concurrency as a first-class design principle.

Delegation of work to computer programs is a trend that can be observed since a long time and is applied even in very complex and sensible domains today [16]. Building such complex and sensible application has several implications for the underlying software concepts. On the one hand the complexity demands rich possibilities for realizing software entities and also for the ways they can interact. Depending on the application scenario that is considered different kinds of entities (e.g. workflows or tasks) and also interaction styles (e.g. message based or method calls) may be appropriate. On the software level this diversity should be reflected by facilitating multiple entity and communication styles. In addition, when business critical domains are considered, the support of non-functional criteria like persistency, transactions and scalability is indispensable. These aspects are concerns that are orthogonal to business functionality and require that entities are under strict control of the execution infrastructure (typically named "managed" entities). Without such a management infrastructure it is very hard not to say impossible to realize the required non-functional mechanisms.

These requirements should be addressed as much as possible already on the underlying software paradigm level to avoid rebuilding solutions on the application level. The systematic realization of an application requires in addition to the conceptual properties of modelled entities also adherence to established software engineering principles. The summarized requirements for a software paradigm being able to build complex distributed applications are shown below:

1. support software engineering principles (e.g. de/composition and reusability)
2. exhibit different kinds of entity behavior (e.g. agent, workflow)
3. having rich interaction styles (e.g. messages, method invocation)
4. can act on their own (autonomously)
5. support non-functional characteristics (e.g. scalability and persistency)

Object orientation, although it has been conceptually extended with remote method invocation, fails in addressing these demands, because it has been conceived with a sequential non-distributed application view in mind. Hence, further paradigms like agents, active objects, components, and services have been devised building on basic object-oriented concepts. These paradigms have specific strengths and weaknesses but none of them is able to address the full range

---

[1] http://en.wikipedia.org/wiki/Amdahl's_law

of problems in distributed systems. The idea of this paper is integrating the strengths of promising paradigms into a new one called *active components*.

The next Section 2 provides an analysis of promising software engineering paradigms and lays down the foundations for the design choices of active components. Thereafter, in Section 3, the basic concepts of active components are described and in Section 4 their implementation and runtime infrastructure is presented. Highlighting the usefulness of the approach, Section 5 presents an example application, which realizes a workflow management systems using active components. Section 6 discusses related work and Section 7 concludes the paper.

2   Paradigms for Complex Distributed Systems

The work presented in this paper is a unification of the concepts of active objects, agents and components. These three paradigms have been selected, because they exhibit interesting technical properties with respect to the development of complex distributed systems. The paradigms will be analyzed with respect to the criteria elicited in the introduction. Other paradigms, such as service-oriented computing, may offer additional beneficial properties, but the inclusion of these properties is left to future work.

For mapping the criteria to technical properties of the paradigm entities, the categories *structure*, *interaction* and *execution* have been introduced. The structure category deals with the inner workings of an entity. The hierarchical aspect of structure addresses criteria 1 (software engineering principles) and demands that entities may need to be decomposed into smaller entities themselves. The second important aspect of entity structure are so called internal architectures, which conceptually capture different kinds of entity behavior as suggested by criteria 2. Criteria 3 requires supporting rich interaction styles as represented in the interaction category. With message-based interaction and object-oriented method invocation, the two most important interaction styles have been included as sub-properties in this category. The execution category considers how entities are embedded into a runtime environment. On the one hand, entities should be able to act autonomously as stated in criteria 4. On the other hand, the non-functional characteristics of criteria 5 (e.g. persistence and scalability) can only be achieved when entities are managed by an infrastructure.

2.1   Software Agents and Multi-Agent Systems

Software agents are a paradigm for open, distributed and concurrent systems [12]. An agent is commonly characterized as being *autonomous* (independent of other agents), *reactive* (advertent to changes in the environment), *proactive* (pursues its own goals), and *social* (interacts with other agents) and may be realized using *mentalistic notions* (e.g. beliefs and desires)[16]. Typically, an agent-based software application is realized as a multi-agent system (MAS), which is a set of agents that interact using explicit message passing, possibly following sophisticated negotiation protocols.

Advantages of the agent paradigm for building complex distributed systems can be found on the intra- and inter-agent level. Intra-agent level concepts allow defining the behavior of a single agent. Agents naturally embrace concurrency, as each agent is autonomous and can decide for itself about its execution. Moreover, many agent architectures have been developed [4], partially based on theories from disciplines such as philosophy and biology. They provide ready-to-use solutions for defining system behavior, that fit well to different problem settings (e.g. simple insect-like agents vs. complex reasoning agents). The inter-agent level deals with concepts to describe interactions among agents in a MAS. Agent interaction is primarily message-based, although other forms exist, such as environment-based interaction (e.g. pheromones for ant-like agents). Regarding message-based interaction, agent research has defined many ready-to-use interaction patterns for open distributed systems (e.g. for negotiation).

Limitations of the agent paradigm can be found in conceptual as well as technical aspects. An obvious conceptual limitation is that message-passing communication is not well suited for all application areas. Building such applications using message-oriented agents leads to cumbersome design with poor performance and maintainability. On the technical level, many existing frameworks provide no management infrastructure and therefore do not address non-functional properties. Moreover, often no sophisticated concepts for modularization on the intra-agent level are available.

2.2   Active Objects

Active objects [10] are a design pattern in the context of object-oriented software development, addressing issues of multi-threading and synchronization. The active object is an abstraction concept for concurrency. A scheduler in the active object manages the execution of method calls on the object's own thread. The pattern increases the concurrency of an application and also avoids synchronization issues, because local data is always accessed from the same thread.

The active object pattern excels at providing method-based interaction. From a developers perspective it may even be transparent, if a method is called on an active object or a conventional passive object. Additionally, the pattern provides some autonomous execution. The pattern decouples caller from callee and lets the active object decide, in which order requests are processed.

The pattern is not a fully-fledged paradigm for distributed computing and thus does not address the other properties. While it seems reasonable to have a hierarchical decomposition of active objects and also to equip active objects with message-based interaction capabilities, it is not obvious how internal architectures or a managed execution could be incorporated into the metaphor.

2.3   Software Components

The component metaphor [15] is inspired from the manufacturing industry, where preproduced components (potentially provided by an external supplier)

	structure		interaction		execution	
	hierarchical	int. arch.	msg-based	meth.call	auton.	managed
agents	partially	yes	yes	no	yes	partially
active objects	no	no	no	yes	yes	no
components	yes	no	yes	yes	no	yes

Fig. 1. Technical properties of paradigm entities

are assembled into a complete product. From a technical viewpoint software components facilitate forming a software application by composing independently developed subsystems on top of some substrate (component platform).

Regarding interaction, component models support message- as well as method-based interaction styles. Existing component platforms further simplify system implementation by providing a ready-to-use component management infrastructure. In this respect, many component platforms such as Java EE application servers address non-functional properties like persistence and replication, which easily allows achieving robustness and scalability of implemented systems.

A major drawback of using software components for distributed systems is the lack of a concept for representing concurrency. Most component models regard component instances as passive (i.e. non-autonomous) entities that only act on request (e.g. when a user performs an action through a web interface). Some infrastructures such as Java EE even prohibit the use of threads by the developer, as this would break transaction or replication functionality. Moreover, component models focus on the interfaces of components and do not address the internal structure apart from a hierarchical decomposition.

2.4   Summary

In Figure 1 it can be observed that each of the analyzed approaches handles the criteria, which have been set out in the introduction, to a different extent. On the one hand, agents and components are conceptually rich metaphors with only a few weaknesses. Agents have some weaknesses with respect to hierarchical decomposition and management infrastructure and do not support object-oriented method interaction. Components lack sophisticated internal architectures and do not support autonomous execution. On the other hand, active objects are not as conceptually rich as the other approaches. Yet, active objects are interesting, because they achieve a combination of method call interaction with autonomous execution. The analysis result motivates the unification of the paradigms into a new conceptual framework as described in the next section.

3   Active Component Concepts

In the following the main concepts for the active components approach will be laid down according to the earlier introduced categories execution, interaction

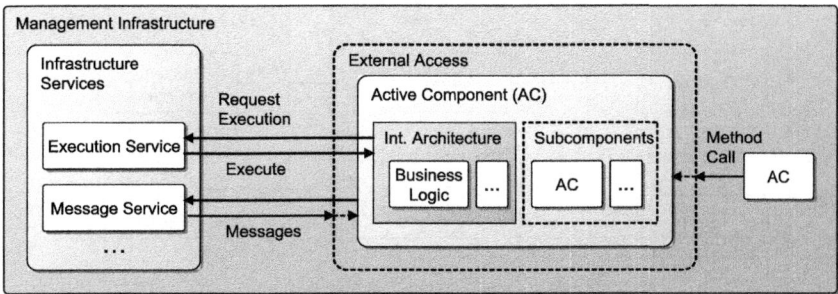

Fig. 2. Active Components (AC) architecture

and structure. The overall architecture is depicted in Figure 2 and consists of a *management infrastructure* containing *infrastructure services* and the *active components* themselves. In this respect the management infrastructure represents a container for all active components and is responsible for their operation.

The characteristics of *autonomous* and *managed* entities seem to be contradicting at first. Autonomous components are entities that want to decide on their own about their execution while the management infrastructure needs to have control about which and when components are executed. This means a management infrastructure always imposes the inversion of control principle (IOC), which puts the control flow responsibility to the infrastructure layer. For bringing together autonomy and management, active components need to follow implicitly the IOC principle by announcing execution requests to the infrastructure layer. Thus, for the programmer IOC is not visible as components can act autonomously, but internally are managed and follow the IOC of the platform.

The interaction of components can be *message-based* as well as *method-call-based*. Message based interaction is asynchronous (possibly remote) and uses unique component identifiers for addressing receiver components. Hence, it is very similar to agent based communication with the exception that no specific message format is imposed by the infrastructure. As result message formats can follow agent related specifications such as FIPA ACL[2] as well as other formats. For synchronization of method-call-based interaction, active components employ a similar scheme as active objects and provide a decoupling layer called *external access*. The layer separates the execution from the calling component and thus avoids inconsistent component states and reduces the possibility of deadlocks.

The behavior of an active component is determined by its *internal architecture* while the structure may include a *hierarchical* decomposition into subcomponents. Internal architectures allow making use of different active component types, thus letting the developer choose for each part of an application, which component type may be a good fit for the desired business functionality. Therefore heterogeneous applications consisting of a mix of component types can be built and interaction between these is easily possible due to the standard interaction means for all active

---

[2] http://www.fipa.org/specs/fipa00061/

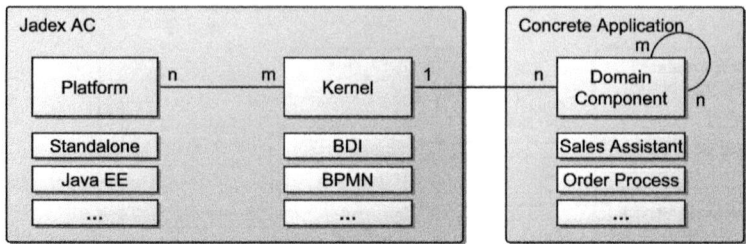

Fig. 3. Elements of the Jadex AC platform

components. Any component may further contain an arbitrary number of child components, which may follow the same or different internal architectures than their parent component. The hierarchy does not impose an execution policy such that child components are concurrent to all other entities. One key benefit of hierarchical components is that management commands can be applied to the whole hierarchy of a component allowing e.g. the termination or suspension of an application as a whole.

In summary, active components integrate successful concepts from agents, components as well as active objects and make those available under a common umbrella. Active components represent autonomous acting entities (like agents) that can use message passing as well as method calls (like active objects) for interaction. They may be hierarchically structured and are managed by an infrastructure that ensures important non-functional properties (like components).

4   Active Components Infrastructure

The active component concept has been realized in the Jadex AC (active components) platform. The implementation distinguishes the basic execution platform from the kernels, which represent different internal architectures. This separation allows developing kernels independently of the execution environment and also providing different execution environments that suit different application contexts. Figure 3 depicts the elements of the platform. The platform provides the infrastructure services (cf. Section 3) to the component instances. Different platform implementations are already available that allow executing components in a *Standalone* Java application as well as on top of the well-known *JADE* agent framework [2]. Furthermore, a platform for executing active components in *Java EE* application servers is currently under development.

4.1   Kernels

Several different internal architectures have already been realized as kernels, which can be categorized into agent kernels, process kernels and other kernels. The *BDI kernel* supports the development of complex reasoning agents, that follow the belief-desire-intention model [14]. Additionally, for insect-like agents,

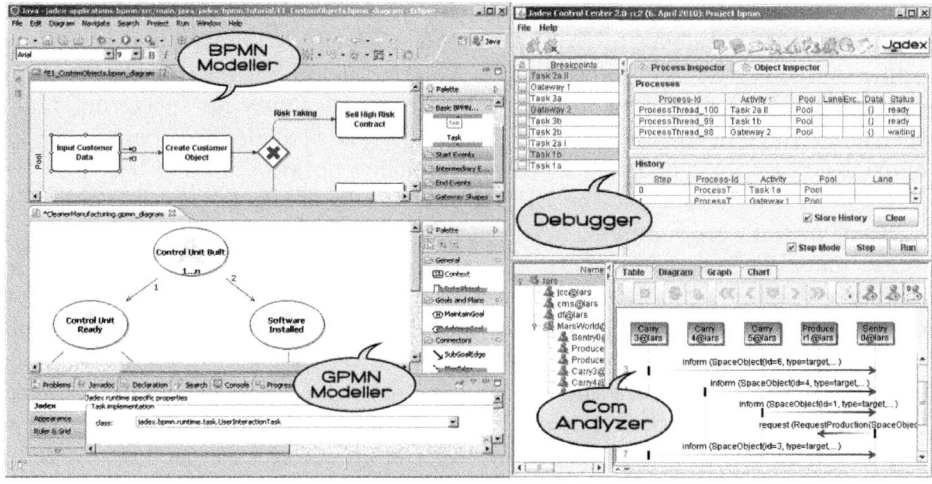

Fig. 4. Modeling tools (left) and runtime tools (right)

a so called *micro-kernel* is provided, which provides a simple programming style and supports the execution of large numbers of agents (>100000 in a desktop Java VM) due to a very low memory footprint. The *Task kernel* is in between the other agent kernels in terms of programming constructs and memory consumption and is best suited for agents performing a fixed set of tasks.

The execution of workflows modeled in the business process modeling notation (BPMN) is realized by a corresponding *BPMN kernel*. Moreover, the *GPMN kernel* interprets the so called goal process modeling notation, which is a unification of BDI agent and BPMN process concepts [6]. Finally, an *application kernel* is provided, that features configuration mechanisms for subcomponents as well as extension points for non-component functionality; so called spaces [13]. As indicated by the m:n-relation between kernel and platform, each kernel may run on any platform and each platform is capable of executing components based on any kernel. This facilitates building heterogeneous systems with different component kinds that interoperate seamlessly.

The right side of the figure represents the domain components, i.e. that a developer builds for a specific application. Each domain component is based on exactly one kernel as indicated by the 1:n-relation. Moreover, components may have an arbitrary number of subcomponents of any kernel. For example, an application based on Jadex AC allows seamless interaction between a *Sales Assistant* implemented as BDI agent and an *Order Process* modeled in BPMN.

4.2   Tool Support

Developing applications with the Jadex active component platform is supported by a suite of tools that can be coarsely divided into modelling and runtime tools (see Figure 4). Programming agents can be done using the Java and XML support of a standard development environment, while modeling workflows is supported by particular tools. For BPMN as well as GPMN diagrams, two eclipse-based editors are available. The *BPMN Modeller* is based on an existing eclipse BPMN plugin[3], and adds a custom properties view for specifying Jadex specific settings of diagram elements. The *GPMN Modeller* is a custom development for supporting the goal process modeling notation, and is based on the EMF/GMF framework like the BPMN modeller for a consistent look and feel.

Runtime tools are combined in the so called Jadex control center (JCC), which allows managing the components on a running platform. The JCC is built up by separate plugins, each of which addresses a specific tool need. All of the tools can be used for any of the previously described kernels. For space reasons, only some of the available tools are presented. The *Starter* (not shown) allows browsing existing component models and is used for creating component instances. Moreover, existing component instances are shown and may be stopped (destroyed) as well as suspended/resumed. The *ComAnalyzer* monitors and visualizes ongoing message-based communication among components and is a powerful tool for analyzing complex interactions. Recorded messages can be shown in different views (table, sequence diagram, 2D graph, bar/pie chart) and filtered according to rules entered by the developer. Finally, the *Debugger* supports stepwise execution of components as well as specifying execution breakpoints. Additionally, the different kernels provide specific extensions to the debugger allowing detailed component introspection, such as current activities of a BPMN process or current goals of a BDI agent. Descriptions of further tools can e.g. be found in [14].

4.3   Usage

The complete Jadex active component platform including kernels, tools and example applications is available as open source software via the project home page[4]. At the University of Hamburg, the platform is currently used in two externally funded DFG research projects as well as in a teaching course. The next section describes an example application from one of the research projects.

5   Example Application

An interesting research area is the application of agent concepts to implement and improve workflow concepts. Workflows often require a workflow management system (WfMS) for interaction with workflow participants and software they use, such as CAD applications and word processors. Since the users generally have their own workstations, the interaction with the workflow management system must be able to interact with the client software remotely using message passing. Such a WfMS was developed as part of the DFG project "Go4Flex", which deals with flexible workflows in areas like change management and production in cooperation with Daimler AG. The WfMS architecture is largely based on the

---

[3] http://www.eclipse.org/bpmn/

[4] http://jadex.informatik.uni-hamburg.de/

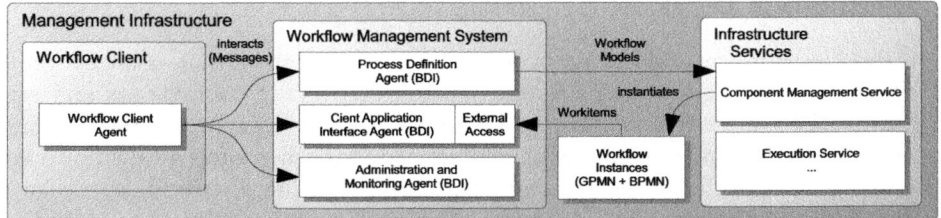

Fig. 5. The basic structure of the workflow management system

reference model of the Workflow Management Coalition and uses three kinds of active components as can be seen in Figure 5.

The system is based on three BDI agents each providing an interface exposing a specific subset of the WfMS functionality. The first agent provides access to stored workflow models and allows a user to add and remove models that are available to the WfMS. Workflow tasks which require user interaction (work items) are generated by the active workflows and are managed by the Client Application Interface Agent. The third agent provides monitoring and administrative capabilities.

The functionality of the agents is accessed by a workflow client using its own active component to exchange messages with the aforementioned agents. This active component can be of any type as long as it adheres to the communication protocol, which employs FIPA ACL messages and FIPA interaction protocols, like the FIPA Request Protocol for requesting a new workflow instance and the FIPA Subscribe Protocol to be informed about new work items. The use of messages and protocols allows a workflow client to be distributed and interact with the WfMS remotely. The current standard client is based on a BDI agent, however, using a different active component such as a micro-agent or a BPMN workflow would be possible. Using agents as workflow clients allows the implementation of features like cooperation between multiple workflow clients.

Due to the active component concept, the creation of new workflow instances can be delegated to the component management service of the Jadex platform so that the WfMS can handle any kind of workflow regardless of the concrete type. As a result, the WfMS automatically supports all types of workflows for which active component implementations are available, which currently includes both BPMN and GPMN workflows, but can be extended with additional workflow models like BPEL by simply providing a corresponding kernel.

The active component approach enables the workflow management system to use seemingly disparate concepts like agents and workflows seamlessly, allowing interesting new approaches of interaction between workflows and agents. The WfMS itself uses such interactions to implement functionality like passing of work items from workflows to the managing agent and finally to the application component where it will be processed. In addition, the use of active components allows the WfMS to abstract from the workflow type, thus allowing easy extensibility and avoiding explicit management of separate workflow engines.

6   Related Work

In the literature several attempts that aim at an integration of agent concepts with other paradigms can be found, whereby especially components and services have been considered. In this paper we focus on components so that first general comparisons of component and agent approaches will be taken into account. Thereafter, concrete integration attempts will be discussed. These have been structured according to their primary underlying paradigm, i.e. extending component approaches with agent ideas and vice versa.

One of the first discussions about components and agents can be found in [8]. It basically considers agents as next generation software components and explains potential advantages of multi-agent system technology. A deeper look into both paradigms has been revealed by Lind in [11], who compares them according to key characteristics of the conceptual entities, the interaction modes as well as the problem solving capabilities. The paper advocates that agent technology provides advantages with respect to flexibility and loosely-coupled interactions and can profit from component orientation by adopting software technical development ideas and execution infrastructure.

With respect to approaches that extend component concepts with agent ideas first Fractal [5] will be discussed. The framework itself provides sophisticated means for realizing hierarchical components distinguishing between client and server interfaces and providing a membrane metaphor that shields internals of a component from the outside. For parallel and distributed component execution Fractal has been extended in the Dream[5] and ProActive [1] projects, which aim at the integration of active object ideas. All Fractal programming principles are also valid within the extensions and the interaction style remains based on method-calls. The decoupling between caller and callee is achieved by using futures in the method signatures. The approaches are promising, but have some limitations due to the exclusive use of method-based interactions, making it hard to realize application cases that e.g. require negotiation mechanisms.

Another strand of development is targeted at the technical integration of components with agents. The main objective consists in executing normal agent software in a component infrastructure. A core advantage of this approach is that agent applications become managed software entities and thus inherit the non-functional properties from the underlying component execution environment. Companies like Whitestein [3] and Agentis[6] have built their commercial agent platforms on basis of such a proven infrastructure, which additionally alleviates the barriers of agent technology adoption. It has to be noted that this form of technical integration does not contribute much to a conceptual combination of both paradigms as agents remain the only primary entity form.

True conceptual integration approaches have been conducted in [9] and [7]. The first proposes so called AgentComponents, which represent agents internally built out of components. Externally, agents are slightly componentified

---

[5] http://dream.ow2.org/dreamcore/
[6] The company does no longer exist.

by wiring them together using slots with predefined communication partners, whereby communication is only handled using message passing. Other important aspects of component models regarding hierarchical composition or method-call based interaction forms have been neglected. In SoSAA [7] the architecture consists of a base layer with some standard component system and a superordinated agent layer that has control over the base layer. Typical reflective mechanisms of the component layer, like explicit binding controllers, facilitate the way the agent layer may exert changes on the components of the lower layer e.g. for performing reconfigurations. Although the overall combined architecture of components and agent contributes to promoting the strengths of both paradigms the approach treats components and agents as completely distinct entities and does not contribute much in consolidating both.

In summary, the possible positive ramifications of combining ideas from components and agents have already been mentioned in early research works. Despite this fact, only few concrete conceptual integration approaches have been presented so far. On the one hand, approaches that enhance component frameworks with active objects only support simple method-based interaction styles. On the other hand approaches leveraging agents with component concepts fail until now in providing a unified view on an agent-component software entity.

7   Summary and Outlook

In this paper paradigms for developing complex distributed systems have been analyzed. Agents, components and active objects have been contrasted with respect to their properties in the categories structure, interaction and execution. The notion of an active component has been proposed as a combination of the properties, which are deemed advantageous for building complex distributed systems. Most importantly, an active component combines autonomous acting (like an agent) with managed execution (like a component). Furthermore, active components support message-based and method call-oriented interaction and allow hierarchical decomposition as well as elaborated internal architectures. The Jadex active component platform has been presented as a freely available implementation of the active component concept. As an example application, a WfMS has been put forward, which is based on the different active component types and is developed in cooperation with Daimler AG.

Future work on the technical level will target the integration of the Jadex AC platform into Java EE application server environments. On the conceptual level, the active component concept can be extended in several directions by including properties of other paradigms, e.g. looking at the area of service oriented computing or considering extensibility as prevalent in plugin systems.

References

1. Baude, F., Caromel, D., Morel, M.: From distributed objects to hierarchical grid components. In: Meersman, R., Tari, Z., Schmidt, D.C. (eds.) CoopIS 2003, DOA 2003, and ODBASE 2003. LNCS, vol. 2888, pp. 1226–1242. Springer, Heidelberg (2003)
2. Bellifemine, F., Caire, G., Greenwood, D.: Developing Multi-Agent systems with JADE. John Wiley & Sons, Chichester (2007)
3. Brantschen, S., Haas, T.: Agents in a J2EE World. White paper, Whitestein Technologies (2002)
4. Braubach, L., Pokahr, A., Lamersdorf, W.: A universal criteria catalog for evaluation of heterogeneous agent development artifacts. In: Proc. of AT2AI-6, IFAAMAS (2008)
5. Bruneton, E., Coupaye, T., Leclercq, M., Quéma, V., Stefani, J.-B.: The fractal component model and its support in java: Experiences with auto-adaptive and reconfigurable systems. Softw. Pract. Exper. 36(11-12), 1257–1284 (2006)
6. Burmeister, B., Arnold, M., Copaciu, F., Rimassa, G.: Bdi-agents for agile goal-oriented business processes. In: Proceedings of AAMAS'08 (2008)
7. Dragone, M., Lillis, D., Collier, R., O'Hare, G.M.P.: Sosaa: A framework for integrating components & agents. In: Proc. of SAC 2009. ACM Press, New York (2009)
8. Griss, M.: Software Agents as Next Generation Software Components (2001)
9. Krutisch, R., Meier, P., Wirsing, M.: The agent component approach: Combining agents, and components. In: Schillo, M., Klusch, M., Müller, J., Tianfield, H. (eds.) MATES 2003. LNCS (LNAI), vol. 2831, pp. 1–12. Springer, Heidelberg (2003)
10. Lavender, G., Schmidt, D.: Active object: An object behavioral pattern for concurrent programming. In: Pat. Languages of Prog. Design, vol. 2, Add.-Wesley, Reading (1996)
11. Lind, J.: Relating agent technology and component models (2001)
12. Luck, M., McBurney, P., Shehory, O., Willmott, S.: Agent Technology: Computing as Interaction (A Roadmap for Agent Based Computing). AgentLink (2005)
13. Pokahr, A., Braubach, L.: The notions of application, spaces and agents — new concepts for constructing agent applications. In: Proc. of MKWI'10 (2010)
14. Pokahr, A., Braubach, L., Lamersdorf, W.: Jadex: A BDI Reasoning Engine. In: Multi-Agent Programming: Languages, Platforms and Applications. Springer, Heidelberg (2005)
15. Szyperski, C., Gruntz, D., Murer, S.: Component Software: Beyond Object-Oriented Programming, 2nd edn. ACM Press and Addison-Wesley (2002)
16. Wooldridge, M.: An Introduction to MultiAgent Systems. John Wiley & Sons, Chichester (2001)

Impact of Competition on Quality of Service in Demand Responsive Transit

Ferdi Grootenboers[1], Mathijs de Weerdt[1], and Mahdi Zargayouna[2]

[1] Delft University of Technology,
P.O. Box 5031, 2600 GA Delft, The Netherlands
[2] INRETS Institute, Gretia laboratory, Building "Descartes II",
2 rue de la Butte Verte, 93166 Noisy le Grand Cedex, France
`fgrootenboers@gmail.com, M.M.deWeerdt@tudelft.nl, zargayouna@inrets.fr`

Abstract. Demand responsive transportation has the potential to provide efficient public door-to-door transport with a high quality. In currently implemented systems in the Netherlands, however, we observe a decrease in the quality of service (QoS), expressed in longer travel times for the customers. Currently, generally one transport company is responsible for transporting all customers located in a specified geographic zone. In general it is known that when multiple companies compete on costs, the price for customers decreases. In this paper, we investigate whether a similar result can be achieved when competing on quality instead. To arrive at some first conclusions, we set up a multiagent environment to simulate the assignment of rides to companies through an auction on QoS, and the insertion of allocated rides in the companies' schedules using online optimization. Our results reveal that this set-up improves the quality of the service offered to the customers at moderately higher costs.

Keywords: Dial-a-ride, multi-company, quality of service, auction.

1 Introduction

Demand-Responsive Transit (DRT) services are a form of transport that is a compromise between public transportation and individual taxis. The principle of these systems is to define the itineraries and schedules of the vehicles based on the requests of the users. Customers are thus provided with relatively cheap door-to-door transportation insofar as they accept to share their ride with others and tolerate a certain detour from their direct trip. The main problem with current DRT services as organized in the Netherlands is that the quality of service (QoS) cannot be guaranteed over longer periods of time. A strong competition for the right to serve for a period of usually three years promises a reasonable quality at a low price, but has the effect that a company that is too optimistic in the contracting phase receives the assignment, but subsequently cannot meet the quality objectives without incurring serious losses. Heavily penalizing such a company for a low QoS will soon lead to bankruptcy, and therefore an even lower QoS until a new company has been found.

J. Dix and C. Witteveen (Eds.): MATES 2010, LNAI 6251, pp. 113–124, 2010.

QoS is usually not specifically addressed in the allocation of rides. The minimization of company's costs is treated as a primary objective, while imposing a minimal QoS [1]. The idea put forward in this paper is to let companies compete on QoS on a day to day basis given a price per kilometer that is fixed in advance. Given known results that competition can reduce the total costs, the question is can we use it to improve the QoS instead, and at what costs? Here we divert from research on using auctions and other price-based mechanisms for task allocation in that not the company with the lowest price receives the task, but the company that guarantees the highest QoS. Our main hypothesis is that this approach significantly increases the QoS without much additional costs.

To test our hypothesis, we implement the proposed approach in a multiagent environment (see Section 3), simulate series of requests, simulate the bidding and scheduling process of the companies (in Section 4), and compute the resulting costs and QoS in Section 5. We compare these results to a single-company setting where the company optimizes costs with and without a guaranteed QoS level.

2   Background

DRT services are usually modeled as a Dial-a-Ride Problem with Time Windows (DARPTW), an extension of the Vehicle Routing Problem. A DARPTW is defined by a set of customers and a fleet of vehicles. Each customer desires to be transported from an origin location to a destination. Customers can impose a time window which includes the earliest possible time and the latest possible time they can be either picked up or delivered. The dynamic DARPTW (D-DARPTW) is NP-hard, which can be proven by a translation from the Traveling Salesman Problem (TSP) [2]. The problem can be solved exactly by modeling it as a Mixed Integer Program (MIP) [3], or by applying heuristics [4]. The disadvantage of using exact algorithms in a dynamic environment is that these algorithms take too much computation time. The disadvantage of using heuristics is that in some cases the solutions are significantly far from the optimal solution.

In a technique called *on-line optimization* the optimal solution is searched for with exact algorithms, but only taking into account that part of the problem that is relevant for the moment [5]. For instance, when searching for the best departure times of the locations of a request to insert into a current schedule, only that part of the current schedule that can be influenced by inserting the new request needs to be considered in the solution process. This results in smaller problems as input for exact algorithms, which implies less computation time. In our simulations of the multi-company environment we apply this online optimization for the insertion of a ride into the schedule of one of the companies.

3   The Multi-company DARPTW

In this section, we define a DARPTW where multiple companies compete for requests. The general principle is that the companies announce an offer to the customer, who chooses the company that will serve its request. Conditioned on

some negotiated constraints, the winning company can then insert the request
into its schedule.

3.1 Problem Definition

The DARPTW can be represented by a directed graph of locations and rides
between these locations, $G = (L, R)$. The set of locations L contains two vehicle depots for each company, that serve as start and end vertex of all vehicles
(denoted by 0 and $2n + 1$), n pickup locations $P = \{1, \ldots, n\}$, and n delivery
locations $D = \{n + 1, \ldots, 2n\}$. This implies that $L = \{0, 2n + 1\} \cup P \cup D$.

A request is a combination of a pickup location $i \in P$ and a delivery location
$n + i \in D$. Time windows are associated with a location i as $[s_i, e_i]$, with s_i the
earliest possible time the request can be served at that location (either pickup or
delivery), and e_i the latest possible time the request can be served. Each location
i has an associated load q_i, which denotes the number of passengers that are to
be pickup up or delivered at that location. We define $q_0 = q_{2n+1} = 0$, $q \geq 0$ for
$i = 1, \ldots, n$, and $q_i = -q_{i-n}$ for $i = n + 1, \ldots, 2n$. Each company has a set of
vehicles denoted by K, and with each vehicle $k \in K$ a maximal capacity Q_k and
a maximal route duration T_k are associated. The cost of a ride from location i
to j with vehicle k is denoted by c_{ij}^k, and the travel time of a ride between i and
j is denoted by t_{ij}. To account for service time at locations (i.e. time to get in
and out the vehicle), we associate with every location i a service duration $d_i \geq 0$
and $d_0 = d_{2n+1} = 0$.

3.2 Mechanism Overview

A customer announces its request to the center, and this is forwarded to all
known companies. Once a company receives a new request, it checks whether it
is possible to insert it into one of its vehicle schedules. If it is not possible to
insert the request into one of the company's vehicle schedules, the company will
not place a bid in the current auction. Otherwise, a bid value is calculated for this
request. When the center has received all bids, it determines the best one (the
highest QoS) and sets the conditions that have to be met by the winning company
in serving the request. The winning company is informed of the determined
conditions, and all other companies are sent a message that they have not won
the auction. The winning company then inserts the request into the schedule
of one of its vehicles. We assume there is always the possibility to have the
request served by a taxi company outside the system at a (usually high) so-called
reservation price. This is done when no bid is offered below this reservation price.
The following subsections detail the elements of this process, starting with the
computation of the QoS calculation.

3.3 Bidding Service Quality

Usually, the additional costs needed to serve a request is used as a bid [6], and to
minimize overall costs, the request is assigned to the vehicle that has announced

the bid with the lowest additional costs. In our work, we let the companies compete on the QoS for an incoming request. Therefore, the bid value in our setting contains the QoS that a company promises to provide. We define QoS as the ratio of the actual ride time to the direct ride time. For instance, when the time to travel from A to B directly (i.e. with no detours) is equal to 5 minutes, and the vehicle drives from A to B via C, in 7 minutes, then the QoS is $\frac{5}{7}$. For customers, this measure emphasizes one of their biggest complaints, namely large detours. For companies, this ratio is a measure of how efficiently different rides are combined.

A vehicle's route is modeled by a sequence of locations i with associated service times d_i and departure times t_i. Furthermore let the minimal time needed to drive from location i to location j be denoted by t_{ij}. The QoS for a request with pickup location i and delivery location j can then be calculated as follows:

$$QoS_{ij} = \frac{t_{ij} + d_i + d_j}{t_j - t_i} \qquad (1)$$

3.4   Auction on QoS and Pre-determined Payments

The mechanism that we propose is based on a *reversed sealed-bid second-price auction*, using QoS instead of prices. In such an auction, each bid is private to the company that submits it, and the winner of the auction has to meet the details of the second-highest bid value. The auction is *reversed*, because there are multiple sellers (the companies) and a single buyer (the customer). This single buyer announces the details of its request, and then the companies can determine a bid value. The winning company is the company that announces the highest QoS, and if multiple companies announce the same highest bid, one of these companies is arbitrarily selected as winner. The request that has been auctioned is allocated to the winning company, which then has to serve the request with the amount promised by the second-highest bidder.

In our setting, the payment for the service is not defined by the auction, but must be set on forehand. We set the payment equal to a *price per kilometer* C_{km} multiplied by the direct distance between the pickup and the delivery location of the customer's request. The profit of a company is then defined as the total *income* a company receives from serving requests minus the total *costs* needed to serve these requests. Clearly, C_{km} essentially determines the income of the companies.

Let for each request $(i, j) \in R$ the direct distance t_{ij} be given. For this problem, we define solutions for two hypothetical situations with complete knowledge of the requests during the day (in advance). We let $OPT(R)$ denote the transportation costs when all rides are optimally combined (in hindsight), and $OPT^{1.0}(R)$ denote the transportation costs when each request is served with a QoS of 1.0.

Proposition 1. *If an auction on QoS is used for multiple companies, and the (fixed) price per kilometer C_{km} is below $\frac{OPT(R)}{\sum_{(i,j) \in R} t_{i,j}}$ few people will be transported. If C_{km} is above $\frac{OPT^{1.0}(R)}{\sum_{(i,j) \in R} t_{i,j}}$, everyone will be transported separately.*

Proof. The lower bound for C_{km} is the minimal total costs needed to serve all requests divided by the total direct distance traveled by all customers. When C_{km} is set below this value, companies have more costs than income, except when a ride largely overlaps with an existing ride (which is never the case when the schedule is still empty). Companies will thus not bid in the auction. Therefore few people will be transported. On the other hand, when C_{km} is set above the average cost of transporting everyone separately, every company makes a net profit for each customer. Therefore, every company will bid a QoS of 1.0 for every request, because it then has the highest chance to win the auction. Since this holds for all companies, all requests have to be served with QoS 1.0.

4   Computations for the Companies

The computations of the transport companies are based on online optimization for the insertion of rides, and for bid determination use a look-ahead on possible future requests via a Monte Carlo simulation in combination with an insertion heuristic. Both approaches are detailed below.

4.1   Online Optimization

Every company has to solve a DARPTW problem to find the set of routes for their vehicles. We define a planning horizon H, which is the time period for which the routes are planned. A solution for one company is represented as follows. Let u_i^k be the time at which vehicle k starts servicing at a location i, w_i^k the load of vehicle k upon leaving location i, and r_i^k the ride time of a customer that places the request to travel from i to $n + i$. In the model that follows, x_{ij}^k is equal to 1 if and only if a ride from location i to j is allocated to vehicle k.

In Figure 1 the entire model is given, in which the objective function is to minimize total routing costs (see Equation 2). Constraint 3 ensures that all requests are served only once and Constraint 4 ensures that every vehicle will once drive to the start and end depot. Together with 5 and 6 this guarantees that every request is served once by the same vehicle and that each vehicle starts and ends its route at a depot. Constraint 7 states that the arrival time at a location must be higher or equal to the start time of servicing at the starting location, plus the service duration at that location, plus the time of the ride from start to end location. It is also obvious that the load of a vehicle at the end location of a ride is higher than or equals the load of that vehicle at the start location (Constraint 8).

The travel time of a user is higher than or equals the time the vehicle is at his delivery location minus the time he picked up the user and minus the duration of servicing at the pickup location; this is ensured by Constraint 9. Constraint 10 states that the duration of a vehicle to drive from the start depot to the end depot must be less than or equal to the total route duration specified for that vehicle, while Constraint 11 ensures that every location is visited within the specified time horizon. The ride time of a passenger is specified to be at least as

Minimize

$$\sum_{k \in K} \sum_{i \in L} \sum_{j \in L} c_{ij}^k x_{ij}^k \tag{2}$$

subject to

$$\sum_{k \in K} \sum_{j \in L} x_{ij}^k = 1 \qquad\qquad (i \in P), \tag{3}$$

$$\sum_{i \in L} x_{0i}^k = \sum_{i \in L} x_{i,2n+1}^k = 1 \qquad (k \in K), \tag{4}$$

$$\sum_{j \in L} x_{ij}^k - \sum_{j \in L} x_{n+i,j}^k = 0 \qquad (i \in P,\ k \in K), \tag{5}$$

$$\sum_{j \in L} x_{ji}^k - \sum_{j \in L} x_{ij}^k = 0 \qquad (i \in P \cup D,\ k \in K), \tag{6}$$

$$u_j^k \geq (u_i^k + d_i + t_{ij}) x_{ij}^k \qquad (i,\ j \in L,\ k \in K), \tag{7}$$

$$w_j^k \geq (w_i^k + q_j) x_{ij}^k \qquad (i,\ j \in L,\ k \in K), \tag{8}$$

$$r_i^k \geq u_{n+i}^k - (u_i^k + d_i) \qquad (i \in P,\ k \in K), \tag{9}$$

$$u_{2n+1}^k - u_0^k \leq T_k \qquad (k \in K), \tag{10}$$

$$s_i \leq u_i^k \leq e_i \qquad (i \in L,\ k \in K), \tag{11}$$

$$t_{i,n+i} \leq r_i^k \leq H \qquad (i \in P,\ k \in K), \tag{12}$$

$$\max\{0, q_i\} \leq w_i^k \leq \min\{Q_k, Q_k + q_i\} \quad (i \in L,\ k \in K), \tag{13}$$

$$x_{ij}^k = 0 \text{ or } 1 \qquad (i,\ j \in L,\ k \in K). \tag{14}$$

Fig. 1. Mixed Integer Program formulation to allocate requests to vehicles within a company. The objective function minimizes costs.

big as the time of a direct ride between its pickup and delivery location and at most as big as the planning horizon (Constraint 12). The load of a vehicle can never be higher than the highest possible load specified. Note that the load of a vehicle increases at a pickup location and decreases at a delivery location, so we can state Constraint 13. The last constraint ensures that we deal with binary variables, so that a variable denotes whether a ride is allocated to a vehicle or not, and we cannot specify that half of that ride is allocated to another vehicle. For the insertion of requests by a company, we use the mathematical model that we have just defined. This formulation evolves over time ignoring (previously inserted and) serviced requests.

4.2   Bid Calculation

To check whether an incoming request can be inserted, we use the insertion heuristics developed by Jaw et al. [4] and Solomon [7]. This is done before a bid value is calculated, and can save expensive computation time. If the request is feasible, the company can propose a bid to the customer.

A company wants to maximize its profit, defined as income minus costs. The company can gain income by serving requests (winning auctions) and it can decrease costs by combining requests. Combining requests often leads to a lower QoS (because there are less direct rides), which can lead to winning less auctions. Promising a higher QoS results in a higher probability to win the auction, but decreases the flexibility to insert future requests.

There are different costs associated with the different QoS values that a company can bid. In general, a company can bid a low QoS for low internal costs, or a high QoS for higher internal costs. For a single-shot second-price auction, it can be shown that it is optimal to bid the highest price possible. However, this is not the case in our (repeated) auction on quality.

Proposition 2. *If each company bids the highest QoS possible, all rides will be transported at QoS of 1.*

Proof. When a company bids the highest QoS possible for the first request, this bid will be a QoS of 1, since its vehicles have empty routes so far. When all companies follow this behavior, the second "price" will also be a QoS of 1, so the ride is accepted at a QoS of 1. When a route contains only rides with a QoS of 1, a next ride cannot be combined, so the highest QoS possible will also be 1. With induction, all rides will be transported at a QoS of 1.

To avoid this side effect of using QoS as a bid for the companies, we allow them to incorporate knowledge about future requests in their bid calculation. This way, they reason about the future possible combinations of the current request while bidding the promised QoS, instead of reasoning only about the current request. To incorporate the expected profit of future requests, the companies must have some knowledge about the distribution in time and space of future requests. From this distribution, they can calculate the expected profit for an incoming request, based on future requests that can give the companies possibilities to combine rides and lower costs. To this end, we use a Monte Carlo [8] simulation in combination with an insertion heuristic.

Estimating expected profit. The idea is to estimate the *expected profit* that a company would make assuming that the current request is inserted into the schedule. To calculate the expected profit, a distribution has to be known on the arrival location and time of future requests. With the help of these distributions, a set of possible future requests can be generated and inserted into the schedule. Once this is done, the total costs needed to insert these requests, and the total income gained by inserting them can be calculated. This expected profit is calculated by using an insertion heuristic based on the works of Jaw et al. [4] and Solomon [7].

Monte Carlo simulations. The specific set of generated future requests can have a big influence on the calculated expected profit. Therefore, a Monte Carlo simulation [8] is performed. The above algorithm is repeated a number of times, and the final expected profit is taken as the average expected profit of these repetitions. To obtain the highest QoS level for the current request, taking into account future requests, Monte Carlo simulations are performed for different levels of QoS. The level for which the expected profit is closest to zero is taken as the bid value.

5 Experiments and Results

The main hypothesis to be tested is the following.

Hypothesis 1. *When multiple companies compete on QoS, the average QoS is higher than in a situation with a single company which minimizes costs. Transportation costs are also higher.*

But also for a single company we expect that transportation costs are higher when the QoS is higher:

Hypothesis 2. *A higher required QoS is more expensive (for a single company).*

As discussed before, requiring a higher QoS from a single company fails in practice, because in general, a higher QoS is more expensive, and for example penalties are not sufficient to incentivize a company to meet the agreed QoS. Our main thesis is that competition can be used to realize a higher QoS, and we expect that this can be done at approximately the same additional cost as for a single company, leading to a third hypothesis.

Hypothesis 3. *When multiple companies compete on QoS, the costs are not significantly higher than in a situation with a single company which minimizes costs with the same average QoS.*

5.1   Experimental Setup

To test these hypotheses, we run the mechanism and algorithms proposed in the previous section on a set of benchmarks. The size of these benchmark problems is chosen such that each one takes at most about 1 hour computation time to solve. This decision resulted in a set of 100 problem instances, each containing 16 customers, in which the coordinates and the pickup and departure times of the requests are distributed following a uniform distribution. We consider these instance over a planning period of 4 hours. The considered network is a continuous map, defined by a square area of 20 by 20 km with a node on every km. To make the problem instances dynamic, we add to each customer the moment at which it becomes available to the system. This is done by randomly choosing a number in the interval $[e_i - 90, e_i - 60]$ (i.e. between 90 and 60 minutes before the earliest pickup or delivery time). We choose these values because we want the instances as dynamic as possible. This means that customers announce their requests quite late, but such that vehicles are able to respond to schedule

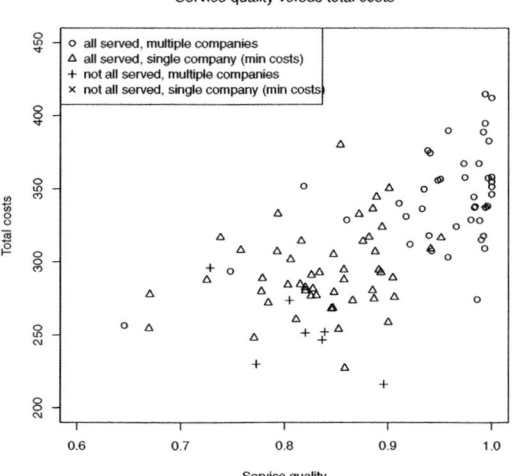

Fig. 2. QoS versus total costs for a multiple company setting and a single company

changes. The maximum capacity for each vehicle is set to 3 passengers. All the experiments have been performed in Java and Java Agent DEvelopment Framework (JADE) [9] on an Intel Xeon E5345 2.33GHz with 16 Gb RAM. Each company uses the MIP-solver SCIP to insert assigned requests. SCIP is one of the fastest non-commercial solvers [10].

To test the hypotheses, we run the system two times for each problem instance. The first time two companies have two vehicles each and compete on QoS. The second time, there is only a single company, having four vehicles and minimizing costs. In a single-company setting, the company does not have any incentive to bid high QoS, because it knows already that it contractually gets assigned all the requests.

5.2 First Experiment

In Figure 2, a plot is given for the comparison of QoS and total costs between a situation with a single and a situation with multiple companies. Two clouds of points can be distinguished. The cloud of points of instances with multiple companies is situated with relative high QoS and high total costs. The other cloud of points has less quality and less total costs and mainly contains instances with a single company. A paired t-test is performed for both average QoS and total costs. The mean difference for QoS is 0.097 with a higher quality in the multi-company setting. The confidence interval is $[0.071, 0.122]$ and the probability that these results are obtained assuming that there is no difference between the two settings is 5.98×10^{-10}. A t-test gives us a mean difference of 37.5 higher total costs for the multi-company setting with a confidence interval of $[25.3, 49.8]$, and a p-value of 1.25×10^{-7}.

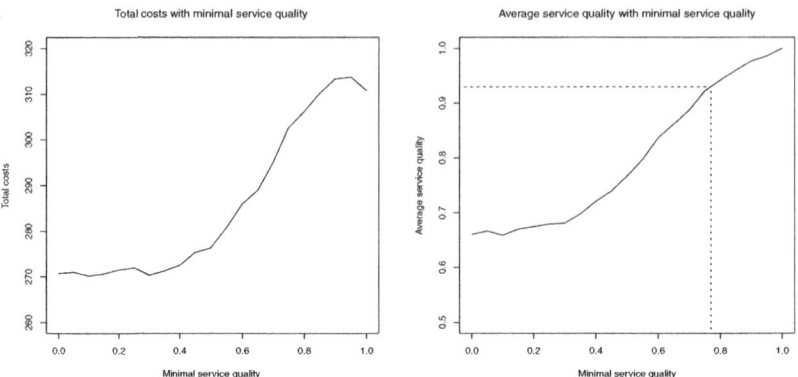

Fig. 3. Average total costs (left) and QoS (right) for instances with a minimal QoS

In conclusion, we have discovered that total costs are about 13% higher in the multi-company setting than in the single-company setting. The fact that companies in a multi-company setting have the incentive to bid higher service quality instead of minimizing costs, results in a higher average service quality. This follows from the results of the paired t-test showing that the QoS of the multi-company setting is 12% higher. Both differences are (very) significant, confirming Hypothesis 1.

5.3   Second Experiment

In the previous experiment, the single company did not take any required level of QoS into account. However, to make a fair comparison of costs (to establish the second hypothesis), we would like to have the same average QoS for the single company as the multiple companies obtain by competition. To arrive at a certain average QoS, we ensure that each ride of the single company has a certain minimal QoS. To determine how to set the required QoS to arrive at such a desired *average* QoS, we first run the experiments for a single company for a required QoS of $\{0.00, 0.05, \ldots, 1.00\}$. We then investigate the relation between these required QoS levels and the average QoS, and at the same time the relation between the required QoS levels and the total costs, to test Hypothesis 2.

In Figure 3 (left), it is shown that the average total costs are increasing as from a QoS level of 0.4, with a slight decrease at level 1.0. This last decrease of average total costs can be interpreted by the fact that if the minimal QoS level is 1.0, less requests can be served, which leads to lower total costs. The non-increasing part of the figure (from level 0.0 to 0.4) can be explained by the fact that the levels do not influence the outcome, because even when a single company minimizes costs, it still serves requests with an average QoS of about 0.66. This is also shown in Figure 3 (right), in which we see no increase in QoS at this interval.

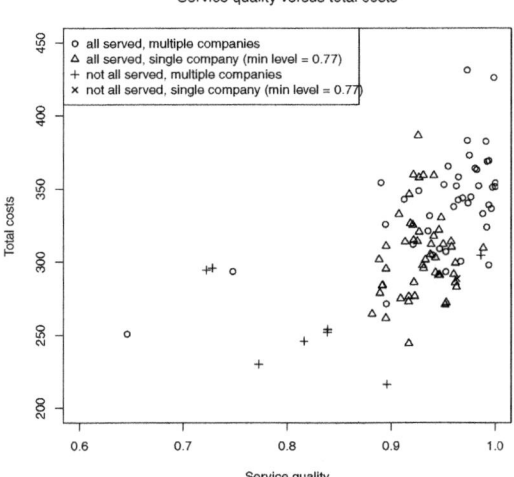

Fig. 4. QoS versus total costs for a multiple company setting and a single company setting in which the single company acts like a company in a multi-company setting

Besides these two exceptions, overall there is a strong correlation between total costs and minimal QoS. The correlation coefficient over the complete range 0.93, confirming Hypothesis 2. When we take only the interval from 0.40 to 0.95 into account, the correlation coefficient is even 0.99. The minimal QoS level that is needed in order to let the company in the single-company setting serve requests with an equal average QoS as in the multi-company setting is derived by searching in Figure 3 (right) for the corresponding level. The average QoS over all instances in the multi-company setting is 0.93 and when we search for the corresponding minimal QoS level we find a value of 0.77.

Subsequently, we run the first experiment again, but now requiring a QoS of 0.77 for the single company. In Figure 4 a scatter plot is shown in which QoS is plotted against total costs, for the multi-company and single-company setting. From this we observe that the costs are somewhat higher in the multi-company setting, but the points in the plot are too close to each other to give a proper judgment about this measure. The paired t-test gives us a mean difference of 23.5 total costs, a 95%-confidence interval of $[11.9, 35.0]$, and a p-value of 1.71×10^{-4}, with higher total costs in the multi-company setting. Another paired t-test is performed to verify that the difference in average QoS between the two settings is not significant. The results of this test confirm this with a mean difference of 0.0013 (higher in the multi-company setting), and a p-value of 0.92.

We thus conclude that compared to the multi-company setting, the total costs in a single-company setting are less, even if this single company provides equal QoS, rejecting Hypothesis 3.

6 Discussion

We conclude that if the price per kilometer is fixed within a reasonable range (Proposition 1), and expectations about the future are somehow taken into account (see also Proposition 2), it is indeed possible to obtain a higher QoS in door-to-door transportation by letting multiple companies compete on QoS (Hypothesis 1). However, in our experiments, the costs are about 7% higher than in the idealistic case where a single company always meets a required QoS while minimizing costs.

For future work, we aim to study other definitions of QoS. For instance, we are thinking about taking into account deviations from desired departure/arrival time. We also plan to consider more realistic generation of requests, based on real data. Besides, we plan to define mechanisms where companies compete both on QoS as well as on costs. In addition, we believe better results can be obtained if the mechanism allows for bidding on combinations of requests. Finally, this paper focused mainly on an experimental evaluation of the idea of competing on quality. It would be very interesting to also provide a theoretical analysis. This is particularly challenging, since the mechanism is in fact a sequential auction.

References

1. Cordeau, J.F.: A branch-and-cut algorithm for the dial-a-ride problem. Operations Research 54, 573–586 (2006)
2. Karp, R.M.: Reducibility among combinatorial problems. In: Miller, R.E., Thatcher, J.W. (eds.) Complexity of Computer Computations, pp. 85–103. Plenum Press, New York (1972)
3. Ropke, S., Cordeau, J.F., Laporte, G.: Models and branch-and-cut algorithms for pickup and delivery problems with time windows. Networks 49, 258–272 (2007)
4. Jaw, J.J., Odoni, A.R., Psaraftis, H.N., Wilson, N.H.M.: A heuristic algorithm for the multi-vehicle advance request dial-a-ride problem with time windows. Transportation Research Part B: Methodological 20, 243–257 (1986)
5. Mahr, T., Srour, J., de Weerdt, M.M., Zuidwijk, R.: Can agents measure up? a comparative study of an agent-based and on-line optimization approach for a drayage problem with uncertainty. Transportation Research: Part C 18, 99–119 (2010)
6. Mes, M.: Sequential Auctions for Full Truckload Allocation. PhD thesis, Universiteit Twente, Enschede, The Netherlands (2008)
7. Solomon, M.: Algorithms for the vehicle routing and scheduling with time window constraints. Operations Research 15, 254–265 (1987)
8. Metropolis, N., Ulam, S.: The monte carlo method. Journal of the American Statistical Association 44, 335–341 (1949)
9. Bellifemine, F., Poggi, A., Rimassa, G.: JADE - a FIPA-compliant agent framework. In: Proceedings of the Practical Applications of Intelligent Agents (1999)
10. Achterberg, T.: SCIP - a framework to integrate constraint and mixed integer programming. Technical Report 4-19, Zuse Institute Berlin (2004)

Towards Distributed Agent Environments for Pervasive Healthcare

Stefano Bromuri[1], Michael Ignaz Schumacher[1], and Kostas Stathis[2]

[1] Institute of Business Information Systems
University of Applied Sciences Western Switzerland (HES-SO)
TechnoArk 3, CH-3960 Sierre, Switzerland
{stefano.bromuri,michael.schumacher}@hevs.ch
[2] Department of Computer Science
Royal Holloway University of London (RHUL)
Egham, UK
kostas.stathis@rhul.ac.uk

Abstract. In this paper we present a prototypical pervasive health care infrastructure, whose purpose is the continuous monitoring of pregnant women with gestational diabetes mellitus. In this infrastructure, patients are equipped with a body-area network made of sensors to control blood pressure and glucose levels, where the sensors are connected to a smart phone working as a hub to collect the data. These data is then fed to a pervasive GRID where abductive agents provide a diagnosis for the actual reading of the sensors and contacting health care professionals if necessary. We also show how, by applying the concept of agent environment, we are facilitated in defining a pervasive GRID for roaming agents that monitor continuously the health status of the patients.

1 Introduction

If current trends in mobile phone technologies, personal digital assistants, and wireless networking are indicative of the way people will interact between them in the future, then our everyday activities is likely to be based upon an abundance of devices and applications providing the computational resources of a complex ubiquitous computing environment. Although the potential of combining these numerous applications and devices is very promising, many different current applications leave the environment's functionalities unexplored and only a small fraction of the environments potential is utilised.

Of particular relevance to the intelligent environment area is the problem of healthcare monitoring using ICT. As cures for life threatening conditions are being discovered, life expectancy increases significantly. As a consequence, the cost for healthcare will grow significantly due to the rise of the number of people that have permanent or chronic health conditions.

Diabetes is a very common chronic illness that is the fourth leading cause of death in most developed countries [1]. Amongst all the conditions related to diabetes, the case of gestational diabetes mellitus (GDM) is of particular interest

J. Dix and C. Witteveen (Eds.): MATES 2010, LNAI 6251, pp. 125–137, 2010.

as it occurs during pregnancy due to increased resistance to insulin but the precise mechanisms underlying it remain unknown. About 4% of pregnant women incur in this sort of complication. The current approach includes a planned diet, exercise and self-blood glucose monitoring tests that can be administered at home. In several cases the doctor requires that the patient visits the dietitian twice per week. However, often two checks every week are not enough: as if the hyperglycemia last for more than one day, this may cause macrosomia (excessive growth of the foetus). Thus, in these cases it is important to act as fast as possible to prevent any serious complication to the mother and the baby, by normalising the blood pressure and glucose levels with appropriate and quick treatments.

To achieve continuous monitoring, we propose a prototypical pervasive healthcare infrastructure, to collect data, monitor and alert GDM patients and inform their caretakers with historical values. Our primary goal is to break the boundaries of the hospital care, allowing patients to be monitored while living their day-to-day life and to keep in touch with healthcare professionals. The importance and significance of the proposed study is to show how by using the mechanisms proposed by distributed agent environments, we can model a distributed infrastructure to provide continuous monitoring to GDM affected women, by means of situated cognitive agents programmed using abductive logic programming. It is important to say that the focus of this study is not on creating a new cognitive model for agents, rather than showing how to model pervasive healthcare applications by means of distributed agent environments. In particular, this paper proposes an early stage prototype of the infrastructure. A first in-lab prototype has been developed, defining the agents functionalities, running simulators of sensors, using Android [9] and testing on single computer. The evaluation of the prototype in real settings and its extensions are subject of future work.

The reminder of the paper is structured as follows: Section 2 presents a background on the problem of GDM; Section 3 is a description of the system we developed; Section 4 presents the relevant related work; finally Section 5 concludes this paper and draws the lines for future work.

2   Motivating Scenario: Gestational Diabetes Mellitus

During pregnancy, some women have such high levels of glucose in their blood that their body cannot produce enough insulin to absorb it all [15]. As specified in [18], GDM affects approximately 4% of pregnant women. GDM is frequently associated with age, pregnancy weight, family history and ethnicity. GDM can increase the risk of health problems developing in an unborn baby, so it is important that the glucose levels in the pregnant woman blood are under control. If untreated or poorly controlled, GDM can cause the baby to: have macrosomia (excessive weight at birth); develop hypoglycemia at birth; develop jaundice (yellow skin); develop respiratory distress syndrome; die after week 28 of pregnancy; die in infancy. As Van Wootten and Turner specify in [18], it is estimated that in normal pregnancies the rate of macrosomia occurrence is about 10%, while in pregnancies where GDM is involved, this rate is around 44% [17], but when a woman with GDM has some sort of basic nutrition counseling with glucose monitoring, this rates drops to 14%-18%.

In GDM, if the blood pressure keeps high for a long time and the patient experiences stomachache, headache or oedema, there is a high risk of preeclampsia which is a pregnancy induced hypertensive state. Preeclampsia may develop from the 20th week of gestation and it is characterised by high blood pressure and about 300 mg of proteins in the urine in a 24h sample, a condition called protenuria. Preeclampsia is different from a condition called Pregnancy Induced Hypertension (PIH), which involves developing high blood pressure without protenuria. Preeclampsia is generally asymptomatic but it may evolve to eclampsia, a life-threatening complication characterised by seizures and eventually coma or death. Both preeclampsia and PIH are considered very serious conditions to keep under control [12].

It is clear that in the scenario of GDM, having a system that allows for continuous monitoring would be of great benefit to reduce the rates of macrosomia in women affected by GDM and to reduce the risks of preeclampsia, but there are some assumptions that is necessary to make and some requirements that it is necessary to consider: (a) pregnant women are usually young and they are used to technologies such as smart phones; (b) pregnant women want to maintain their lifestyle and carry on their day-to-day activities; (c) GDM is characterised by blood pressure, glycemia, body weight and a set of symptoms and complications that are inter-related between each other.

3   The Pervasive Healthcare Infrastructure

As the basis for the definition of our prototype, we utilised a pre-existing distributed agent platform called GOLEM [3,4,6,5] which is based on the concept of agent environment. First of all it is better to specify what we mean with *agent environment* and *environment*. In general with the term *environment* we mean the world that is external to the agents and that the agents can inspect by using the *agent environment*. On one hand we define the *agent environment* as an entity that mediates the interaction between the agents and resources deployed in the system, working as medium of interaction. On the other hand the *agent environment* hides to the agents the complexity of dealing with the state of the environment, by providing standard interfaces and standard descriptions to the resources in the external environment. In the scope of this paper we use *environment* in terms of a place or a set of places delimited by borders defined in terms of longitude and latitude in the real environment, and that are mapped to a *distributed agent environment* for monitoring purposes, where every node of the distributed agent environment has an assigned area of the real environment.

As specified in [4], the GOLEM platform models a distributed environment in terms of the patterns proposed by distributed event based systems (DEBS) [2]. Thus, the advantage of GOLEM is that we can utilise a platform that handle the dispatching of events in a distributed environment where the entities deployed on top of the platform are publishers and subscribers of events. GOLEM models four main entities which are objects, agents, avatars and containers.

Objects are passive reactive entities that encapsulate a service. Such objects can be used by *agents*, which represent the cognitive part of the agent environment. *Avatars* are particular kind of agents that represent users in the agent environment. Agents, objects and avatars are deployed within *containers*. Containers represent a portion of the distributed agent environment and they work as mediators for the interaction happening between agents and objects in the distributed settings. The container behaviour in GOLEM can be defined declaratively by means of the Ambient Event Calculus (AEC). The AEC is a particular dialect of Event Calculus [11] that allows to handle the concurrent modification of objects states and agent states in distributed settings.

The AEC also allows to define topologies of GOLEM containers in terms of neighbours containers and super and sub containers. The purpose of the pervasive healthcare environment we deployed is to deliver continuous monitoring to GDM patients outside the boundaries of hospital care, allowing healthcare professionals to keep in touch with the patients and allowing the patients to keep their life style. The pervasive healthcare infrastructure is associated to a real environment where the patients can move using a mobile phone to connect to GOLEM containers in form of avatars. Every GOLEM container in the network represents a different area of the city where the patient resides. For example Fig. 1(a) shows a portion of a network associated to an area of the city of Lausanne, around the Centre Hospitalier Universitaire Vaudois (CHUV).

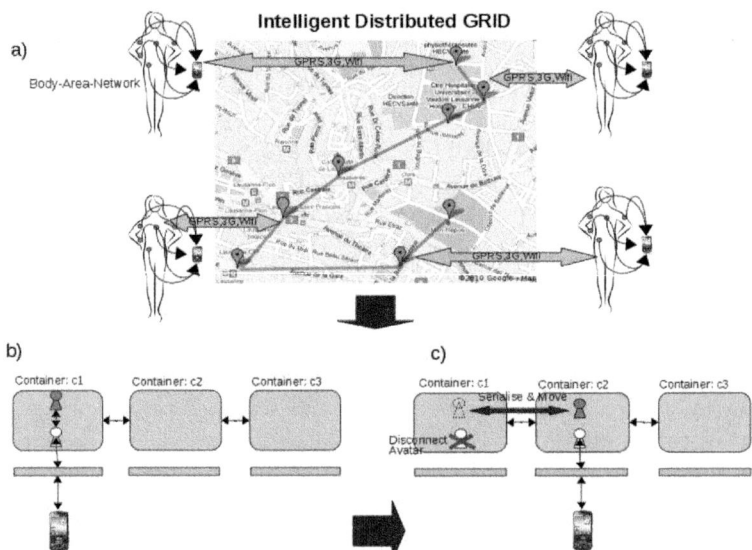

Fig. 1. a) Intelligent Environment fo Diabetes Monitoring b) and c) show how mobility of avatars and agents take place due to the mobile phone changing location in the real environment

Utilising an agent environment to communicate with a smartphone brings a set of advantages with respect to smartphone-only based solutions. First of all despite the fact that modern smart phones have a lot of computational power, computation and communication intensive applications tend to consume their battery very quickly, while in our case we only have to deal with communication with the network. Secondly, having an agent environment at support of the application allows us to introduce new and personalised services at runtime, decoupling the analysis of the data from its production. Thirdly, we can decouple the reasoning, embedded in the agents, from the actual services, embedded in the objects available to the agents in a particular location. Finally, modelling the pervasive healthcare environment as a distributed agent environment, allows us to reuse the mediation capabilities of the agent environment to define coordination and communication patterns between the agents when needed, while with a hub only based solution this kind of interaction would be technically difficult to support.

To represent the state of a GOLEM container, such as the ones shown in Fig. 1(b) and Fig. 1(c) we use the object-based notation of C-logic, a formalism that describes objects as complex terms that have a straightforward translation to first-order logic [7] and can be queried using the AEC. For example the following C-logic term specifies that

```
pervasive_golem_node:c1[
  uri ⇒ "container://one@134.219.7.1:13000", type ⇒ open,
  latitude ⇒ 46.5253, longitude ⇒ 6.6438,
  location_name ⇒ 'Centre Hopitalier Universitaire Vaudois Lausanne',
  neighbours ⇒ { pervasive_golem_node:c2, pervasive_golem_node:c3},
  entities ⇒ { agent:a1, agent:a2}]
```

a GOLEM container c1 has been deployed, it is identified by the URI container://one@134.219.7.1:13000, is an open container, it is associated with a certain latitude and longitude in the real environment, it represents the location named 'Centre Hopitalier Universitaire Vaudois Lausanne' and it has a set of neighbours in the distributed agent environment. To deal with the distributed topology presented in Fig. 1(a) we use the predicates of the AEC. For example, the following two AEC rules (see [4] for a more detailed description):

```
happens(Event,T)← attempt(Event,T), possible(Event,T).
happens(Event, T)← attempt(Event, T), necessary(Event, T).
```

specify that an action in the GOLEM agent environment happens only if it has been attempted and it is possible or necessary, where possible/2 and necessary/2 rules are application dependent rules. In other words, possible/2 rules specify what are the actions that is possible to perform in the environment given its current (possibly distributed state), while the necessary/2 rules specify what are the actions that happens as a consequence to previous events.

Moreover, to provide the mediation necessary to handle events in the distributed setting in [4] we presented the locally_at/8, neighbouring_at/9 and regionally_at/9 primitive predicates to link the state of distributed containers, following a logic programming approach. Briefly, the definition of locally_at is as follows:

```
locally_at(Cld, Path, Path*, Id, Cls, Att, V, T)←          locally_at(Cld, Path, Path*, Id, Cls, Att, V, T)←
  holds_at(Cld, container, entity_of, Id, T),                instance_of(SCId, container, T),
  holds_at(Id, Cls, Att, V, T),                              holds_at(SCId, container, super, Cld, T),
  append(Path, [Cld], Path*).                                append(Path, [Cld], NewPath),
                                                             locally_at(SCId, NewPath, Path*, Id, Cls, Att,V,T).
```

The definition of locally_at/8 states that the state of an entity can be inferred either from the top-level container or from a sub-container. If the states is inferred in the top-level container, then the predicate holds_at/5 is applied to infer the attribute Att of value V of an entity of class Cls and identifier Id. If the first predicate fails, then the second predicate moves the computation in a sub-container. In this way containers can be recursively embedded inside other containers as objects, according to the topology needed, and deployed on different hosts. The neighbouring_at/9 and the regionally_at/9 predicates have a similar behaviour but allow to query adjacent and super-containers respectively. Finally, to specify how the state of an entity modifies over time, we utilise initiates/5 and terminates/5 rules. For example, the following initiates/5 rule specifies when the position of an agent changes to the one the agent moves to:

```
initiates(E, avatar, A, position, Pos) ← do:E [actor ⇒ A, act ⇒ move:M [destination⇒ Pos]].
```

The complete description of the event's effects also requires to terminate the attribute holding the old position of the agent by means of a terminate/5 rule. In the current prototype the agent environment takes care of pairing agents and avatars as well as defining the mobility rules (i.e. what are the conditions that move an agent from one container to another) that implement the behaviour shown in Fig. 1(b) and Fig. 1(c). We define the following rules for mobility purposes:

```
possible(E,T)←                                    possible(E,T)←
  move:E[actor⇒avatar:A, move ⇒ Pos],               instance_of(Id,topology,T),
  instance_of(Id,topology,T),                        holds_at(Id,topology,borders,Borders,T),
  holds_at(Id,topology,borders,Bdr,T),               outside_borders(Bdr, Pos),
  inside_borders(Bdr, Pos).                          neighbouring_at(this, [], [C], 1, Id, topology, borders, Bdr, T),
                                                     inside_borders(Bdr,Pos).
```

The first one states that it is possible to move in the space represented by a container only if this space is within the borders controlled by the container. Otherwise, the second rule specifies that it is possible to move outside the borders only if there is another container that is responsible for a certain area where the patient is currently moving. The following AEC rules:

```
necessary(E, T)←                                  necessary(E, T)←
  happens(E*, T),                                    happens(E*, T),
  deploy:E* [deploy⇒avatar:Av],                      disconnect:E* [actor⇒A, new_container ⇒ C],
  not neighbouring_at(this, [], [C], 1, Av, caretaker, _, T),   holds_at(A,avatar,caretaker,Id,T),
  deploy:E[agent⇒caretaker:A].                       physical_act:E[move_to⇒ C agent⇒ Id].
```

State respectively that whenever an avatar is deployed in the agent environment (event E*), also its caretaker agent is deployed (event E), and that whenever an avatar disconnects from the agent environment to connect to a new container, the agent associated to the avatar is also serialised and moved to the new container. Finally, a further necessary/2 rule defines that an avatar is moved to a different container when outside the boundaries of the current container, but we omit the details as it is simpler than the ones presented above.

3.1 The Body-Area Network

In addition to objects and agents, GOLEM allows the embodiment of users by means of avatars in the distributed agent environment. In this prototype every patient is equipped with a smart phone loaded with a software capable to read the data produced by the sensors worn by the patient. The smart phone then allows the patient to interact with the GOLEM agent environment by means of their avatar as shown in Fig. 2.

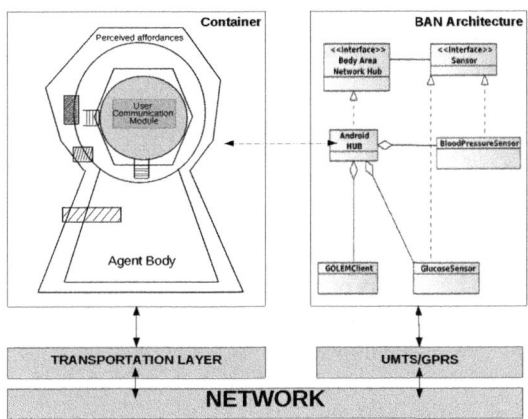

Fig. 2. The BAN Architecture

Users of the network have a wearable body-area network (BAN) that monitors periodically the blood pressure and the glucose levels of the patient. In the current prototype, the sensors are simulated and the values are entered directly by the patients, but in the future BAN will be built in term of Bluetooth sensors that monitor the physiological signs of the patient. In more details, the BAN monitors the variation in time of three values which are systolic blood pressure, diastolic blood pressure and glucose levels.

Moreover the terminal allows the patient to specify the symptoms that are being experienced during the day, through the interface shown in Fig. 3.

Thanks to the fact that the users are embodied in the agent environment as avatars, they can produce events in the agent environment as the following one:

pressure_reading:e1[avatar ⇒ avid1, caretaker_agent ⇒ ag1,systolic_pressure ⇒ 120, diastolic_pressure ⇒ 80].
location:e2[avatar ⇒ avid1,latitude ⇒ Lat, longitude ⇒ Lon].

The event specified above is pressure_reading event with identifier e1, produced by the avatar avid1 for the caretaker agent ag1, and it contains a systolic pressure value of 120 and a diastolic pressure value of 80, while the event e2 is used by the system to keep track of the patient in the real environment and to move her from one container to another when the necessary/2 rules previously explained are triggered.

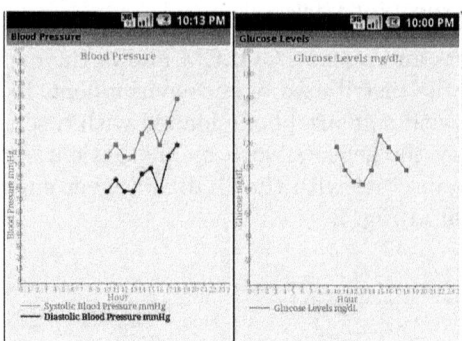

Fig. 3. The Smart Phone UI

3.2   The Caretaker Abductive Agents

In this paper we focus on agents that can diagnose the current condition of a GDM affected patient by means of abuctive logic programmed agents, differently from [6], where we focused on the navigation in the environment. In particular in this section we will describe the current prototypical cognitive model, exemplifying the behavior of the agent given a particular situation or event by showing extracts of the agent mind code.

Abductive logic programming (ALP) is a high level knowledge-representation framework that can be used to solve problems declaratively based on the idea that a set of seemingly unrelated observed facts (results), are somehow connected according to well known laws, thus offering an explanation of what might be true. As defined in [10], given a background theory T, and an observation G, the task of ALP is to compute a set of ground atoms Δ called explanation, and a ground substitution θ such that $\Delta \cup T \models G\theta$. Moreover, the set of atoms contained in Δ belongs to a set of predicates A, also called abducibles that are predicates for which there is not complete information. More formally we can say that an abductive framework is expressed in terms of a tuple $< T, \Delta, IC >$ where T is a knowledge base, Δ a set of abducibles and IC a set of integrity constraints on the abducibles. We utilise the abductive locic agent mind architecture depicted in Fig. 4.

Such an agent mind is based on the following cycle, which is an extension of the model presented in [5]:

```
cycle(T)← see(Percept, T), revise(Percept, T), choose(Action, T), execute(Action, T), now(Tn), cycle(Tn).
```

Briefly, the see/2 stage takes a percept out of the queue of percepts at a certain time T and it passes it to a revise/2 stage which in turns updates an event calculus database keeping the state of the world that is of interest for the agent (in this case the patient status). The most important stage is the choose/2 stage, of which we show the specification below:

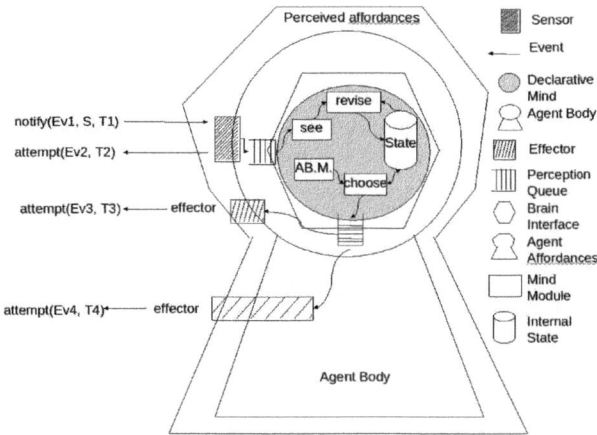

Fig. 4. Abductive Agent Mind Cycle

choose(Action, T)←
    instance_of(AvatarID, avatar, T),
    findall(S, holds_at(AvatarID,symptom,S,T), Symptoms),
    findall(A, select(Symptoms,A,T), Acts),
    higher_priority(Acts, Action, T).

higher_priority(ActList, Act, T)←
    member(Act, ActList), priority(Act, P, T),
    not (member(ActX, ActList), not ActX = Act,
    priority(ActX, PX,T),
    PX > P).

The choose stage selects a possible action by means of the select/3 and higher_priority/3 predicates. The select/3 predicate chooses then the best action to perform (such as contacting a doctor), given a diagnosis produced by the abductive module. For example a subset of the rules for GDM within the abductive module of the agent mind, can formalised as follows:

DomainKnowledge :

oedema←preeclampsia(yes), protenuria(yes).

blood_pressure(S,D)← preeclampsia(yes), protenuria(yes), pih(no), sys(160, S, 240), dias(100, D,150).
blood_pressure(S,D)← preeclampsia(no), protenuria(no), pih(yes), sys(160, S, 240), dias(100, D,150).

glucose(G)← macrosomia(yes), G > 150.
glucose(G)← hypoglicemia(yes), G < 80.
bmi(BMI)← macrosomia(yes), BMI >30.

IC :

← preeclampsia(yes), protenuria(no).
← preeclampsia(yes), pih(yes).
← pih(yes), protenuria(yes).

where the head of the rules in the domain knowledge represents the symptoms observed, while the body represents the abducible predicates that are part of the explanation associated to the symptoms observed.

The select/3 rules define the best action to take given a certain diagnosis produced by the demo/2 predicate, that queries the abductive module. The implementation of demo/2 predicate is based on Prologica [13] and it takes the symptoms, which correspond to the observations set G in ALP, to find an explanation, that corresponds to Δ in ALP. The knowledge base T of ALP is implicitly represented by the domain knowledge and the integrity constraints queried by the demo/2 predicate. For instance, we can define the following select/3 rule for the case when pre-eclampsia is diagnosed with very high blood pressure (which means that there is a high risk of eclampsia):

```
select(Symptoms, A, T)←
    demo(Symptoms, Explanation),
    M = m[diagnosis ⇒ eclampsia, diastolic ⇒ D, systolic ⇒ S, patient ⇒ ID, location ⇒ Loc],
    A = email:act1[actor ⇒ AID,doctor_email ⇒ DE, message ⇒ M, priority ⇒ 10],
    subset_of([preeclampsia(yes),sys(160, S, 240), dias(100, D,150)], Explanation),
    instance_of(ID,patient, T), holds_at(ID, doctor_email, DE, T),
    holds_at(ID, current_location, Loc, T),
    myID(AID).
```

The rule above specifies that, given a diagnosis of pre-eclampsia with high blood pressure (D stands for diastolic, S stands for systolic), the action to perform is to send an email to the current doctor of the patient for which the agent is in charge, specifying the current diagnosis.

4   Related Work

There have been several attempts to deal with the issues here presented. For example, Schaeffer-Filho et al. [14] define the concept of *Self Managed Cell* (SMC). Schaeffer-Filho defined the concept of SMC as a recursive structure that goes from the body-area network for health monitoring of the patient to the SMC to handle the household of the patient to the SMC of the healthcare professionals in charge of the patient. Such SMCs are structured with an event bus designed to follow the publisher/subscriber pattern [2]. The BAN is modelled as a virtual complex node that abstracts a set of sensors and publish events in the form of health records in the upper level SMC. The doctor SMC works as a subscriber for the events produced by the BAN. Thus, it could happen that the events published by the SMC are then retrieved by the doctor SMC to have a better view on the condition of the patient. From a certain perspective we can relate the concept of SMC to the concept of agent environment. As shown in our prototype, SMCs are based on DEBS patterns for the notification and dispatching of events. The most relevant difference between the approach proposed by SMCs and ours is that we utilise cognitive agents to prefilter the data produced by the BAN and that we model the behaviour of the agent environment as a declarative structure that evolves over time.

Another attempt to model an infrastructure for pervasive healthcare is presented by Wagner and Nielsen in [16]. Wagner and Nielsen envision an architecture based on 4 logic tiers: Public Tier, Central Tier, Home Tier and Mobile Tier. The Public Tier is publicly available as a SOA-based infrastructure which comprises a set of services for professional caretakers, nurses and doctors. The central tier models the domain model, specifying how the data are exchanged/accessed by the various actors of the system. The Home Tier is represented as a touch screen available in every house that the patient can use and a Mobile Tier take care of those situations when the patient leaves his house. With respect to Open-Care, our infrastructure embeds cognitive agents that can be programmed to monitor the patients according to the condition affecting them. Moreover, the use of the GOLEM infrastructure allows us to define a clear topology for the environment, which is missing from the OpenCare project.

In [8] Ciampolini et al. present a distributed MAS based on the ALIAS language to deal with distributed diagnosis. The agents of such a system are programmed according to the principles of abductive logic programming. Of particular relevance is the fact that Ciampolini et al. define a procedure to combine the results of different diagnosis produced by multiple expert agents in a single combined diagnosis. Moreover, in Ciampolini's approach the diagnosis is provided in term of probabilities. With respect to the work proposed by Ciampolini et al. we have a simpler reasoning procedure as we do not combine the diagnosis proposed by multiple agents. The contribution of our prototype with respect to the work proposed by Ciampolini is the introduction of the agent environment to foster continuous monitoring of the patients and to coordinate the interaction between the user and the agent environment to allow the agent to produce complex actions, such as sending an alert to the patient and to healthcare professionals when needed.

5   Conclusion

In this paper we presented a novel prototypical pervasive healthcare infrastructure to monitor patients affected by GDM in their day-to-day activities. The protype is defined in terms of a Body-Area Network based on a smart phone and on a set of sensors to check the physiological signs of a patients. Such physiological signs are then sent as events to the GOLEM agent infrastructure where roaming mobile agents, capable to perform abductive reasoning, check the events produced in the agent environment. Thus, if a critical situation occurs, the agents notify the healthcare professionals in charge of the patient.

One of the advantages of our simulated infrastructure using the GOLEM and Android mobile phone platforms is that it can be deployed in a real setting by further extending the knowledge of the agents, the topology of the containers, and the body sensor network functionalities. In such a setting, an important issue is how to store and retrieve the information produced in the pervasive healthcare agent environment. Such information is of medical importance as the data retrieved could help to uncover unknown patterns of certain illnesses, thus storing it in an appropriate manner is an important direction for future work. The next steps of the project include: (a) substitute the simulated sensors with real ones; (b) deploy the infrastructure in real settings; (c) evaluate the platform with a pilot study at CHUV.

Acknowledgement

This work was partially supported by the COST Action on Agreement Technologies. The authors would like to thank Dr Ruiz and the Department of Endocrinology and Diabetes at CHUV for the support during the definition of the prototype.

References

1. The effect of intensive treatment of diabetes on the development and progression of long-term complications in insulin-dependent diabetes mellitus. The Diabetes Control and Complications Trial Research Group. N. Engl. J. Med. 329, 977–986 (September 1993)
2. Blanco, R., Wang, J., Alencar, P.: A Metamodel for Distributed Event-based Systems. In: DEBS '08: Proceedings of the Second International Conference on Distributed Event-Based Systems, pp. 221–232. ACM, New York (2008)
3. Bromuri, S., Stathis, K.: Situating Cognitive Agents in GOLEM. In: Weyns, D., Brueckner, S.A., Demazeau, Y. (eds.) EEMMAS 2007. LNCS (LNAI), vol. 5049, pp. 115–134. Springer, Heidelberg (2008)
4. Bromuri, S., Stathis, K.: Distributed Agent Environments in the Ambient Event Calculus. In: DEBS '09: Proceedings of the Third International Conference on Distributed Event-Based Systems. ACM, New York (2009)
5. Bromuri, S., Urovi, V., Stathis, K.: Game-based E-retailing in Golem Agent Environments. Journal of Pervasive and Mobile Computing 5(4) (2009) (in Press)
6. Bromuri, S., Urovi, V., Stathis, K.: iCampus: A Connected Campus in the Ambient Event Calculus. International Journal of Ambient Computing and Intelligence 2(1), 59–65 (2010)
7. Chen, W., Warren, D.S.: C-logic of Complex Objects. In: PODS '89: Proceedings of the Eighth ACM SIGACT-SIGMOD-SIGART Symposium on Principles of Database Systems, pp. 369–378. ACM Press, New York (1989)
8. Ciampolini, A., Mello, P., Storari, S.: Distributed medical diagnosis with abductive logic agents. In: ECAI 2002 Workshop on Agents in Healthcare, Lione (2002)
9. Google Inc. What is Android? (2008), Home Page, http://code.google.com/android/what-is-android.html
10. Kakas, A.C., Kowalski, R.A., Toni, F.: Abductive logic programming. J. Log. Comput. 2(6), 719–770 (1992)
11. Kowalski, R., Sergot, M.: A logic-based calculus of events. New Gen. Comput. 4(1), 67–95 (1986)
12. Petit, P., Top, M., Chantraine, F., Brichant, J.F., Dewandre, P.Y., Foidart, J.M.: Treatment of severe preeclampsia: until when and for what risks/benefits? Rev. Med. Liege. 64, 620–625 (2009)
13. Ray, O., Kakas, A.: Prologica: a practical system for abductive logic programming. In: Dix, J., Hunter, A. (eds.) 11th International Workshop on Non-Monotonic Reasoning, pp. 304–312 (May 2006)
14. Schaeffer-Filho, A., Lupu, E., Sloman, M.: Realising management and composition of self-managed cells in pervasive healthcare, pp. 1–8 (April 2009)

15. Serlin, D.C., Lash, R.W.: Diagnosis and management of gestational diabetes mellitus. Am. Fam. Physician 80, 57–62 (2009)
16. Wagner, S., Nielsen, C.: OpenCare project: An open, flexible and easily extendible infrastructure for pervasive healthcare assisted living solutions, pp. 1–10 (April 2009)
17. Warren, J.M.: Pregnancy outcomes in women with gestational diabetes compared with the general obstetric population. Obstet. Gynecol. 91, 638–639 (1998)
18. Van Wootten, W., Elaine Turner, R.: Macrosomia in neonates of mothers with gestational diabetes is associated with body mass index and previous gestational diabetes. Journal of the American Dietetic Association 102(2), 241–243 (2002)

Context-Aware Route Planning

Adriaan W. ter Mors, Cees Witteveen, Jonne Zutt, and Fernando A. Kuipers

Delft University of Technology, The Netherlands

Abstract. In context-aware route planning, there is a set of transportation agents each with a start and destination location on a shared infrastructure. Each agent wants to find a shortest-time route plan without
colliding with any of the other agents, or ending up in a deadlock situation. We present a single-agent route planning algorithm that is both
optimal and conflict-free. We also present a set of experiments that compare our algorithm to finding a conflict-free *schedule* along a *fixed path*.
In particular, we will compare our algorithm to the approach where the
shortest conflict-free schedule is chosen along one of k shortest paths. Although neither approach can guarantee optimality with regard to the total set of agent route plans — and indeed examples can be constructed to
show that either approach can outperform the other — our experiments
show that our approach consistently outperforms fixed-path scheduling.

1 Introduction

Consider a transportation problem in which each agent wants to reach its destination location in the shortest possible time, while avoiding collisions and deadlocks involving other agents. This problem arises in the deployment of Automated
Guided Vehicle Systems (AGVSs), for instance in manufacturing where the vehicles carry materials between production stations, or at container terminals such
as Hamburg and Singapore, where they carry containers to and from ships [1].
Another application domain of multi-agent transportation is taxi routing at air-
ports [2,3], where aircraft have to taxi, e.g. from a runway to a gate, while avoiding
close proximity with other aircraft.

Avoiding collisions and deadlocks can be achieved by constructing a set of
conflict-free route plans[1]. A route plan for a single agent specifies which infrastructure *resources* (such as roads and intersections) the agent will visit, and at
which times it will visit these resources. The set of agent route plans should
ensure that there are never more agents in a resource than its *capacity* allows.
Finding an optimal set of conflict-free route plans is an NP-hard problem [4],
and optimal centralized approaches have difficulty finding plans for more than
a handful of agents (four agents, in [5]). Fortunately, there exist ways to trade
off plan quality for reduced computation times.

---

[1] Other ways of preventing collisions and deadlocks, such as assigning agents to non-
overlapping parts of the infrastructure, are described in the AGV survey paper by
Vis [1].

J. Dix and C. Witteveen (Eds.): MATES 2010, LNAI 6251, pp. 138–149, 2010.

In *context-aware* route planning (CARP), agents plan one after another, with agent n finding an optimal (shortest-time) route that does not create a conflict with any of the $n - 1$ existing plans (the context). Kim and Tanchoco [6] presented a context-aware route planning algorithm with a worst-case complexity of $O(|\mathcal{A}|^4|R|^2)$ (i.e., for a single agent), where $\mathcal{A}$ is the set of agents that already have a plan and R is the set of roads and intersections from the infrastructure. A further trade-off between plan quality and computation time can be achieved by finding an optimal *schedule* along a *fixed path*. In fixed-path scheduling (FPS), an agent has one or more pre-determined paths from its start location to its destination location, and it will choose the path along which it can find the shortest-time conflict-free schedule. Hatzack and Nebel [2] presented a fixed-path scheduling algorithm which they applied in an airport taxi routing scenario, with each agent always choosing the shortest path (i.e., the shortest-distance path) from start to destination. Lee et al. [7] suggest finding a conflict-free schedule along one of k shortest paths, determined using Yen's algorithm [8]. The fixed-path scheduling approach cannot guarantee individually optimal route plans, because it may be faster to take a longer but less congested path.

In this paper we present a context-aware routing algorithm with a significantly lower worst-case complexity of $O(|\mathcal{A}||R|\log(|\mathcal{A}||R|) + |\mathcal{A}||R|^2)$. Although no complexity results have been published for fixed-path scheduling approaches, we can convert our own CARP algorithm to an FPS algorithm, and the resulting worst-case complexity is $O(|\mathcal{A}||R|\log(|\mathcal{A}||R|))$. Hence, fixed-path scheduling is faster, but it is not easy to rank both approaches in terms of plan quality, especially if we consider global plan cost, i.e., the cost of a set of agent plans. In this paper we will therefore present a set of experiments that show the performances of both methods on a variety of inputs.

This paper is organized as follows. In section 2, we present a model for the multi-agent route planning problem. The main idea is that the infrastructure is a graph of *resources*, each with a capacity that specifies how many agents may simultaneously occupy a resource. In section 3 we will present our route planning algorithm, which is based on the idea of performing a search through a graph of free time windows. Section 4 describes experiments that try to determine the relative performances of context-aware routing and fixed-path scheduling on a variety of infrastructures, including a realistic airport taxi routing scenario. Finally, section 5 concludes this paper.

2 Model

We assume a set $\mathcal{A}$ of agents that each have to find a quickest-time path from one location in the infrastructure to another. We model the infrastructure as a *resource graph* $G_R = (R, E_R)$, where resources in R can be roads, intersections, or interesting locations that the agents can visit. An agent can directly go from resource $r \in R$ to resource $r' \in R$ if the pair (r, r') is in the *successor relation* $E_R \subseteq R \times R$. A resource r has a capacity $c(r)$, denoting the maximum number of agents that can simultaneously make use of the resource, and a duration $d(r) > 0$

which represents the minimum time it takes for an agent to traverse the resource. An agent's plan consists of a sequence of resources, and a corresponding sequence of intervals in which to visit them.

Definition 1 (Route Plan). *Given a start resource r, a destination resource r', and a start time t, a route plan is a sequence $\pi = (\langle r_1, \tau_1 \rangle, \ldots, \langle r_n, \tau_n \rangle)$, $\tau_i = [t_i, t_i')$, of n plan steps such that $r_1 = r$, $r_n = r'$, $t_1 \geq t$, and $\forall j \in \{1, \ldots, n\}$: (i) interval τ_j meets interval τ_{j+1} ($j < n$), (ii) $|\tau_j| \geq d(r_j)$, (iii) $(r_j, r_{j+1}) \in E_R$.*

The first constraint states that the exit time of the jth resource in the plan must be equal to the entry time into resource $j + 1$. The second constraint requires that the agent's occupation time of a resource is at least sufficient to traverse the resource in the minimum travel time. The third constraint states that if two resources follow each other in the agent's plan, then they must be adjacent in the resource graph. The cost of a single agent's plan is defined as the difference between the start time and the end time. For the cost of a set of agent plans, we define two measures. The *makespan* is the difference between the earliest starting time and the latest finish time; the *joint agent plan cost* is simply the sum of the individual agents' plan costs.

In sequential route planning, an agent must respect the plans of all the agents that came before it. From the set of existing agent plans, we can infer how many agents will be in each of the resources for each point in time.

Definition 2 (Resource load). *Given a set Π of agent plans and the set of all time points T, the resource load λ is a function $\lambda : R \times T \to \mathbb{N}$ that returns the number of agents occupying a resource r at time point $t \in T$: $\lambda(r, t) = |\{\langle r, \tau \rangle \in \pi \,|\, \pi \in \Pi \wedge t \in \tau\}|$*

An agent may only make use of a resource in time intervals when the resource load is less than the capacity of the resource. In such a *free time window*, an agent can enter a resource without creating a conflict with any of the existing agent plans.

Definition 3 (Free time window). *Given a resource-load function λ, a free time window on resource r is a maximal interval $w = [t_1, t_2)$ such that: (i) $\forall t \in w : \lambda(r, t) < c(r)$, (ii) $(t_2 - t_1) \geq d(r)$.*

The above definition states that for an interval to be a free time window, there should not only be sufficient capacity at any moment during that interval (condition (i)), but it should also be long enough for an agent to traverse the resource (condition (ii)). Within a free time window, an agent must enter a resource, traverse it, and exit the resource. Because of the (non-zero) minimum travel time of a resource, an agent cannot enter a resource right at the end of a free time window, and it cannot exit the window at the start of one. We therefore define for every free time window w an *entry window* $\tau_{\text{entry}}(w)$ and an *exit window* $\tau_{\text{exit}}(w)$. The sizes of the entry and exit windows of a free time window $w = [t_1, t_2)$ on resource r are constrained by the minimum travel time of the resource: $\tau_{\text{entry}}(w) = [t_1, t_2 - d(r))$, and $\tau_{\text{exit}}(w) = [t_1 + d(r), t_2)$.

An agent that wants to go from resource r to (adjacent) resource r' should find a free time window for both of these resources. By definition 1 of a route plan, the exit time out of r should be equal to the entry time into r'. Hence, for a free time window w' on r' to be *reachable* from free time window w on r, the *entry* window of w' should overlap with the *exit* window of w.

Definition 4 (Free time window graph). *The free time window graph is a directed graph $G_W = (W, E_W)$, where the vertices $w \in W$ are the set of free time windows, and E_W is the set of edges specifying the reachability between free time windows. Given a free time window w on resource r, and a free time window w' on resource r', it holds that $(w, w') \in E_W$ if: (i) $(r, r') \in E_R$, and (ii) $\tau_{exit}(w) \cap \tau_{entry}(w') \neq \varnothing$.*

The free time window graph encodes the relevant information of the plans of the first $n-1$ agents (allowing agent n to plan its route), but it does not contain any information on the possible movements of agents $n + j$, $j \geq 1$. To ensure that agent n will not make a plan that will make it impossible for any subsequent agent to find a plan, we need to make some simplifying assumptions regarding the start and destination locations of each agent: these locations must either have sufficient capacity to hold all the agents that might need it, or we need to assume that agents arrive and depart from the infrastructure, like airplanes landing on and taking off from an airport.

3   Route Planning Algorithms

In classical shortest path planning, e.g. using Dijkstra's algorithm, if a node v is on the shortest path from node s to node t, then a shortest path to v can always be expanded to a shortest path to t. This implies that once we have found a shortest path to v, then no other paths to this node need be considered. In context-aware route planning, it is not the case that a shortest route to an intermediate resource can always be expanded to the destination, as illustrated in figure 1. In figure 1 we see an agent A_1 that wants to go from r_1 to r_5, and an agent A_2 with source-destination pair r_5, r_3. All resources have unit capacity. Let us assume that A_2 has already made a plan, and now A_1 wants to find a plan. If the minimum traversal times of all resources are the same, then A_1 could reach r_2 before A_2 needs it. However, this shortest partial plan to r_2 cannot be expanded, because then the agents would meet head on. Agent A_1 must therefore find an alternative route to r_2, which is to wait in r_1 until A_2 has reached r_3. Hence, multiple route plans to an intermediate resource must be considered. A naive approach that would try all different routes to an intermediate resource would require exponential time to execute. The idea behind our algorithm is that we only need to consider shortest partial plans to the free time windows on a resource: if we have a partial plan that arrives at resource r at time t that lies within free time window w, then all other partial plans to r that arrive at time t', $(t' \geq t) \wedge (t' \in w)$, can be simulated by waiting in resource r from time t to time t'. This waiting is possible because no conflict will be introduced as long as the agent exits r before the end of w.

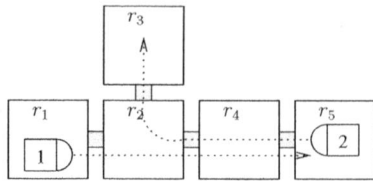

Fig. 1. If A_1 respects the plan of A_2, then the earliest route to r_2 cannot be expanded

Our route planning algorithm performs a search through the free time window graph that is similar to A*: In each iteration, we remove a partial plan from an open list of partial plan plans with a lowest value of $f = g + h$, where g is the actual cost of the partial plan, and h is a heuristic estimate of reaching the destination resource. We cannot directly apply an algorithm like A* to G_W, because the existence of a pair $(w, w') \in E_W$ does not guarantee that a partial plan, ending in w, can be expanded to free time window w'. The reachability of w' from w implies that there exists a time point $t \in (\tau_{\text{exit}}(w) \cap \tau_{\text{entry}}(w'))$, not that *all* time points in $\tau_{\text{exit}}(w)$ are also in $\tau_{\text{entry}}(w')$. Hence, when expanding a plan that ends in window $w = [t_1, t_2]$ at time t to free time window w', we must verify that $[t, t_2] \cap \tau_{\text{entry}}(w') \neq \varnothing$. We will write $\rho(r, t)$ to denote the set of free time windows (directly) reachable from resource r at earliest exit time t.

In line 1 of algorithm 1, we check whether there exists a free time window on the start resource r_1 that contains the start time t. If there is such a free time

---

Algorithm 1. Plan Route

Require: start resource r_1, destination resource r_2, start time t; free time window graph $G_W = (W, E_W)$
Ensure: shortest-time, conflict-free route plan from (r_1, t) to r_2.
1: **if** $\exists w \left[w \in W \mid t \in \tau_{\text{entry}}(w) \wedge r_1 = \text{resource}(w) \right]$ **then**
2:     mark(w, open)
3:     entryTime$(w) \leftarrow t$
4: **while** open $\neq \varnothing$ **do**
5:     $w \leftarrow \text{argmin}_{w' \in \text{open}} f(w')$
6:     mark(w, closed)
7:     $r \leftarrow \text{resource}(w)$
8:     **if** $r = r_2$ **then**
9:         **return** followBackPointers(w)
10:     $t_{\text{exit}} \leftarrow g(w) = \text{entryTime}(w) + d(\text{resource}(w))$
11:     **for all** $w' \in \{\rho(r, t_{\text{exit}}) \setminus \text{closed}\}$ **do**
12:         $t_{\text{entry}} \leftarrow \max(t_{\text{exit}}, \text{start}(w'))$
13:         **if** $t_{\text{entry}} < \text{entryTime}(w')$ **then**
14:             backpointer$(w') \leftarrow w$
15:             entryTime$(w') \leftarrow t_{\text{entry}}$
16:             mark(w', open)
17: **return** null

window w, then in line 2 we mark this window as open, and we record the entry time into w as the start time t. In line 5, we select the free time window w on the open list with the lowest value of $f(w)$. As in the original A* algorithm, the function $f(w) = g(w) + h(w)$ is a combination of the actual cost $g(w)$ of the partial plan to w, plus a heuristic estimate $h(w)$ to reach the destination from w. If the resource r associated with w equals the destination resource r_2, then we have found the shortest route to r_2, for the following reason: all other partial plans on Q have a higher (or equal) f-value, and if the heuristic is consistent[2], expansion of these partial plans will never lead to a plan with a lower f-value. We return the optimal plan in line 9 by following a series of backpointers.

If r is not the destination resource, we prepare to expand the plan. First, in line 10, we determine the earliest possible exit time out of r as the cost of the partial plan: $g(w) = \text{entryTime}(w) + d(r)$. Then, in line 11, we iterate over all reachable free time windows that are not closed. When expanding free time window w to free time window w', we determine the entry time into w' as the maximum of the earliest exit time out of resource r, and the earliest entry time into w'. We only expand the plan from w if there has been no previous expansion to free time window w' with an earlier entry time (initially, we assume that the entry times into free time windows are set to infinity). In line 14, we set the backpointer of the new window w' to the window w from which it was expanded. Then, we record the entry time into w' as t_{entry}, and we mark w' as open. Finally, in case no conflict-free plan exists, we return null in line 17.

The worst-case complexity of algorithm 1 is $O(|W| \log(|W|) + |E_W|)$: the while-loop in line 4 runs for at most $|W|$ iterations (every free time window is expanded at most once), and removing the smallest element from a priority queue can be done in $O(\log(W))$ time. All other operations between lines 4 and 10 can be performed in constant time. The for loop in line 11 could inspect every connection between two free time windows exactly once, so lines 12 to 16 can run at most $|E_W|$ times. If we assume that agents are not allowed to make cyclic plans, then one resource can hold at most $|A|$ reservations, and consequently $|A| + 1$ free time windows. Hence, $W \leq (|A| + 1)|R|$, and the complexity of algorithm 1 is $O(|A||R| \log(|A||R|) + |A||R|^2)$, which has been proved in [4], where the correctness is also proved[3].

3.1 Fixed-Path Scheduling Algorithms

Algorithms to find a shortest-time schedule along a fixed sequence of resources can be found in [2] and [7]. It is also possible to use algorithm 1 to schedule along a fixed path, by presenting it with a reduced version of the free time window

---

[2] Because we make use of a closed list, it is not sufficient to require that the heuristic is merely admissible (i.e., that it would never overestimate the cost of reaching the destination). For a consistent heuristic, it should hold that $h(w) \leq g(w, w') + h(w')$, where $g(w, w')$ is the actual cost of getting from w to w'.

[3] Complexity analysis and correctness proof of an earlier version of algorithm 1 can be found in [9].

graph. In particular, the set of edges E_W should only contain a pair (w, w') in case the respective resources r and r' are successors in the path along which we want to find a conflict-free schedule. The complexity of running algorithm 1 on such a reduced free time window graph is $O(|\mathcal{A}||R|\log(|\mathcal{A}||R|))$. The reduction in complexity is achieved because a partial plan is only expanded to a single successor resource, rather than considering expansion to all adjacent resources. As a result, the for-loop in line 11 runs only for a single iteration (per partial plan). The while loop from line 4 runs for at most $|\mathcal{A}||R|$ iterations, and none of the lines in the algorithm contribute more than $O(\log(|\mathcal{A}||R|))$ time.

3.2   Examples

We will now present two examples to compare the context-aware approach to the fixed-path scheduling approach. The first example shows how a central resource can become a bottleneck in the fixed-path approach, while the second example demonstrates that a context-aware planner can sometimes select plans that make it harder for subsequent agents to find efficient plans. In figure 2 we see an infrastructure with a central resource r_c, and agents A_i with respective start locations r_s^i and destination locations r_d^i. For each agent, the shortest path from start to destination is via the central resource r_c. Each agent also has the option of taking a path that is one resource longer. A fixed-path scheduling approach (with $k = 1$) will select the shortest path for each agent, resulting in tremendous congestion on the central resource. A context-aware approach will result in one or two agents using r_c, while the other agents will take the alternative route.

In figure 3 we see an infrastructure with two long corridors of resources. Three agents in resource $r_{s,1}$ want to go to resource $r_{d,1}$, while the three agents in resource $r_{s,2}$ want to go to resource $r_{d,2}$. All locations, except for the start and

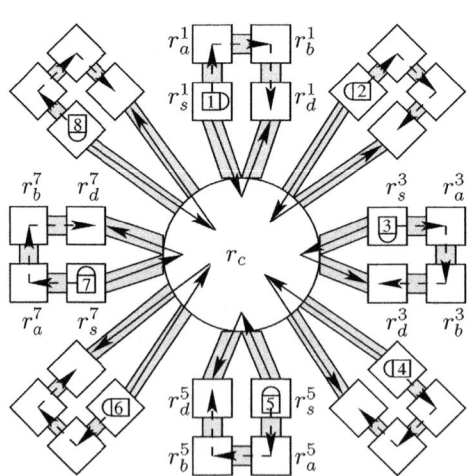

Fig. 2. FPS, with $k = 1$, always makes use of r_c, which leads to congestion

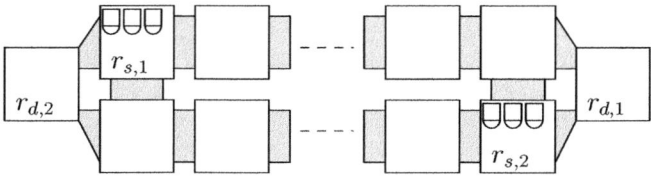

Fig. 3. An optimal multi-agent plan is for all agents to stay in their respective corridors

destination locations, have capacity one. The shortest path for each agent is to travel to its destination along its initial corridor. The fixed-path approach with $k = 1$ will therefore direct each agent along its initial corridor, which will result in the optimal multi-agent plan. The behaviour of the context-aware approach depends on the order in which the agents plan. If all agents from one group are allowed to plan first, then for either the second or the third agent it will be fastest to select the other corridor; then all agents from the other group must wait until a corridor is empty.

4 Experiments

In this section we will compare the global plan cost resulting from k-shortest path scheduling and context-aware routing, and see how they compare to lower bounds on the cost of an optimal global plan. A lower bound on the makespan is the longest of the shortest paths between any of the agents' source-destination pairs, while a lower bound on joint plan cost is the sum of the lengths of the shortest paths between the agents' source-destination pairs.

One problem instance consists of an infrastructure, a set of agents each with randomly chosen start and destination locations, and a random ordering of the agents in which they will plan (in section 3.2, we saw that agent orderings can have an impact on global plan quality). In our experiments we varied the number of agents from 50 to 500, with steps of 50, and for each number of agents 400 different problem instances: 20 different sets of agent start and destination locations, and 20 different agent orderings for each 'task set'.

The first infrastructure we used is a model of Amsterdam Schiphol airport (see figure 4(a)), on which the start location of each agent was a gate (or a runway), and the destination location a runway (or a gate). Of the six runways available at Schiphol, three were randomly chosen to be departure runways, the remaining three arrival runways[4]. There are a total of around 200 gates in the Schiphol infrastructure, and around 800 taxiway resources, for a total of a little over 1000 resources. We generated two types of infrastructures: lattice networks, which are like grids only with variable-length connections between intersections, and random graphs, which are constructed by first creating a random spanning

---

[4] At Schiphol airport, runways are not operated in *mixed mode*, which is to say they are never used for departure and arrival at the 'same' time.

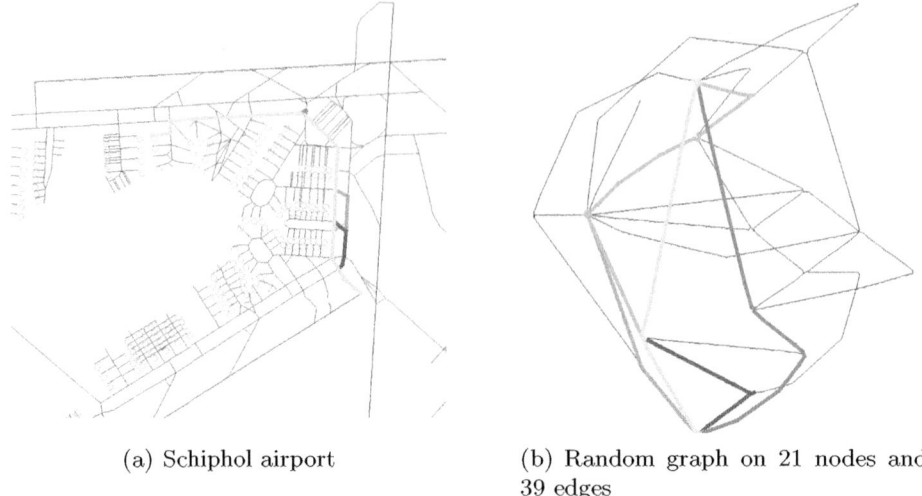

(a) Schiphol airport

(b) Random graph on 21 nodes and 39 edges

Fig. 4. The thicker lines indicate the 5 shortest paths between two locations

tree[5], and then adding edges between randomly chosen, as yet unconnected nodes (until the desired number of edges in the graph has been reached). See figure 4(b) for an example of a random graph. The minimum travel times of the resources were determined by setting the length of the median-length resource to 150 meters, and setting the maximum agent speed to 40km/h (as in the airport experiments). In figure 4, we see two examples of the kind of paths that the k-shortest paths algorithm returns. Figure 4(a) shows a section of the Schiphol infrastructure, and we can see that all five paths have much in common with the shortest paths: two alternative paths take a parallel taxiway, while two other paths make a very small detour. In figure 4(b), we see that the five paths found on a random graph are significantly different from each other, and they might constitute alternatives for an agent that tries to avoid congested roads.

4.1   Results

In figure 5, we can see that although fixed-path scheduling is faster, context-aware routing still manages to find plans for all 500 agents within half a second of computation time, when planning on random graphs[6]. On the larger Schiphol infrastructure, finding all 500 agent plans required around 5 seconds. Figure 6 shows the results from the comparison between context-aware routing and fixed-path scheduling on the Schiphol infrastructure. The most important conclusion

---

[5] We create a random spanning tree by iterating through the set of nodes, and in iteration i we connect the node with index i with a randomly chosen node with index smaller than i.

[6] All experiments were run on 4GB dual-CPU 2.4 GHz AMD Opteron machines.

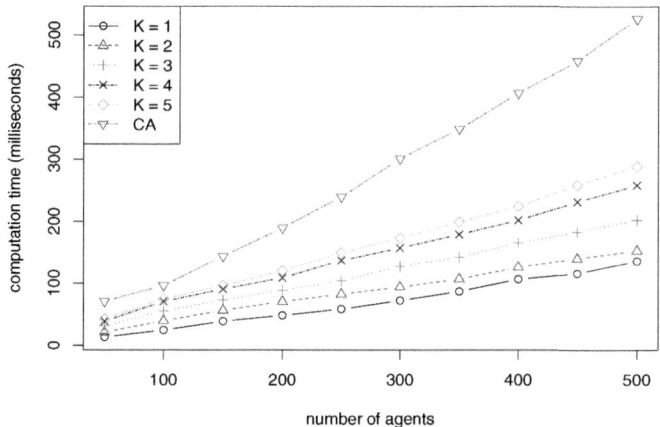

Fig. 5. CPU times for CARP and FPS (k = 1, 2,...,5) on random infrastructures

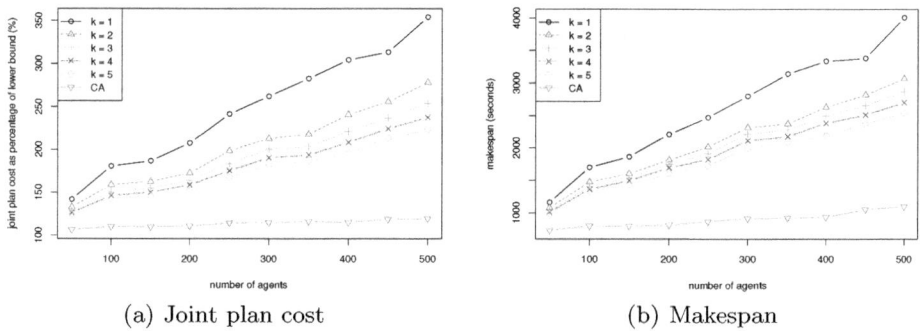

(a) Joint plan cost   (b) Makespan

Fig. 6. Global plan cost of CARP and FPS on the Schiphol infrastructure

we can draw from figure 6 is that context-aware routing outperforms fixed-path scheduling, for all k between 1 and 5, for both makespan and joint plan cost. Figure 6 also shows that for $k = 1$ (i.e., when agents always choose the shortest path), fixed-path scheduling can perform quite badly. Apparently, if each agent chooses the shortest path, then some resources become overused, resulting in long waiting times, even if alternative routes are available, which a context-aware planner would choose. The reason that for higher values of k fixed-path scheduling still does not approach the performance of context-aware is that, on the Schiphol infrastructure, a standard k-shortest path algorithm does not find useful alternatives, as we can see in figure 4(a). A second conclusion that we can draw is that context-aware routing stays quite close to the lower bounds on global plan cost. For 500 agents, the cost of the multi-agent plan (whether measured in makespan or in joint plan cost) is only 30% more expensive than the lower bounds. Figure 7 shows the results in terms of joint plan costs for the other types of infrastructures. A quick glance reveals that fixed-path scheduling fares

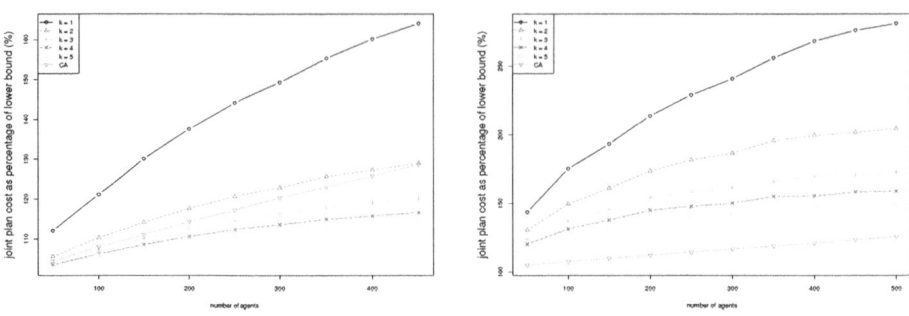

(a) Random graphs on 180 nodes and 300 (b) Lattice graphs of around 450 resources
edges

Fig. 7. Joint plan cost for CARP and FPS, on lattice and random infrastructures

no better on the generated instances. Because of space considerations, we only
show the joint plan cost results here, but for the makespan measure the same
holds as for the Schiphol infrastructure: fixed-path scheduling performs even
worse than for the joint plan cost measure. It seems that fixed-path scheduling
is unable to find useful alternative paths, because the nature of Yen's [8] k-
shortest path algorithm is such that all shortest paths are found by making
minimal deviations from the same shortest path.

5   Conclusions

In this paper we presented our context-aware route planning algorithm, which
finds an optimal (shortest-time) route plan that is conflict-free with regard to a
set of existing agent plans. We compared our algorithm to an approach that finds
an optimal *schedule* along a fixed path. The advantage of fixed-path scheduling
is that it requires less computation time than context-aware routing. In practice,
however, this may not be of great importance, as context-aware routing can often
find plans for hundreds of agents within a second.

   With regard to the global plan cost resulting from the application of either
context-aware routing or fixed-path scheduling, in our experiments context-
aware routing consistently outperforms fixed-path scheduling. The fixed-path
scheduling approach, in which we can choose from one of k shortest paths, seemed
to suffer from the fact that the k shortest paths returned by Yen's algorithm [8]
(which was also used by the fixed-path scheduling approach of Lee et al. [7])
are too similar. Using the k shortest disjoint paths (cf. [10]) can remove that
concern, but there may not always be many disjoint paths.

   Given the speed of context-aware routing, we do not believe, however, that
trying to revive fixed-path scheduling by finding alternative sets of k paths is the
most fruitful direction of future research. Instead, we could focus on determining
which routes a context-aware route planner should *not* take. From our examples

we know that context-aware route planners sometimes select routes that make it very difficult for subsequent agents to find good plans. In analogy to Stackelberg games (cf. [11]), if the first few agents select routes that are beneficial to others, then subsequent agents may join existing flows of agents on the infrastructure, which might lead to efficient global plans.

References

1. Vis, I.F.: Survey of research in the design and control of automated guided vehicle systems. European Journal of Operational Research 170(3), 677–709 (2006)
2. Hatzack, W., Nebel, B.: The operational traffic problem: Computational complexity and solutions. In: ECP'01, pp. 49–60 (2001)
3. Trüg, S., Hoffmann, J., Nebel, B.: Applying automatic planning systems to airport ground-traffic control - a feasibility study. In: Biundo, S., Frühwirth, T., Palm, G. (eds.) KI 2004. LNCS (LNAI), vol. 3238, pp. 183–197. Springer, Heidelberg (2004)
4. ter Mors, A.W.: The world according to MARP: multi-agent route planning. PhD thesis, Delft University of Technology (March 2010)
5. Desaulniers, G., Langevin, A., Riopel, D., Villeneuve, B.: Dispatching and conflict-free routing of automated guided vehicles: An exact approach. International Journal of Flexible Manufacturing Systems 15(4), 309–331 (2004)
6. Kim, C.W., Tanchoco, J.M.: Conflict-free shortest-time bidirectional AGV routing. International Journal of Production Research 29(1), 2377–2391 (1991)
7. Lee, J.H., Lee, B.H., Choi, M.H.: A real-time traffic control scheme of multiple AGV systems for collision-free minimum time motion: a routing table approach. IEEE Transactions on Man and Cybernetics, Part A 28(3), 347–358 (1998)
8. Yen, J.Y.: Finding the K shortest loopless paths in a network. Management Science 17(11), 712–716 (1971)
9. ter Mors, A.W., Zutt, J., Witteveen, C.: Context-aware logistic routing and scheduling. In: ICAPS, pp. 328–335 (2007)
10. Suurballe, J.: Disjoint paths in a network. Networks 4(2), 125–145 (1974)
11. Korilis, Y.A., Lazar, A.A., Orda, A.: Achieving network optima using Stackelberg routing strategies. IEEE/ACM Transactions on Networking 5(1), 161–173 (1997)

Social Conformity and Its Convergence for Reinforcement Learning

Juan A. García-Pardo, J. Soler, and C. Carrascosa

Universidad Politécnica de Valencia
Camino de Vera s/n. 46022 – Valencia, Spain
{jgarciapardo,jsoler,carrasco}@dsic.upv.es

Abstract. A dynamic environment whose behavior may change in time presents a challenge that agents located there will have to solve. Changes in an environment e.g. a market, can be quite drastic: from changing the dependencies of some products to add new actions to build new products. The agents working in this environment would have to be ready to embrace this changes to improve their performance which otherwise would be diminished. Also, they should try to cooperate or compete against others, when appropriated, to reach their goals faster than in an individual fashion, showing an always desirable emergent behavior. In this paper a reinforcement learning method proposal, guided by social interaction between agents, is presented. The proposal aims to show that adaptation is performed independently by the society, without explicitly reporting that changes have occurred by a central authority, or even by trying to recognize those changes.

1 Introduction

Learning is in general desirable since it will allow an agent to fit better in the environment, either because by design they were not 100% accurate in their parameters and they had to adjust them, or just because some of the parameters of the environment were unknown or vary through time.

When talking about learning in multi-agent systems there are some situations in which there is no other way to know how the environment is going to react to agents' actions but to actually perform them. In these cases multi-agent learning (*MAL*) reinforcement learning (RL) techniques [1] are useful to discover how the universe in which the MAS is located works. This phase aims to learn the parameters which steer the *mental model of the universe*, and usually ends when some error measure between the *real* behavior of the universe and the *expected* or *modeled* one is small enough to neglect it. The learning phase can stop after this, and the exploitation phase can mainly be used from this point on.

One approach to RL in the MAL community is taken from the Game Theory framework [2,3], in which the agents in the system act rationally to achieve their goals. The algorithms found in the research papers from this area usually focus on the equilibrium (Nash-equilibrium) of the solution, i.e. the solution is *good enough* for all the parties involved (cooperating or competing). One of

J. Dix and C. Witteveen (Eds.): MATES 2010, LNAI 6251, pp. 150–161, 2010.

the problems of these kind of approaches is the consideration of rationality of the agents, which may not be true [4]. In fact, humans do not usually behave rationally [5], in the sense described by Nash [6] equilibrium.

On the other side, there are cooperative learning algorithms which allow to obtain an optimal policy common to the whole set of learning agents (e.g. see [7]), with no need from them to behave rationally in the Nash sense, but the algorithm must know the whole set of agents which are learning the policy under discussion, and has some other constraints. The environment covers the *mechanical* part (the one which is independent to the MAS) and also the *social* part (actually, the MAS itself, including every agent capable of performing changes in the environment, both social or mechanical).

When the environment is dynamic learning is going to be essential. The agents will require to learn a set of parameters which were not present at design time. Changes in the environment usually require them to learn again. But some changes require something beyond a parameter estimation. They require adaptation by the agents. An example of this adaptation would appear in some *self-healing* systems [8].

If the agents could self-adapt to the environment, depending only on the interactions with the agents that inhabit in the same universe, and re-adapt every time significant changes would appear, the system would auto-control itself, and would not need a centralized logic trying to figure out whether there was a significant change or not, and which actions would be the most appropriate to take to improve the outcome.

Our goal in this paper is to study the behavior of self-adaptive agents immerse in an unknown dynamic environment, which is open and heterogeneous. Enabling self-adaptation through social interaction between certain agents will show that it is possible to have adaptive agents with no central control at all.

The rest of the paper is structured as follows: Section 2 presents the formal basis behind reinforcement learning and its limitations. Section 3 presents an introduction to the problematic of adapting in dynamic systems and a proposal based on social reinforcement to tackle the problem of detecting significant changes. Section 4 proves the convergence of Q-learning using that approach. Section 5 introduces the testbed used to check the feasibility of such approach, with some results made in simulation. Lastly, Section 6 presents the evaluation of the results and indications of which is going to be the next steps in this research.

2   Theoretical Background

Learning how environment behaves through interaction is a well studied method to obtain policies that yield optimal behaviors. Reinforcement Learning techniques [1] allow precisely to obtain optimal policies once the agents are trained enough time in the environment. These techniques are in the classical view limited to its use in centralized control systems. In this case, the *environment* does not take into account the rest of agents that may interact simultaneously while our agent is exploiting the values it has learned so far.

For each time instant t, we will call s_t, $s_t \in S$ the state of the universe, $a_t, a_t \in A$ the action which is executed by the agent, and $r(s_t, a_t)$, $r : \{S, A\} \to \mathbb{R}$ the reward (or feedback from the system) obtained by executing a_t while being in the state s_t. All of them in a discrete time model.

The agent must learn the optimal action policy π^* only through the rewards over time. A policy π is just a function $\pi : S \to A$ which indicates the agent which is the action with the best accumulated reward over time, taking into account the rewards and the transitions to other states. The policy π has a cumulative reward value V^π

$$V^\pi \equiv r_t + \gamma r_{t+1} + \gamma^2 r_{t+2} + \ldots = \sum_{i=0}^{\infty} \gamma^i r_{t+i} \tag{1}$$

being $r_t \equiv r(s_t, a_t)$, the reward of the universe at moment t and $r_{t+1} \equiv r(s_{t+1}, a_{t+1})$ the reward at the next discrete temporal instant (time step), s_{t+1} being determined by the transition δ as $s_{t+1} = \delta(s_t, a_t)$. Policy π determines which actions to take at every state, $\pi(s_t) = a_t$. The symbol γ is called the *discount factor*, $0 \leq \gamma < 1$, usually constant $\forall t$; the closer γ to 1 the greater emphasis future rewards are given with respect to immediate rewards.

The most used algorithm for implementing reinforcement learning is called *Q-Learning* [9,1]. π^* would be the optimal policy:

$$\pi^*(s) = \operatorname*{argmax}_a V^\pi(s) = \operatorname*{argmax}_a [r(s, a) + \gamma \, V^*(\delta(s, a))] = \operatorname*{argmax}_a Q(s, a) = \pi^*(s)$$

being Q a *matrix* holding the values or rewards for state-action pairs.

It has to be taken into account also that the reinforcement learning agents go through a learning stage, in which they estimate the Q-values, and another stage of exploiting the computed optimal policy. One way to split these two different stages is by means of a stochastic function which determines the probability of executing an action from the current optimal policy or a random action.

$$p(a|s) = k \; ; \; \pi^*(s) \neq a \; ; \; 0 \leq k \leq 1$$

The parameter k indicates the probability of an agent choosing randomly an action from the ones it has available, instead of executing the computed one corresponding to π^* according to its Q-table. This way, if $k \to 0$ it is said that the agent is in the *exploiting* stage of the π^* policy, and analogously, if $k \to 1$ the agent is in the *exploration* stage, exploring the Q-values of the universe.

Of course, the value of k does not have to be constant, and can be given by a function of different variables, although the most usual is to be a function of time, satisfying $\lim_{t \to \infty} k = 0$ or some other constant near 0. This way, the agent starts initially in the exploration stage, remains with this behavior for some time (hopefully enough to compute the right Q-values) and later exploits the computed π^* policy through these Q-values.

It has to be noted that in the case of a multi-agent system, the transition function $\delta(s, a) : \{S, A\} \to S$ does not behave as before: the rest of the agents, while interacting simultaneously with the environment, have modified the original state s, and now it is necessary to compose all the actions from all the agents who have executed them, in the right order, to describe the new transition $\delta(\delta(\ldots\delta(s,a)\ldots,a_i),a_j)$. Following this idea, it would be necessary to model the universe around each agent also taking into account the state of each of the remaining agents [7], and the actions now would be a tuple of n individual actions, one for each of the n agents in the MAS. Computational cost of this approach increases exponentially with the number of agents (in the general case), which implies the intractability of the problem when the number of agents is high. Another constraint that must be borne in mind is that each agent should be able to observe the action performed by each of the other agents in the environment, fact that may not be realistic in some environments.

But in environments where the execution of the actions of other agents do not change the state that the transition function would obtain, or the reward, with high probability, the convergence would still be guaranteed, and the agent would be able to obtain the optimal policy. In order to accomplish that it would be of paramount importance the choice of the representation for the states of the universe. It is necessary to maintain a commitment between the ability of expressiveness of the states of the universe [10] (which may be infinite, but enumerable [11]) and the aggregation property which may allow agents to use algorithms for *Q-learning* not explicitly designed for multi-agent environments, but obtaining near optimal policies. A method called *Soft State Aggregation* (SSA) [12] tries to *join* different states of the universe so that after the transformation the states that are semantically similar get *mapped* near. Some other approaches, such as using fuzzy-ART networks [13] bring us the possibility of describing a continuous universe, potentially infinite.

3   Adaptation in Highly Dynamic Systems: Social Reinforcement

In any open multi-agent system that allows heterogeneous agents, the adaptation of part or the whole society is a difficult task [14]. Adaptation should occur when changes that arise are significant enough to yield losses higher than the cost of the adaptation itself to the new conditions. Detection of the importance of changes in the environment is not naive, since the optimal policy is unknown a priori, without which we can not obtain reference values to compare both the individual behavior of each agent and the one of the whole society.

For all non-static environments, we can say that there are certain changes that require dynamism and adaptability of agents. The changes that could lead to an adaptation of the agents can be divided into the following taxonomy:

- *Mechanical Changes:* they happen in the environment, such as changes in rules or characteristics of the environment where agents are located.
- *Social Changes:* they happen in the organization (in the agents):
  - A new intelligent agent appears
  - An existing intelligent agent disappears
  - A new non-deterministic agent appears
  - An existing non-deterministic agent disappears

We will give the name *Self-adaptive Intelligent Agents* to those which have been prepared to automatically adapt themselves to the changes, in an autonomous way, and give the name *Non-deterministic Agents* to the rest, whether they are human controlled or [partially] autonomous, but not self-adaptive. Even though changes in the environment include a variety of situations [15], all possible changes in the system are compositions of the changes mentioned above.

Changes in the transition function and in the rewards can happen, despite our efforts to find a suitable representation, particularly when the environment changes. For example, in a market there may constantly appear new ways to build new products, such as by introduction of new objects (functions) which allow actions unknown until that moment, or by changing prices or dependencies. All this *mechanical* changes will have an effect.

Trying to adapt a multi-agent system in a *bottom-up* way, so, trying to exhibit emergent behavior through the design of the individuals has been always desirable, as long as the the system as a whole gets adapted. We will try to address the problem of detecting significant changes in the system, in an autonomous way, through the *social reinforcement* (R_Σ).

Each agent would care only of maximizing its own benefit until asked to review its behavior. The agent, we expect, will find a niche in the system because there is a need in the organization, which has to be fulfilled, and it is convenient for both the organization and the individual agent (at least in our study case, where the *game* is collaborative). There would be no "central authority" managing the adaptation: the *social reinforcement* would take care of this. By having an agent that is capable of observing the outcome of their actions in the universe, and providing this agent with *social reinforcement* —the latter significant of the opinion that the rest of the organization has about its actions— we can take advantage of the received information, which could show us the social approval with respect to the actions taken by the agent, as an indicative value of the utility of this agent to the society.

These socially sensible agents would use social approval (or disapproval) to determine whether to change its behavior or to continue with the policy which they consider the optimal one, π^*. The parameter of exploration k can be modified from the social reinforcement, being now function of a set of values, which in turn are function of the reinforcements of the environment:

$$K : \{R_\Sigma\} \to \mathbb{R} \ ; \ R_\Sigma : R \to \mathbb{R} \qquad (2)$$

We need to define the social reinforcement in order to compute the exploration probability. The social reinforcement is computed as shown in (3).

$$r_{\Sigma,t}(s_t, a_t) = \sum_a \rho_a \ \tau_a \ r_{\Sigma,t,a}(s_t, a_t) \qquad (3)$$

This definition the social reinforcement value is not bounded. The parameter τ_a represents the trust that this agent has in agent a being proper and correct in its reinforcement. Usually $0 \le \tau_a \le 1$. The parameter ρ_a represents the reputation of agent a according to the society. Depending on the value of ρ_a and τ_a the opinion of agent a will be more important or not, for each agent a in the society.

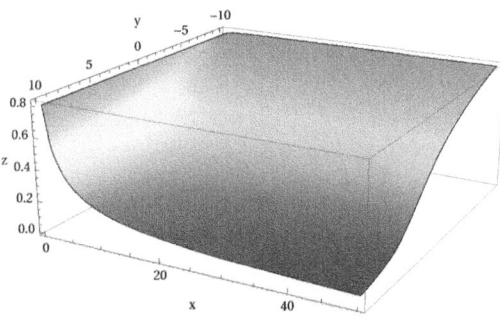

Fig. 1. Evolution of k_t (z-axis) as time (x-axis) and Σ (y-axis) change. $k_0 = 0.8$.

A proposal for the k evaluation function, which takes into account the social reinforcements both positive and negative, is shown in equation (4). The calculation of the exploration parameter k is now done using a series similar to the sigmoid function:

$$k_{t+1} = \frac{k_t}{k_t + 2^{k_t(r_{\Sigma,t}(s_t,a_t)-2)}} \tag{4}$$

Which is bounded between 0 and 1.

The series expressed in equation 4 converges for monotonic values of $r_{\Sigma,t}$ as shown in Sec. 4.

The effect of this k function coupled with the optimal policy π^* searching algorithm is shown by simulation, in Sec. 5. A picture the behavior of the k_t series is shown in Fig. 1.

4   Convergence of Learning

Convergence of the learning process is proven under some assumptions:

- The agent can represent the universe without taking into account other agents. Al least the agent has function of representation which can represent the universe with no ambiguity with a high probability, probability that increases with time.
- The agent knows the set of actions that are available at any time.
- The agent can observe the response of the system to its actions.

To prove that the Q-learning algorithm converges now, the k_t series has to converge as well. Being the k_t series convergent, the Q-learning algorithm will behave as usual, thus converging to the optimal policies (under the former assumptions) if all the states are visited enough. Lets write (4) using $\sigma \equiv r_{\Sigma,t}(s_t, a_t)$ for the sake of clarity:

$$k_{t+1} = \frac{k_t}{k_t + 2^{k_t(\sigma-2)}} \tag{5}$$

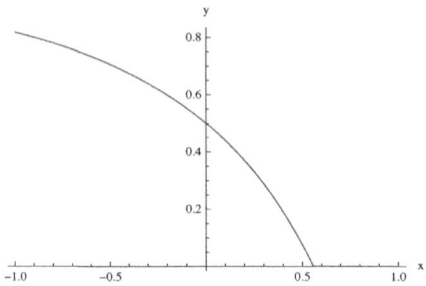

Fig. 2. Convergence of the k_t series (in the y axis) as σ changes (in the x axis)

In the limit when $t \to \infty$ we expect $k_{t+1} = k_t$, thus

$$k_t = \frac{k_t}{k_t + 2^{k_t(\sigma-2)}}$$

$$1 = (1 - k_t)2^{-k_t(\sigma-2)}$$

$$2^{\sigma-2}(\sigma - 2) = 2^{\sigma-2}(\sigma - 2)2^{-k_t(\sigma-2)}(1 - k_t)$$

$$2^{\sigma-2}(\sigma - 2) = 2^{(1-k_t)(\sigma-2)}(1 - k_t)(\sigma - 2)$$

$$ln(2)2^{\sigma-2}(\sigma - 2) = e^{(1-k_t)(\sigma-2)ln(2)}(1 - k_t)(\sigma - 2)ln(2)$$

$$(1 - k_t)(\sigma - 2)ln(2) = W(ln(2)2^{\sigma-2}(\sigma - 2))$$

$$k_t = 1 - \frac{W(ln(2)2^{\sigma-2}(\sigma - 2))}{(\sigma - 2)ln(2)} \qquad (6)$$

In (6) the $W(x)$ stands for the Lambert-W function such that for every number $x \in \mathbb{R}$, $x = W(x)e^{W(x)}$.

In Fig. 2 the convergence of k_t is shown for $-1 \leq \sigma \leq 1$ in a graphical way. Note that approximately when $\sigma > 0.55$ the value of k_t drops to zero and stays there. This allows for systems with a high probability of exploitation as long as the social reinforcement is positive and not too small (> 0.55).

Since the convergence of the exploration probability is proven, the convergence of the Q-learning algorithm follows easily:

An agent will cast a *ballot* in the range $[-1, +1]$ depending on the rewards obtained by the *mechanical* part of the universe. Using for example the following rule while in a given state s and after executing action a: When $Q_{n+1} > Q_n$ cast $+1$; when $Q_{n+1} < Q_n$ cast -1; in case $Q_{n+1} = Q_n$: cast $+1$ if $\delta_{n+1} = \delta_n$ and cast -1 otherwise. This all in the case the environment is deterministic. When it is not, and has an stochastic transition function, the expressions $\delta_{n+1} = \delta n$ have to be replaced by the corresponding ones $p(\delta_{n+1}|\delta n)$. The higher the probability of the transition, the closer the value would be to $+1$.

5   Study Case

To study the effects of social learning on a practical level we have proposed a simple collaborative game: a market economy in which the production line has different types of units, and the agents should build some or consume certain products for their survival. In this scenario the agent competes with other for survival, or by obtaining as many points as possible. These points may be named *life*, since below 0 agents disappear. In the event of a player disappearance, the market automatically removes all products which were unsold and belong to that player. If the agent reenters the market, it spawns with the initial values of *life* and *money*. The market hosts the products that the agents build. Any product can have dependencies of n_i, $i \in [0, m]$ units of m different products, and need some specific time to be built. This base time can be slightly modified depending on each agent features, but not the dependencies.

Finally, the price of the products is fixed by each one of the agents. To get a product from the market the player must pay in advance. Negative balances are not allowed, but agents are able to modify the price of the products they built even when they are already on the market.

In this environment the actions of other players are not observable, but its results may be: they cannot tell if an agent is making a product, but they notice the agent did build it when it puts it on sale on the market.

The system (the market) may change the production rules of the system at any time. The variations allowed are the creation and deletion of product types, changes on the dependencies (both the amount and the type) and the modification of the base time needed for production. Also the possibility of agents entering and leaving the market at any time.

The environment can simulate supply chain processes, where demand can vary and rules can be altered. This way, a good agent would adapt itself to the variations automatically and, with some time, come back with a good behavior competing and collaborating with other agents inside the environment.

5.1   Simulation

Different techniques of intelligence can get different strategies to follow: collaborate to eliminate certain players so that there are less competitors, control prices according to some strategy, estimate and predict the behavior of other agents... Since it is an open and heterogeneous system, some techniques such as finding the Pareto-optimal equilibrium or Nash equilibriums are not (theoretically, but not tested in this paper) the appropriate ones [16,17]: each agent may act in a non rational way, and may follow very particular policies.

As seen in section 2, reinforcement learning in a multi-agent system cannot be applied unless some conditions are given. For the simulation the agents use a well-known technique for grouping states (Soft State Aggregation, or SSA) which allow them to represent an infinite space of continuous values, with D' dimensions, in a D-dimensional finite space (clusters) [12]. For the exposed study case this space is seen as a D-dimensional matrix, grouping the states ($\in \mathbb{R}^D$) in an exponential way. The discrete position (or index of the cluster) i for the continuous variable x is computed as:

$$i = log_2(x + 2^s) \rightarrow log_2(x + 1) \tag{7}$$

Bounding i on some number (ω) which is to be considered near to the maximum that is to be seen for that variable, for D dimensions that are taken into account for the environment representation. Therefore the total set of states which every agent must represent is $\omega^D \times |A|$. The number of actions $|A|$ is known by every agent (although may change with time).

Two different types of agents will be differentiated; those who can receive and understand social reinforcement and those which not. It is expected to observe a better adaptation of the social-aware agents compared to the non-social ones (traditional reinforcement learning).

Three types of products where loaded: *Wheat*, with no dependencies and needing 1 cycle. *Flour*, requiring 2 units of *flour* and 2 cycles. And *Bread*, eatable, providing 10 units of life, requiring 2 units of *flour* and 2 cycles.

Learning of the Q-table was done individually for both the social-aware agents and the non-social. Parameter ω was fixed at 4, which means that the last state for each dimension will represent values of $x \in [7, +\infty]$. The dimensions (or variables) taken into account to represent the environment are the number of products of each kind in the market plus agent's *life* and *balance*.

The actions available to the agents are the creation of any kind of the products plus another one called *eating*. The total space of representation needed by each agent is only of $(4)^{(3+2)} \times 4 = 4096$ states. Learning stage has taken $1,000,000$ cycles, with a probability of exploration ≈ 1, hopping to explore as many states as possible, as many times they could. Every agent starts with exactly the same Q-matrix at the beginning of the simulation. Four different experiments were carried out: (1) No changes in the environment. (2) One of the products loses dependencies. (3) One of the products increases its dependency constrains. (4) A mixture between 2 and 3.

5.2   Results

Since the target for this study was adaptability, the work has been concentrated around this issue. The cases involved changes in the environment, one was prepared to test adaptation when easing the production process (thus a human would be happily adapting), the second one was carried out testing agents when the environment hardens quite a lot and the last one was a mixture, to check the relationship between the former two. Results are partially as we expected.

The test results are shown for the simulation of two different multi-agent societies: one formed by agents not social-aware, thus, not self-adaptive (in this simulation, called *non-social*), and another one formed by the agents under study, social-aware ones (called *social*). Values inside the tables represent the amount of re-spawns (deaths and reentries) that the agents have required, for every 1000 cycles, per agent (the less the better). Generally speaking the results are encouraging (see table), although the fact that every *re-spawn* means in a real system the agent to be thrown out by non compliance of the rules.

We can see at table 1 how the social agent is more likely to adapt than the non-social one. Adaptation in the first case (with the title *No variation*) is needed as the other agent may interact with the environment, modifying partially the

Table 1. Re-spawns of the agents for every adaptation case

Case	# of Agents	Steps	Non-social	Social
(1) No variation	2	10000	7.05	3.6
	4	10000	10.55	2.38
(2) Small variation	2	10000	7.4	1.85
	4	10000	14.05	1.35
(3) Mild variation	2	10000	14.35	12.6
	4		19.23	11.53
	2	100000	18.91	12.37
	4		18.42	11.59
(4) Combination	2	10000	16.85	11.15
	4	10000	17.28	10.6

sequence of actions of our π^* (as seen in section 2 it must hold $\lim_{t \to \infty} p(a|s) \approx 0$; $\pi^*(s) \neq a$ for every agent, and in this simulation the grouping function (7) is just not robust enough, they collide when positioned on states with low index).

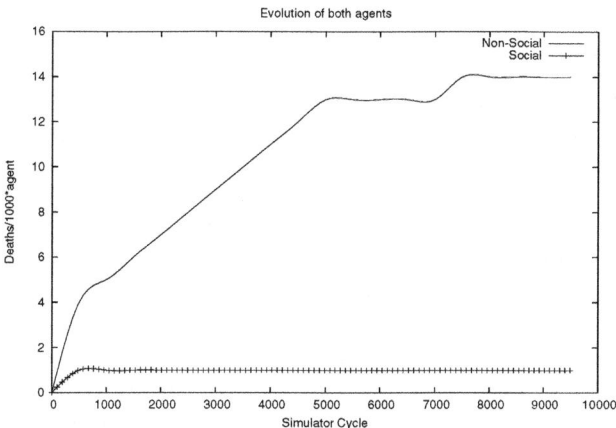

Fig. 3. Evolution of the re-spawn of both agents when Flour changes to no dependencies

We can see as well how the result improves when the number of social-agents increases. This is due to the increase of the social reinforcement, as there are more agents to reward others.

Case 2 shows that what it is supposed to be a relaxation of the requirements for the system, disturbs a lot the learned policies. Agents do not need to go through the states which pointed the existence of the product *Wheat*, but they still try to produce it, even though *Wheat* is now an useless product, and should not be built and non-social agents will follow this behavior unaware of the existing change.

Detail of the evolution of the re-spawns along time is also included (figure 3) in order to observe how non-social agents cannot amend the policy they were using, while the social agents find very quickly an equilibrium which they manage to hold. Furthermore, since now the rules for food creation are less tight they have even better score than before evolution of the environment.

Case 3 shows an odd result: we expected to see the social aware agents to improve its score while staying longer on the system, supposedly learning new policies. It came out that it did not improve at all its behavior. The restrictions imposed were squeezing too much the agents, since they do not have time to actually build all the required products using less *life* that the one that the *Bread* will gave them back. Anyway we see a better performance as the number of social-aware agents increase in the society, making it easier to adapt faster to the new (squeezing) conditions.

Case 4 shows that the mixture of the two previous experiments do not average results on the scores. Adaptation is a bit more complicated than that. The policy that was learned for the experiment in case 2 is not the same as the one in this experiment, nor the one in case 3.

Still, in all cases the social-aware agents have perform better when there were more of them that with a small population, which supports the assumption that social-aware agents behave better as their number grow.

6   Conclusions and Future Work

The results of these experiments, although do not prove better performance in adaptation of the social-aware agents for the general case, are very encouraging. The case of study was chosen independently as part of another ongoing work, meaning that was not *prepared* for these new agents to perform better. We can see that with very little modifications to a well-known algorithm the agents have achieved self-adaptation in this case of study without any central control.

Our aim to design an intelligent agent who can adapt itself to the environment seems to be achievable in the medium term. Further simulation with other mapping functions will have to be carried on to ensure that the state space is representable by a social reinforcement learning agent. In order to achieve this medium term goal, the future work mentioned below should be carried out:

• Special interest, we believe, is to take in the search for different methods of state aggregation, stochastic ones (as SSA) or not, and to study if the use of such mapping functions is going to be powerful enough by itself, and under what circumstances, to apply individual reinforcement learning in multiagent systems.

• The simulation did not use any particular algorithm to adapt the Q-matrix. Instead, the agents kept the wrong values for some time (the non-social ones for a very long time), but the creation of new policies could have been speeded up if an adaptation of the values would have been made. Finding algorithms able to adapt this values in this fashion would be very desirable.

• We have no real knowledge of which proportion of social-aware agents needs the system to work in a proper way. There is the chance that the agents can be fooled by some other agents which know about the way they work to be adaptive. Research in this direction could show interesting results in terms of robustness and, in the end, adaptability of the system as well.

Acknowledgements

This work has been partially funded by TIN2009-13839-C03-01, TIN2008-04446, PROMETEO/2008/051, GVPRE/2008/070 projects, CONSOLIDER-INGENIO 2010 under grant CSD2007-00022.

References

1. Sutton, R.S., Barto, A.G.: Reinforcement learning i: Introduction (1998)
2. Vidal, J.: Learning in multiagent systems: An introduction from a game-theoretic perspective. Adaptive Agents and Multi-Agent Systems, 562–562
3. Akchurina, N.: Multiagent reinforcement learning: algorithm converging to nash equilibrium in general-sum discounted stochastic games. In: AAMAS '09: Proceedings of The 8th International Conference on Autonomous Agents and Multiagent Systems, pp. 725–732 (2009)
4. Shoham, Y., Powers, R., Grenager, T.: Multi-agent reinforcement learning: a critical survey. In: AAAI Fall Symposium on Artificial Multi-Agent Learning, Citeseer (2004)
5. López-Paredes, A., Hernández-Iglesias, C., Gutiérrez, J.P.: Towards a new experimental socio-economics: Complex behaviour in bargaining. Journal of Socio-Economics 31(4), 423–429 (2002)
6. Hu, J., Wellman, M.P.: Nash Q-learning for general-sum stochastic games. The Journal of Machine Learning Research 4, 1039–1069 (2003)
7. Melo, F.S., Ribeiro, M.I.: Coordinated learning in multiagent MDPs with infinite state-space. Autonomous Agents and Multi-Agent Systems, 1–47
8. Ghosh, D., Sharman, R., Raghav Rao, H., Upadhyaya, S.: Self-healing systems–survey and synthesis. Decision Support Systems 42(4), 2164–2185 (2007)
9. Hu, J., Wellman, M.P.: Multiagent reinforcement learning: Theoretical framework and an algorithm (1998)
10. Tsitsiklis, J.N., Van Roy, B.: Feature-based methods for large scale dynamic programming. Machine Learning, 59–94 (1994)
11. Gordon, G.J.: Stable function approximation in dynamic programming (1995)
12. Singh, S.P., Jaakkola, T., Jordan, M.I.: Reinforcement learning with soft state aggregation. In: Advances in Neural Information Processing Systems, vol. 7, pp. 361–368. MIT Press, Cambridge (1995)
13. Tateyama, T., Kawata, S., Shimomura, Y.: A Reinforcement Learning Algorithm for Continuous State Spaces using Multiple Fuzzy-ART Networks. In: International Joint Conference on SICE-ICASE, pp. 2445–2450 (2006)
14. Helleboogh, A., Vizzari, G., Uhrmacher, A., Michel, F.: Modeling dynamic environments in multi-agent simulation. Auton. Agents Multi-Agent Syst. 14(1), 87–116 (2007)
15. Dignum, V., Dignum, F., Sonenberg, L.: Towards dynamic reorganization of agent societies. In: Proceedings of Workshop on Coordination in Emergent Agent Societies, pp. 22–27 (2004)
16. Hu, J., Wellman, M.P.: Multiagent reinforcement learning in stochastic games (1999), citeseer.ist.psu.edu/hu99multiagent.html
17. Claus, C., Boutilier, C.: The dynamics of reinforcement learning in cooperative multiagent systems. In: Proceedings of the Fifteenth National Conference on Artificial Intelligence, pp. 746–752. AAAI Press, Menlo Park (1998)

COLYPAN: A Peer-to-Peer Architecture for a Project Management Collaborative Learning System

Hanaa Mazyad and Insaf Tnazefti-Kerkeni

Laboratoire d'Informatique, Signal et Image de la Côte d'Opale,
Université de Lille Nord de France
50 rue Ferdinand Buisson BP 719, 62228 Calais Cedex, France
{mazyad,kerkeni}@lisic.univ-littoral.fr

Abstract. In this paper, we present a project management collaborative learning system that tries to respond to the requirements of a motivating learning process. In this system, learner, group learners and tutors are in an environment where each one teaches and learns, by interacting with others. Peer-to-peer (p2p) network reflects and supports this relationship between users in a collaborative learning community. We propose a p2p agent-based system for their management and sharing.

Keywords: Collaborative learning communities, Knowledge management, Peer-to-Peer, Agent-oriented architecture.

1 Introduction

The evolution of Information and Communication Technology (ICT) helped in the development of systems dedicated to learning. Today, the computer became a simple element of a more complex system involving the cooperation of various human and artificial entities that share a set of teaching resources.

Recently, we have been interested, in our laboratory, in the field of collaborative learning. Collaborative learning is a learning process for the progressive acquisition of knowledge within a group in an appropriate environment. This work resulted in the definition of a teaching method called MAETIC equipped with ICT [1]. The main purpose of the deployed pedagogy is to provide real support to knowledge acquisition while doing a project by a group of learners. To this end, our objective is to develop a learning platform that offers learners a support for their projects development and progress monitoring by the tutor.

In the context of e-Learning, it is essential to avoid the failure and/or desertion of learners. So, it is important to propose for tutors automatic or semiautomatic tools, with assistance and decision support. These tools help to keep traces of all interactions related to learners belonging to a given group and report the indicators of progression status in this learners group and its durability. Multi-agent systems (MAS) come as a solution for knowledge organization and exploitation problems and also for problems of the coordination and communication in such environments.

J. Dix and C. Witteveen (Eds.): MATES 2010, LNAI 6251, pp. 162–172, 2010.

This paper presents COLYPAN, a web-based peer-to-peer system that supports collaboration among learners, learners groups and tutors. This system allows the implementation of additional functionalities in order to keep a detailed history of all groups' actions when learners access their accounts in order to assess the group's life and its evolution. Thus, COLYPAN allows students to learn while collaborating in order to achieve their projects and provides tutors with tools to trace the activity of their students. In this paper, we start, in section 2, by briefly introducing the MAETIC method before discussing some related works. In section 3, we describe the Peer-to-peer architecture proposed for a project management collaborative learning system. A case study is presented in section 4 to illustrate our architecture. Finally, some directions for future work and conclusions are presented in section 5.

2   MAETIC Method

2.1   Description of the Method

MAETIC (from french "Méthode pédAgogique InstrumentEe par les TIC": a pedagogic method instrumented by the ICT) is a teaching method which, as part of pedagogy for project learning, describes a set of formalized and applied procedures according to defined principles. Thus, the objective of MAETIC is to allow a learner to develop requested knowledge and skills by the implementation of a developing process of a "product" and lead to technical project management. For the tutors, MAETIC's objective is to promote the establishment of a process that will facilitate their educational activities.

MAETIC is based on five stages commonly adopted in the process of project management [2]: the initialization, the preparation, the planning, the project monitoring and the revenue. Each stage establishes activities, requires the production of one or more deliverables, and takes place over one or several sessions. Since the work is collective, MAETIC advocates the establishment of an organization in the group project (description of roles) that promotes the acquisition or enforcement of transversal skills needed for teamwork. The fact of making the group produce deliverable develops qualities related to the written production.

Thus, each project team must establish its weblog. This weblog aims to describe the life of the project. Besides the general information on the project (subject, members), it is responsible of storing all the notes concerning the project's life and is also responsible for collecting developed deliverables.

The learning activity in this device is defined by the tutor. Learners must join groups to accomplish this activity. Learners in each group have the same responsibility: the commitment to finish the work, time management and the respect of deadlines. There are no predefined roles or division of tasks.

2.2   Contribution of Multi-agents System

Contrasting with traditional education practices, which view tutors as *producers* and learners as *consumers* of knowledge, in collaborative learning, both tutors and learners are seen, at the same time, as producers and consumers, gathered in an environment where everyone has something to teach and something to learn. This way, instead of playing the role of detaining and transmitting knowledge, the tutor assumes other functions, such as those of *motivator, guide* and *collaborator*. Meanwhile, the learners become more active and responsible for their own learning.

There is a critical need, in such context, for tools : (1) supporting collaboration among distributed users with similar interests, or who are part of the same workgroup; (2) organizing information for facilitating access in various contexts; (3) managing traces of all interactions related to learners belonging to a given group and report the indicators of progression status in this learners group and its durability. Multi-agent systems (MAS) are involved in the modelling of interactions in complex societies of artificial or human individuals. They bring an interesting resolution for knowledge organization and exploitation problems and also for problems of the coordination and communication mechanisms.

2.3   Related Works

Before discussing the proposed architecture, we review the approaches presented in the literature that provide multi-agents platforms for collaborative learning. In the field of Artificial Intelligence and education, several approaches have been developed. For example, Guizzardi and al. [3] have developed a Peer-to-peer system called "Help & Learn". This system was modeled using an agent-oriented language called AORML [4]. It is an open system that is designed to support the extra-class interactions between learners and tutors. "Help & Learn" is limited to providing assistance to learners who request it. Other systems have been developed. Fougeres and Ospina [5] have proposed a based-agent mediation system for the project management platform called iPédagogique. This system, modeled in AUML, serves as an interface between the human and the application to enhance their relationship and is used to promote collaboration among users. Recently in [6], the authors presented a model for an adaptative multi-agent system for dynamic routing of the grant's activities from a learning environment. This model allows the assignment of activities taking into account the specialization of learners, their experience and the complexity of activities already taken. None of these three systems cares of monitoring learning and therefore, cannot trace user's activities.

Mbala and al. [7] have developed a multi-agent system called SIGFAD to support users in remote education. SIGFAD is modeled using the MASE methodology and uses the JAM model for building agents. It is interested in monitoring learning. However, it is not sufficiently independent and does not start up alerts to prevent tutors if there's a problem with a learner or group.

Hereafter, we present the project management collaborative learning system COLYPAN.

3   COLYPAN : A Multi-agent Architecture for Modeling a Collaborative Learning System

COLYPAN (COllaborative Learning sYstem for Project mANagement) is a system dedicated to project management. It provides users tools to accomplish their project. The users of this system are learners and tutors. In COLYPAN, the learning activity is defined by the tutor. Learners must join groups to accomplish their activities.

In each group, learners have the same responsibility: the commitment to finish the work, time management and the respect of deadlines. There are no predefined roles or division of tasks.

COLYPAN is also a collaborative learning system where users exchange their information and skills and thus learn from each others. The knowledge resources exchanged in the COLYPAN environment isn't differentiated from those exchanged for other purposes :

- There is a share of physical resources, such as: books, articles, and other educational artifacts;
- With the growing use of information technology and the Internet in these settings, there are plenty of electronic documents, references, and web links;
- There is also tacit knowledge, i.e. knowledge found in people's minds and that is usually informally exchanged among them by different means, for instance for persons, through messages, or via Internet communication tools integrated in virtual learning environments.

Another objective of COLYPAN is to provide tutors with tools to enable them to determine the activity level in groups and startup needed mechanisms for remediation and assistance [8]. These objectives can be divided into two categories: those related to user support and objectives dedicated to save and extract interaction data. The aim of the second category of objectives is to review automatically the interaction data in order to alert users when the progress of the work session is not satisfactory or that the group risks a burst.

3.1   Peer-to-Peer Architecture for a Collaborative Learning System

In a collaborative learning system, each member must manage and exchange his knowledge and cooperate with others in order to achieve his goals. Compared to these aspects, a Peer-to-peer system is particularly suitable to develop a collaborative learning system since depicted with the following capabilities :

- Supports autonomy: each member of the system is seen as a peer that manages and has control over a set of local technologies, applications and services;
- Is decentralized : the community of peers is able to achieve its goal independently from any specific member or component;
- Is cooperative : in order to join and use the system, each member must provide resources or services to the others;
- Is dynamic : peers and resources can be added or removed at any time.

In this P2P application, each human is considered as a peer.

We adopted also an agent-oriented design and development approach. Indeed, the multi-agent system (MAS) is an appropriate framework for realizing a P2P application. The characteristics that they have, especially (a) their capability to allow the sharing or distribution of knowledge, and (b) that they assemble a set of agents and coordinate their actions in an environment to accomplish a common goal, are needed in this P2P application.

Thus, COLYPAN is an oriented-agent system, in which several groups of learners interact and collaborate to achieve a given project. System's agents are responsible for managing knowledge exchanged among peers. We have chosen to deploy the system on the multi-agents platform Madkit [9]. This choice is taken owing to the fact that MadKit is intended for the development and the execution of multi-agents systems and more particularly for multi-agents systems based on organizational criteria (groups and roles). However, MadKit does not impose any particular architecture to the agents. We describe below the system agents.

3.2   The Different Agents of the System

We have two types of agents in the system: human and artificial agents (Figure 1).

1. Human agents are Tutors and learners. They are called Peers.
2. Artificial agents are :

    - a_TEACH: the tutor's assistant, it gives him information concerning the data related to the interactions and the tasks to be made.
    - a_LEARN: the learner's assistant, it gives him information concerning the interactions' data and the tasks to be made.
    - a_ACTIV: Supervises actors' activities during a session. It provides statistics concerning the progression of each activity. It reminds learners about deadlines and notifies the late groups by sending alerts.
    - a_GROUP: Supervises groups' space during a session. It dresses a list of present, absent agents in a group. The a_GROUP has a list of all the group members and information about each one like, skills and especially, the other groups to which each peer belongs. This way, if one member p of the group a needs to communicate with another group b, the a_Group agent can find which peer x belongs to both of groups a and b and thus the peer x can help the peer p by joining the group b.
    - a_KB: Manages the knowledge base of the group. Each group has its own knowledge base (KB). The KB contains information about the group members and the project. the a_KB is also responsible of the interactions with the global database.
    - a_TOOL: Supervises the use of tools. It must provide statistics about the use of groups and tutors space tools (Email, Chat, Forum, Weblog...). With each use of the system tools, interactions are sent to the a_KB.
    - a_DB: manages the database and users accounts.

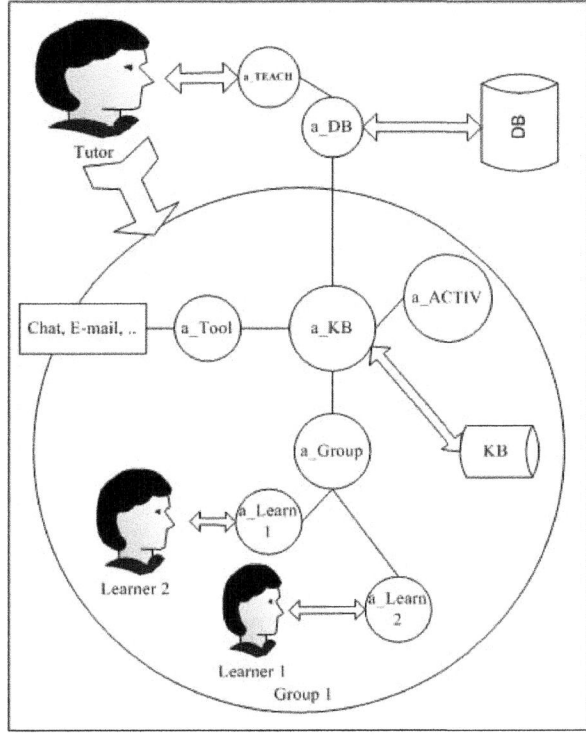

Fig. 1. The System Agent

3.3   The Groups Working Way

In COLYPAN, groups are independent of each other. Each group works on its own project and has its own resources and its own artificial agents. Each group has an agent for each learner "a_LEARN"; an agent supervisor of activities "a_ACTIV"; an agent supervisor of space group "a_GROUP"; an agent supervisor of tools "a_TOOL"; an agent supervisor of knowledge base "a_KB". Only two agents are common to all the groups : the tutors agent "a_TEACH" and the database supervisor agent "a_DB".

Each peer knows only the peers that belong to his/her group and therefore he/she can communicate with them. Thus, groups can communicate or share information only if they have at least one member in common (Figure 2). In fact, there is an overall view of all the groups in the system. Each group knows the number of existing groups, their knowledge and skills. However, there is no direct link between the groups.

Each group has a goal and all the group members must work together in order to achieve it. Collaborative work requires that the members contribute equally for realizing the work. Thus, all of the members must be active for achieving the group's goal. The inactive members affect the group and delay the objectives

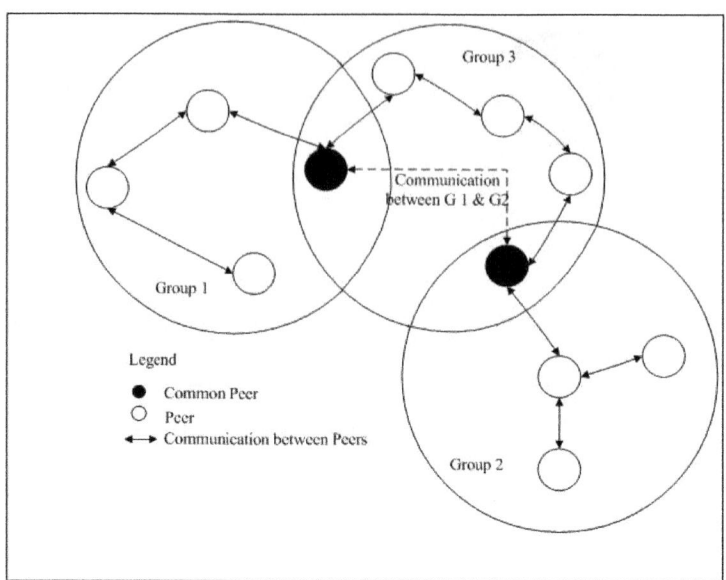

Fig. 2. Intra-group and inter-group communication

achievement. So to ensure the activity of all groups, each inactive group (more than half of its members are inactive) receives first a warning notification sent automatically to all of its members. If after a period determined by the tutor the group remains inactive, the group must stop its inactive members and send a join request to other members or break up the group and in this case, the members may request to join other groups. At the end of each project, the group may, if its members want, start working on another project or the group will be dissolved.

Initially, a person who wants to form a group, sends a join request to all the members. This person becomes the group initiator. Each peer who wants to join a group must submit an admission request to this group. Noting that, a peer can belong to several groups simultaneously.

The group initiator has the right to accept the first member of the group. Once the group is composed of more than one member, a vote to accept/reject a new member becomes mandatory. For this, an email is automatically sent to all the group members and voting will be open after sending the email.

To vote, each member must access his account and accept/reject the candidature. At the vote deadline, the system automatically records the votes. To consider the vote, at least half of the group members have to vote. Depending on the vote result, the candidate is admitted or not. In the case of equality of voices, the group initiator decides to accept/reject the candidate.

Once the groups are formed, tutors suggest different projects. Each group must choose a project. If several groups choose the same project, they must negotiate to reach a mutual agreement.

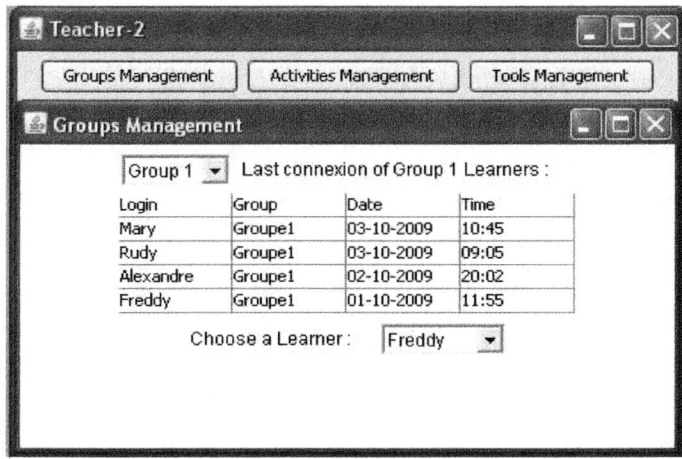

Fig. 3. Tutors support tools interface

The project realisation will be step by step according to the project management method MAETIC. Tutors specify the deadlines for each stage and the final deadline. Note that the tutor's role is to guide and to advice his learners, in addition to his principal role of monitoring and evaluation.

Each group realizes its project alone. On the other side, it could ask help from other groups. In fact, the "a_group" agent has a list of all its group members and the other groups to which each peer belongs.

Each group must provide an estimated planning and the final one. By comparing them, inactive members could be determined. This will be detailed below in the scenario.

Figure 3 shows the tutors support tools interface. Tab "Groups Management" allows tutors to manage learners by providing information on their activities. The tab "Activities Management" provides tutors with statistics on the achievement of activities and thus allows them to monitor the progress of learners in their projects. The tab "Tools Management" provides tutors with statistics on the use of tools by learners. In effect, this allows the tutor to judge the level of social interactions of learners.

4   A Case Study

This pedagogic activity is part of a software engineering course in the second year of computer science. In this activity, 60 learners must form groups to realize a project. To achieve a project, learners have 10 weeks, with one week to join a group and choose a project. The work is divided into five stages. Learners must submit at the end of each stage an electronic document to the tutor via the system.

Each learner must create a personal account. Then, the learner may choose to join one (or more) group or form a new group. In the latter case, he becomes the initiator of the group.

Rudy is one of the learners who have decided to form a group for his database project. He sends a join request to the candidates and specifies the project topic that is the databases. Frederick is pleased, he also has a database project to do, he sends a request to Rudy to join his group. Rudy decides to accept Frederick in the group. Group 1 is now composed of 2 members. The vote is now mandatory. The vote must be based on the candidate's skills and what he can bring to the group. Once the group is formed, it must choose one of the projects suggested by the tutors. Group 1 chooses a project entitled "Hospital Management". Another group chooses the same project. Both groups must negotiate to resolve this conflict: Frederick and Mireille from group 1 wanted to work on another subject and some members from the other group too. So, the group 1 takes the "hospital management" project, Mireille and Frederick left group 1 for the other group and Mary and Alexandre left their group to join group 1.

Group 1 is now formed, the initiator organizes a group meeting to start the work. On the agenda:

- Task identifying
- task assignment to each member
- establishment of an estimated planning.

After this meeting, members must collaborate together to achieve their tasks within the deadline. Failure to complete a task at time by one member causes a delay on the work of the whole group and thus, punishes the whole group. Indeed, in the second stage of the project, Mary had to make a graphic charter to be respected in all documents. However, Mary didn't finish this task at time despite a deadline reminder sent by the system. So, the agent a_ACTIV (Figure 4) sends a warning to all the group members. If such delay occurs, the group may be dissolved.

In the first meeting, an estimated planning had been established. This planning should be modified to produce a real planning at the end of each stage. Thus, it is possible to verify the work done by each learner. The periodically connection to the system is not a sufficient criterion for judging the work of each member. A learner may connect just to check mail or to chat.

At each project stage, the tutor is present to guide and advise learners but he doesn't intervene on the group work and tasks division. He provides learners with documents and resources necessary to accomplish the tasks. Only at the end of each stage, he evaluates the learners.

Tutors and learners must keep a weblog. Learners should consult the tutor weblog before each stage. This allows them to be aware of work progress, tutor comments but also to download documents added by the tutor and needed to carry out further work.

The learner weblog allows learners to upload their documents but also to discuss, ask questions and exchange their information. Each group has its own weblog. Thus, the group is informed of the work of the others members.

Learners and tutors can use private messages or the chat to communicate.

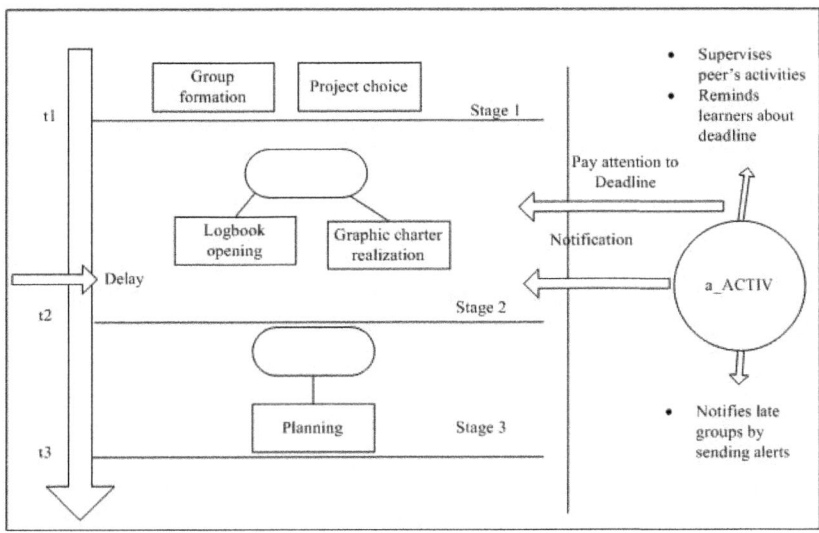

Fig. 4. The a_ACTIV notification for late group

5   Conclusion and Future Work

In this paper, we proposed an agent-based architecture that allowed the implementation of the collaborative project management method : MAETIC. Indeed, our system consists of a population of autonomous agents in interaction where each agent has communication, coordination and collaboration capabilities. However, we need a network to establish communication between agents so, we chose to use the P2P approach to link up agents between them. This choice comes from the fact that in a Peer-to-Peer system, each peer has a significant autonomy and a peer can join different Peers groups to achieve different goals. In addition, some P2P concepts, like peer group and autonomy are typical multi-agent systems concepts. Finally, the concept of a Peers group is adequate to support the dynamic aspect of social organizations in multi-agent systems. So it is appropriate in our work, to suggest the P2P approach in the deployment of an open multi-agent system.

Our system is an opened system that supports the interaction between learners, groups of learners and tutors. It provides users with tools for the project management and allows tutor :

— To know the level of productivity of each learner in terms of realization of pedagogic activities, and its level of communication with the other members of the group;
— To know the progression of each group compared to the realization of the activities and also the present, absent, inactive members;
— To know the levels of realization of the activities by all groups and thus to adjust the calendar if needed.

In addition, it is interesting to note that our system notifies the inactive groups which is not the case of the systems described in section 2. We illustrated our architecture by a case study that describes the behavior of the supervisor agent of activities "a_ACTIV".

One of the main assumptions of multi-agent systems is that their underlying network infrastructure is steady, that is the nodes of the network on which agents are deployed are known, and that there is no break in the execution of agents' protocols. Oppositely, P2P networks define a framework particularly characterized by the fact that the nodes that are dedicated to agents deployment may appear or disappear dynamically in the network or even become unavailable, due to many reasons such as the mobility of the user in its environment or his disconnection. These changes in the system configuration create unusual circumstances that make the current mechanisms of agents reasoning inappropriate. For example, how can we manage the protocols interruptions, the disappearance of a set of agents (and thus of competences), the migration of data according to the context [10],[11]. Thus, our purpose is to develop a scalable negotiation-oriented coalition formation method specifically tailored for large-scale distributed systems where nodes may crash and every agent has a partial view of the system and can only communicate with the agents in its own view, i.e., its neighbors.

References

1. Talon, B., Leclet, D.: Dispositif pédagogique pour un apprentissage de savoir-faire. Revue Internationale des technologies en pédagogie universitaire 5(2), 58–74 (2008)
2. Marchat, H.: Kit de conduite de projet. Organization editions, Paris (2001)
3. Guizzardi-Silva, R., Aroyo, L.M., Wagner, G.: Help&Learn: A peer-to-peer architecture to support knowledge management in collaborative learning communities. Revista Brasileira de Informatica na Educaçao 12(1), 29–36 (2004)
4. Wagner, G.: The Agent-Object-Relationship Meta-Model: Towards a Unified View of State and Behavior. Information Systems 28(5), 475–504 (2003)
5. Fougères, A.J., Canalda, P.: iPédagogique: un environnement intégrant la gestion assistée de projets d'étudiants. In: Colloque TICE 2002, Lyon (2002)
6. Simian, D., Simian, C., Moisil, I., Pah, I.: Computer Mediated Communication and Collaboration in a Virtual Learning Environment Based on a Multi-agent System With Wasp-Like Behavior in Large-Scale Scientific Computing book, pp. 618–625 (2008)
7. Mbala, A., Reffay, C., Chanier, T.: SIGFAD: un système multi-agents pour soutenir les utilisateurs en formation à distance (2003)
8. Mazyad, H., Kerkeni, I.: A Multi-Agents Approach For Modeling a Collaborative Learning System. To appear in WBE 2010 Proceeding, Sharm el-Sheikh (2010)
9. http://www.madkit.org
10. Aknine, S., Mir, U., Arantes, L.B.: Multi-agent Coordination in ad'hoc networks based on coalition formation ICAART, vol. (1), pp. 241–246 (2010)
11. Mazyad, H., Kerkeni, I., Ajroud, H.: Multi-Agent System Architecture for Managing the Coordination in Peer-to-peer Systems. In: ICTTA 2008, DAMAS (2008)

Preference Generation for Autonomous Agents

Umair Rafique and Shell Ying Huang

School of Computer Engineering
Nanyang Technological University, Singapore
{umai0001,assyhuang}@ntu.edu.sg
http://www.ntu.edu.sg

Abstract. An intelligent agent situated in an environment needs to
know the preferred states it is expected to achieve or maintain so that it
can work towards achieving or maintaining them. We refer to all these
preferred states as *"preferences"*. The preferences an agent has selected
to bring about at a given time are called "goals". This selection of preferences as goals is generally referred to as "goal generation". Basic aim
behind goal generation is to provide the agent with a way of getting
new goals. Although goal generation results in an increase in the agent's
knowledge about its goals, the overall autonomy of the agent does not
increase as its goals are derived from its preferences (which are programmed). We argue that to achieve greater autonomy, an agent must
be able to generate new preferences. In this paper we discuss how an
agent can generate new preferences based on analogy between new objects and the objects it has known preferences for.

Keywords: Autonomous Agents, BDI, Goal Generation, Preference
Generation.

1 Introduction and Related Work

Any autonomous agent situated in an environment needs to know the preferred
states it is expected to achieve or maintain so that it can work towards achieving or maintaining them. In approaches centered around BDI model of agency
[2], this information is provided in the form of desires, norms and obligations.
Desires are the preferred states because of the agent's own preferences, norms
are the preferred states because of the social standards the agent has to obey
and obligations are the preferred states because of the responsibilities assigned
to the agent [7]. We refer to all these different types of preferred states collec-
tively as *"preferences"*. The preferences an agent has selected to bring about at a
given time are called "goals" which are defined as "the preferred states an agent
wants to put effort into bringing about" [18]. Having a set of goals, the agent
would deliberate about them (called "goal deliberation" [13]) to determine how
(in what order) these should be achieved.

Goals are distinguished from preferences in the sense that goals have to be
realistic and mutually consistent while preferences need not be. Hence goals
are generally considered as *refined* preferences. [14] refine preferences (desires in

J. Dix and C. Witteveen (Eds.): MATES 2010, LNAI 6251, pp. 173–184, 2010.

their case) for getting goals by resolving conflicts among desires using priority rules. [17] and [6] refine preferences (desires) by prioritizing beliefs over desires whenever a conflict among the two occurs so that the resulting goals are "realistic". [3] and [7] include obligations and norms into the process and resolve conflicts among desires, norms, obligations and beliefs based on agent types (i.e. realistic, selfish, stable and social agents). Each agent type is the result of giving priority to a specific mental attitude. For example the agent giving the highest preference to its beliefs while solving conflicts among its mental attitudes is a "realistic" agent. This process of refining preferences into goals is called "goal generation" [3] [7].

The basic aim behind goal generation is to provide the agent with a way of getting new goals. In other words such a process should *increase* the agent's knowledge about its goals. Keeping in view only the set of goals the agent has, the above mentioned approaches certainly result in an increase in its goals. However the agent's goals are based on its preferences and since these preferences are programmed, goal generation as discussed above does not result in an overall increase in the agent's knowledge about its goals. An agent using such an approach cannot identify goals beyond its programmed preferences and hence has limited autonomy. This ability to generate new goals beyond its programmed knowledge can be crucial in certain domains. We are working with one such domain called "Intelligent Assistance in Smart Homes". Smart Homes are hi-tech home environments where various technologies, including Artificial Intelligence, are used to improve quality of living for the inhabitants [12]. Intelligent Assistance is an important feature in this setting where an intelligent agent assists Smart Home inhabitants in daily life activities and may suggest different activities that it deems appropriate for the inhabitants [9]. These activities can be related to maintenance of the home (e.g. suggesting to get the fan repaired, floor cleaned, carpet dried etc.) as well as about the well being of the inhabitants (e.g. suggesting to go for a walk). Such an agent can be initially programmed with preferences the programmer can foresee the agent coming across and so it can generate goals based on these preferences. However the situations such an agent is expected to encounter are so diverse that it is impossible to cover all of them in advance. Without the ability to increase its knowledge about its goals and preferences, any such agent is of limited usability. Hence to achieve greater autonomy, such an agent must have the ability to increase its knowledge of preferences and must be capable of *"preference generation"*. This means generating new desires, norms and obligations.

To address preference generation, we focus on the question, *"where preferences come from?"*. For example why would an agent prefer floor to be clean and not dirty? Studies in the field of Psychology provide the answer in the form of "motivations". "Motivations are reasons people hold for initiating and performing voluntary behavior" [10]. Motivations are only desired for their own sake and there is no other reason for them. For example a human may have a motivation to gain social status. Human behavior can be described in terms of completing the "behavior chain" where humans perform acts to satisfy their motivations.

Hence at the end of every behavior chain, there is a motivation [10]. This basic idea of motivations being at the core of human behavior is well established in the field of Psychology (see for example [8]) and there is significant amount of work on determining the set of primitive motivations humans may have (e.g. [10] propose a list of 16 motivations). Motivations can also affect a person's perception, cognition, emotion and behavior (for example [11] considers their role in controlling attention). In this paper however we are only concerned about role of motivation in determining behavior.

Considering motivations as the reason behind preferences answers the question we mentioned above. Hence an agent would prefer a clean floor and not a dirty one because clean floor contributes towards its motivation of, say, "Order and Cleanliness". To highlight our interpretation of preferences as satisfying motivations, we refer to them as *motivational preferences*. Generation of motivational preferences in humans can be seen as "identifying" those states as preferred which satisfy their motivations where determining what satisfies their motivations is linked to their feelings. For example a person can feel that a dirty floor is not satisfying. This feel can be different for different people depending upon their personality as for example a cleanoholic person will be more affected by preferences about cleaning than a social person. However as artificial agents cannot "feel" (at least until now) the effect of different states, they cannot generate preferences in the same way as humans do.

Although it may not be possible for artificial agents to generate new preference from scratch, it is possible for them to learn new preferences based on their existing preferences. Existing (programmed) preferences of an agent can be seen as providing it with the information on what satisfies its motivations. For example if an agent has a preference of keeping the floor clean, it implicitly means that this preference satisfies its motivations (that is why it has this preference). Based on this information provided by the existing preferences, we propose that preferences can be generated about new (unknown) entities based on preferences the agent has about objects which are similar to this new one. In other words if keeping an entity in a certain state based on some known motivational preference contributes towards satisfying an agent's motivations, then keeping another *similar* entity in that state would also contribute towards satisfying the agent's motivations. For example if the agent prefers clean floor then it would also prefer clean table top since both are similar in this respect (both have surfaces).

This paper is organized as follows. In Section 2 we discuss our proposed preference generation mechanism in detail. In Section 3 we propose an approach for learning new preferences with its experimental evaluation using the domain of Intelligent Assistance in Smart Homes in Section 4. The paper ends with conclusion and future work in Section 5.

2   Preference Generation

We choose to represent entities in the world as *"objects"* where an *object* is identified with the name of the real world entity it represents and is described using *attributes*. An attribute represents a property of the object (e.g. 'temperature" represents a property of the object "water") and has a value (e.g. temperature of an instance of water can be at 40C). Some example objects are given below in the format <*Object ID; Attributes(Attribute ID:Value)*>.

<*sofa seat;price:200,color:black,material:leather,usage:sitting,surface state:dry*>
<*coffee table;surface type:wood,location:living room,cleaning method:wet cloth*>
<*milk;volume:1,usage:drinking,uht treatment:no,temp to keep:4*>

Based on this representation, motivational preferences can be defined as follows.

Definition 1. *A motivational preference represents the agent's preferred value for an attribute of some object which the agent prefers because this preferred value contributes towards satisfying its motivations.*

Motivational preference for an object depends on the context the object is in. For example an agent may prefer the table in its living room to be clean but may not worry about keeping the table in its store room clean. This context of an object will be captured by its attributes. For example to distinguish between tables in the example above, an attribute "location" can be used which will have different values for both tables ("living room" and "store room" respectively).

Achieving motivational preferences would contribute towards satisfying the agent's motivations. The set of motivations an agent may have is likely to be small (as for example [10] argues in favor of only 16 basic motivations for humans) and hence can be easily programmed. The agent can also be programmed with motivational preferences about the objects which the programmer can foresee the agent coming across. However an agent working in a real environment can be expected to encounter many new objects and must be able to generate preferences for them. Our idea for preference generation is that if keeping an object in a particular state (based on some motivational preference) contributes towards satisfying some motivation, then keeping another "similar" object in the same state will also contribute towards satisfying that motivation. We call this approach of generating new preferences as *"Preference Learning"*.

We assume that satisfaction level of a motivation is represented by a number in the range [0,1] where a motivation is fully dissatisfied when its satisfaction level is 0 while fully satisfied when it is 1. cpm stands for "Contribution of preference p towards satisfying motivation m" and represents how much p contributes towards satisfying m. cpm is also in the range [0,1].

Two different types of motivational preferences, "reactive" and "proactive", can be identified based on the way a motivational preference affects the motivation it contributes towards satisfying. A "reactive motivational preference" is the one which contributes towards satisfying m with cpm as long as it holds. For example a preference representing that floor must be clean contributes towards the motivation of "Cleanliness" as long as it holds and ceases to contribute when it stops to hold (i.e. the floor becomes dirty). We call it reactive because it requires "reaction" from the agent if the agent wants to satisfy the corresponding motivation. A "proactive motivational preference" is the one which contributes towards m with *cpm* every time it is achieved. For example a preference representing the state when the agent has met a friend contributes towards the motivation of "Socialization" is proactive. We call it proactive because the agent can choose to make this preference true "proactively" if it wants to satisfy the corresponding motivation.

An agent can learn both these types of preferences and simply add them to its existing set of preferences. At first it may seem that learning proactive motivational preferences in this way will result in an agent generating a preference for every object similar to the one it already has a preference for (for example generating the preference to buy another car if it already has a preference to buy a similar car). However it is not the case. Motivational preferences simply represent what the agent prefers, they are not "goals". A motivational preference becomes a goal only when the agent *selects* it to be brought about. We call this process "Preference Selection"[1]. For example a motivational preference may require that the agent owns a certain car but it becomes a goal only when the agent selects it to be achieved. Achieving a preference essentially means that the agent would execute a plan that will make this preference hold (e.g. executing the plan of buying the car). Apparently it does not matter how many preferences about buying cars the agent has, what matters is how many cars the agent wants to buy at a given time. In other words it depends on the preference selection strategy, and not on the set of preferences. Hence it is safe to learn new preferences in this way. Details of this preference selection mechanism are beyond the scope of this paper.

We represent motivational preferences by the tuple $<$*type, obj, attr, dValue, motivation, cmp*$>$. For reactive motivational preferences, *type* is "MR" and is "MP" for proactive motivational preferences. *obj* represents the object this preference is for and *dValue* is the desired value for *obj*'s attribute *attr*. *motivation* represents which motivation this preference contributes towards satisfying and *cmp* represents how much this contribution is. The attributes for which the agent may not like to have a specific desired *dValue*, *dValue* will be "DC" (Don't Care) meaning the agent does not care whatever value this attribute may get. Some example preferences are given below.

$<$MR, Floor, Surface, Clean, Cleanliness, 0.5$>$
$<$MP, Movie1, Status, Watched, Entertainment, 0.7$>$
$<$MP, Movie2, Status, Watched, Entertainment, 0.7$>$

A motivational preference represents the state when attribute of the object is at the value suggested by this preference. For example if object refers to a movie and its attribute is "watched" then value "yes" represents the state when the agent has watched the movie. [7] refers to such representation of preferences as "state based" (see [7], Section 2).

---

[1] This selection of preferences as goals is the same thing what existing approaches call "goal generation" as we discussed in Section 1. However we refer to it as *"preference selection"* to emphasize that it is mere selection of preferences not generation of something new.

Having a set of goals (which are essentially the preferences selected to be achieved at a given time) the agent can deliberate about them during "Goal Deliberation" to determine in what order these should be achieved. The basic aim is to achieve as many of these goals as possible and as soon as possible given the agent's limited resources. [4][15][16] discuss different mechanisms to schedule goals keeping in consideration conflicts between plans that are used to achieve these goals. Although goal deliberation is not our focus in this paper, one aspect of it is related to our work on preference learning. We have mentioned above that goals are achieved using plans. Most of the existing approaches allow for more than one plan to be represented for the achievement of a goal so that the agent can choose the one it finds more appropriate in a given situation. In the same way as an agent prefers a certain state of an object over another because it satisfies its motivations, we argue that an agent may "prefer" a certain plan over another also because it contributes towards satisfying its motivations. For example an agent may prefer plans costing least resources because consuming less resources is what satisfies the agent. Another agent (who is rich) may prefer plans providing it more comfort as resources are less important to such an agent. The preferences like "dry-cleaning delicate cloths" (since it would protect them), "vacuum-cleaning carpet" (since it cleans better) or "eating bananas instead of apples" (since bananas taste better) are all examples of cases when an agent prefers certain plan over others since these preferred methods provide the agent with more satisfaction. We call such preferences towards doing an action (or treating an object) in a certain way as *Task Preferences*. "Execution Advice" used by [13] also seems to serve the same purpose.

These preferred ways of achieving a goal can also be represented as attributes of the object. For example "Cleaning Method" can be an attribute of object "carpet" with the preferred value "vacuum-cleaning". Then the preference learning mechanism we discussed above for motivational preferences can also be used to learn these task preferences. Task preferences have the same basic representation as that of motivational preferences which we discussed above. However *type* in this case will be "T" while *cpm* is not relevant. Some examples of task preference are given below.

$<T,\ Floor,\ Cleaning\ Method,\ Mop\text{-}Cleaning,\ Cleanliness,\ NA>$
$<T,\ Chicken,\ Cooking\ Method,\ Roasting,\ Taste,\ NA>$

Figure 1 provides the summary of our discussion in this section. In the next section we discuss how preferences can be learnt.

3   An Approach for Preference Learning

Preference Learning (PL) works in the same way for both motivational and task Preferences and hence we refer to them as only "preference" in this Section. We denote the new object for whose attribute the agent wants to learn a preference as $Object_{obs}$, the attribute as $Attr_{PL}$ and this new, to be learnt preference as *newPref*. We denote the set of all objects the agent knows about as $Objects_{All}$ and the set of its known preferences as *Preferences*. Our approach is to identify

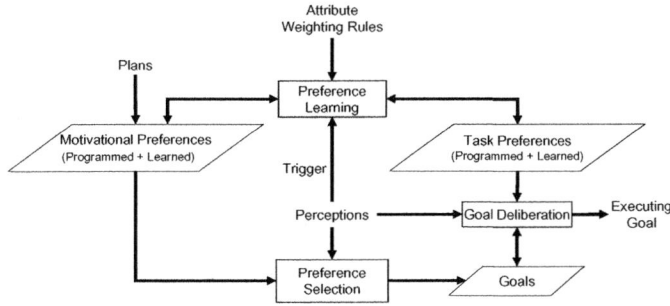

Fig. 1. A Framework for Goals

the most similar object to $Object_{obs}$ from $Objects_{All}$ that has a known preference for $Attr_{PL}$ and then to use information from this preference to learn $newPref$.

One approach can be to have $Objects_{All}$ divided into different classes and then see which class $Object_{obs}$ belongs to whenever a new $Object_{obs}$ is found. However this approach is not feasible for PL. In case of PL our purpose is not only to find the most similar object to $Object_{obs}$ but also to find it in the context of $Attr_{PL}$. Only those objects from $Objects_{All}$ should be considered for finding object similar to $Object_{obs}$ which have $Attr_{PL}$ as an attribute. Hence different $Attr_{PL}$ of the same $Object_{obs}$ would lead to the consideration of different objects for finding the one most similar to $Object_{obs}$ and so general purpose classes where all broadly similar objects are put together will not work. For example a chair with a leather seat can be seen as belonging to class of chairs. But if we want to find most appropriate cleaning method for its seat, a leather sofa is more relevant than other type of chairs in the class of chairs (e.g. wooden chair). Making context specific classes, where objects that are similar only in a particular context are put together, is also not feasible as it is not possible to foresee all different type of objects an agent working in some real environment would come across. Hence we do not pre-classify $Objects_{All}$ and choose to find the most similar object to $Object_{obs}$ whenever a new $newPref$ is to be learned.

The approach of Instance Based Learning (IBL) algorithms [1] suits our purpose well. Here specifically we use the basic idea from a well known IBL algorithm, Nearest Neighbor Algorithm [5]. Nearest Neighbor Algorithm classifies a new sample based on the class of the training sample most similar to it. The similarity between the two samples is found by measuring their distance in the feature space created by their attributes. We use this idea of finding similarity in the feature space for finding the object most similar to $Object_{obs}$ from $Objects_{All}$. As main consideration here is to learn a value for $Attr_{PL}$, an object from $Objects_{All}$ is useful only if it has $Attr_{PL}$ as an attribute. This acts as a filter condition and those objects from $Objects_{All}$ which satisfy this condition are identified during the first step. We call them "neighbors" of $Object_{obs}$. The next step is to find the distance between each of these neighbors and $Object_{obs}$ so that the most similar, or "nearest", neighbor of $Objects_{obs}$ can be chosen.

Many distance measures have been proposed in literature (see for example [20] for a discussion). These measures can be divided into two broad categories as those which use some parameters derived from training data (like for example Mahalanobis, Correlation, Chi-square, Value Difference Metric), and the ones without such parameters (like Euclidean, Manhattan, Camberra) which rely on simple difference calculations between the two samples. The former tend to show higher accuracy but these cannot be used for PL due to lack (rather absence) of training data. Hence we resort to the measures which do not require any training data. Such a measure should be able to work both for nominal as well as continuous attributes as during PL we encounter both. Heterogeneous Euclidean-Overlap Metric (HEOM) [20] is one such measure.

Using HEOM the distance between two objects, X and Y, in the feature space of their attributes can be measured as,

$$D(X, Y) = \sqrt{\sum_{a=1}^{m} d_a(a_X, a_Y)^2} \tag{1}$$

where m is number of attributes of X (or Y) and $d_a(a_X, a_Y)$ is the difference between the values of X and Y for attribute a. $d_a(a_X, a_Y)$ is defined as,

$$d_a(a_X, a_Y) = \begin{cases} 1 & \text{if } a_X \text{ or } a_Y \text{ missing} \\ overlap(a_X, a_Y) & \text{if a is nominal} \\ diff_a(a_X, a_Y) & \text{if a is numeric} \end{cases}$$

$$overlap(a_X, a_Y) = \begin{cases} 0 & \text{if } a_x = a_Y \\ 1 & \text{otherwise} \end{cases}$$

$$diff_a(a_X, a_Y) = \frac{|a_X - a_Y|}{max_a - min_a}$$

HEOM as described above can be used when both X and Y have same attributes (as generally is the case in classification). $d_a(a_X, a_Y) = 1$ hence is used to cater for missing data. However in case of PL the distance is to be measured between different objects which can have different attributes. If the distance between two Objects X and Y is measured in the feature space created by the union of their attributes using $d_a(a_X, a_Y) = 1$ when a_X or a_Y is missing, the distance measure is not very reliable as it will be hugely affected by the absence of attributes for one object or the other and the distance because of difference in attribute values will not be so prominent. Nonetheless considering similarity between two objects because of number of common and different attributes is also very important. If an object X shares more attributes with Y than with Z, then X and Y can be considered more similar as they have more properties in common. On the other hand if X has more attributes different from Y than from Z, then intuitively X is *less* similar to Y than it is to Z. Hence both, distance because of difference in attribute values and similarity or dissimilarity because of number of common or different attributes, are important in case of PL.

We choose to keep these two measures separate. For measuring the distance because of difference in attribute values, we modify HEOM so that the distance between two objects is measured in the feature space of their common attributes. Similarity and dissimilarity because of common and different attributes we handle separately as we discuss below (Equation 4). Our modified D(X,Y) is,

$$D(X, Y) = \sqrt{\sum_{a=1}^{k} d_a(a_X, a_Y)^2 / k} \qquad (2)$$

where k is number of common attributes between X and Y. While determining k, we exclude $Attr_{PL}$ which although $Objects_{obs}$ shares with its neighbors, it does not have a value for it. We normalize this distance with k so that the distances measured between different pairs of Objects with different k are comparable.

It is well known that when comparing two objects in different respects, different attributes have different significance (see for example [19]). For example if we compare seat of a car with seat of a sofa for determining the preferred state of the seat, attributes like price, color and size of the seats are not relevant while the attribute "used for" is highly relevant. On the other hand if a car seat is to be compared with another car's seat to see which one should be purchased, price, color and size become relevant while "used for" is not relevant any more. To handle this we use "Attribute Weighting Rules" which provide information on significance of an object's attributes for determining the value of another attribute of this object. For example if the object is "car seat" and the attribute under consideration is "owner", the Attribute Weighting Rule will describe how significant other attributes of "car seat" are for determining the value of its attribute "owner" (which can be 'yes' or 'no'). The sum of all the weights assigned to an object's attributes for each Attribute Weighting Rule is 1. The reason for using these rules instead of standard methods of Feature Weighting, like the ones discussed in [19], is that in case of PL there is no training data available while all such Feature Weighing methods work based on training data. Hence we further modify $D(X, Y)$ as,

$$D_c(X, Y) = \sqrt{\sum_{a=1}^{k} w_a^c \times d_a(a_X, a_Y)^2 / k} \qquad (3)$$

where $D_c(X, Y)$ is the distance between X and Y, when being compared in the context c (which essentially is represented by $Attr_{PL}$). w_a^c is the weight assigned to attribute a and represents the significance of this attribute for determining the value of $Attr_{PL}$.

We also modify $diff_a(a_X, a_Y)$ (for (1), (2) and (3)) as,

$$diff_a(a_X, a_Y) = \frac{|a_X - a_Y|}{max(a_X, a_Y)}$$

because in case of PL attribute a may not have many values (i.e. not many objects may have a as an attribute). If it is shared only between X and Y (which is quite likely), the range $(max_a - min_a)$ will be the same as the difference between their values which would result in $diff_a(a_X, a_Y) = 1$ always.

To handle the similarity because of number of common attributes and the dissimilarity because of number of different attributes between a pair of objects we define a measure of similarity between two objects X and Y (represented as $Sim(X, Y)$) as,

$$Sim(X, Y) = \left[\frac{AttrCm(X, Y)}{TotAttr(X, Y)} - \frac{AttrDiff(X, Y)}{TotAttr(X, Y)} \right] \tag{4}$$

where $AttrCm(X, Y)$ represents the number of common attributes between X and Y, $AttrDiff(X, Y)$ represents the number of attributes different between X and Y while $TotAttr(X, Y)$ is number of attributes in the union of X and Y.

Equation 3 represents distance because of difference in attribute values while Equation 4 represents similarity because of number of common and different attributes between X and Y. We combine $Sim(X, Y)$ with $D_c(X, Y)$ to get our final measure of similarity between two objects X and Y, denoted as $S(X, Y)$.

$$S(X, Y) = Sim(X, Y) - D_c(X, Y) \tag{5}$$

Using this measure, $Object_{obs}$'s similarity with each of its neighbors will be determined and the most similar one will be declared as the "nearest neighbor" of $Object_{obs}$. The reason for using only the nearest neighbor of $Object_{obs}$, and not k-nearest as is done in K-Nearest Neighbor Algorithm [5], is that the agent can intentionally have different preferences for slightly different objects. For example the agent may prefer to own a car with 4 doors and not to own the one with 2. In the last step the information from the preference this nearest neighbor has about $Attr_{PL}$ will be used to get values of *type*, *dValue* and *cpm* for *newPref*.

4   Evaluation

In this section we evaluate the approach of preference learning we proposed in Section 3. Due to the unavailability of any standard data set that has different objects described using attributes, we have constructed a set of 60 objects ourselves. These are the objects a Smart Home agent may normally encounter. These are referred to as *"Known Objects"*. The agent has a corresponding set of *"Preferences"* for these objects and a set of *"Weights"* which describe the significance of an object's attributes for determining the value of a specific attribute. A fourth set, *"Perceptions"* contains 50 objects that the agent has perceived from the environment. These are the objects whose preference attributes the agent wants to learn preferences for. We have constructed a set of "correct" preferences for these objects, in the same way as we have done for "Known Objects", and use it for evaluating the learnt preferences.

We have tried to include a reasonable number of attributes for each object, mixing nominal and numeric attributes, so that a fair evaluation can be performed. Using this data, we evaluate all five measures we mentioned in Section 3 (i.e. Equation 1 to 5). The purpose is to support the line of reasoning we adopted in the previous section. Summary of the results of our evaluation is given in the table below. The number of objects in each case is 50 (i.e. number of Objects in set *Perceptions*).

Measure Used	Preferences Learnt Correctly (out of 50)
(1)	37
(2)	32
(3)	30
(4)	30
(5)	50

(1) and (2) fail mainly when attributes that do not play any role in determining the value of a given preference attribute are different for similar objects. However (1) gives better results than (2) since it includes similarity and dissimilarity because of number of common and different attributes. (3) includes weights describing significance of attributes and hence is not affected by irrelevant attributes. But since it only includes distance because of attribute values and does not include similarity and dissimilarity because of common and different attributes, it can consider very different objects as similar if they have some common attributes. (4) only takes into account similarity and dissimilarity because of number of common and different attributes and does not consider the difference between attribute values. Hence it cannot distinguish between different objects of the same type and considers all of them as equally similar to each other. Any one of them can be picked randomly as the most similar. Hence although an object found as most similar using this measure is of the right type, it may not be the right object. (3) alone is not adequate as it does not include similarity and dissimilarity because of number of common and different attributes while (4) alone is also not adequate as it does not take into account distance because of attribute values. Combining (3) and (4) into (5) cures both these problems and can correctly learn preferences for all of the perceptions. Based on this preliminary evaluation we can say that (5) is a good starting point as a measure for Preference Learning. However only a thorough evaluation on a real dataset would make it clear how good it is in a real life scenario.

5   Conclusion and Future Work

We have proposed an approach to preference generation that allows an agent to learn new preferences about an object (which can be about its preferred state or about preferred way to achieve such a state) based on its existing preferences about similar objects. Using this approach an agent can learn new preferences beyond its programmed knowledge and hence achieve greater autonomy. One main issue with the usage of this approach is that of describing objects using attributes. An interesting development in this regard can be the development of automated solutions that can construct a database of objects where these objects are described using attributes. It would require some complex analysis of sentences to see what properties are normally ascribed to an object. We take it as part of our future work.

References

1. Aha, D.W., Kibler, D., Albert, M.K.: Instance-based learning algorithms. Machine Learning 6(1), 37–66 (1991)
2. Bratman, M.: Intention, plans, and practical reason. Harvard University Press, Cambridge (1987)
3. Broersen, J., Dastani, M., Hulstijn, J., van der Torre, L.: Goal generation in the BOID architecture. Cognitive Science Quarterly 2(3-4), 428–447 (2002)
4. Clement, B.J., Durfee, E.H.: Theory for coordinating concurrent hierarchical planning agents using summary information. In: Proceedings of AAAI, pp. 495–502 (1999)
5. Cover, T., Hart, P.E.: Nearest neighbor pattern classification. IEEE Transactions on Information Theory 13(1), 21–27 (1967)
6. da Costa Pereira, C., Tettamanzi, A.G.B.: Goal generation with relevant and trusted beliefs. In: Proceedings of AAMAS'08, pp. 397–404 (2008)
7. Dignum, F., Kinny, D.: From desires, obligations and norms to goals. Cognitive Science Quarterly 2 (2002)
8. Maslow, A.: Motivation and Personality. Harper & Row, New York (1954)
9. Rafique, U., Huang, S.Y.: A new action description scheme for informal reasoning. In: Arabnia, H.R., de la Fuente, D., Olivas, J.A. (eds.) Proceedings of ICAI'09, vol. II, pp. 582–588 (2009)
10. Reiss, S.: Multifaceted nature of intrinsic motivation: The theory of 16 basic desires. Review of General Psychology 8(3), 179–193 (2004)
11. Simon, H.: Motivational and emotional controls of cognition. Psychological Review 74(1), 29–39 (1967)
12. Simpson, R., Schreckenghost, D., LoPresti, E., Kirsch, N.: Plans and planning in smart homes. In: Augusto, J.C., Nugent, C.D. (eds.) Designing Smart Homes. LNCS (LNAI), vol. 4008, pp. 71–84. Springer, Heidelberg (2006)
13. Thangarajah, J., Harland, J., Yorke-Smith, N.: A soft COP model for goal deliberation in a BDI agent. In: CP'07 Workshop on Constraint Modelling and Reformulation (2007)
14. Thangarajah, J., Padgham, L., Harland, J.: Representation and reasoning for goals in BDI agents. Australian Computer Science Communications 24(1), 259–265 (2002)
15. Thangarajah, J., Padgham, L., Winikoff, M.: Detecting & exploiting positive goal interaction in intelligent agents. In: Proceedings of AAMAS'03, pp. 401–408. ACM, New York (2003)
16. Thangarajah, J., Padgham, L., Winikoff, M.: Detecting and avoiding interference between goals in intelligent agents. In: Proceedings of the International Joint Conference on Artificial Intelligence, pp. 721–726. Academic Press, London (2003)
17. Thomason, R.H.: Desires and defaults: A framework for planning with inferred goals. In: Proceedings of KR 2000, pp. 702–713 (2000)
18. Birna van Riemsdijk, M., Dastani, M., Winikoff, M.: Goals in agent systems: a unifying framework. In: Proceedings of AAMAS'08, pp. 713–720 (2008)
19. Wettschereck, D., Aha, D.W., Mohri, T.: A review and empirical evaluation of feature weighting methods for a class of lazy learning algorithms. Artificial Intelligence Review 11, 273–314 (1997)
20. Randall Wilson, D., Martinez, T.R.: Improved heterogeneous distance functions. Journal of Artificial Intelligence Research 6, 1–34 (1997)

Evaluation of Techniques for a Learning-Driven Modeling Methodology in Multiagent Simulation

Robert Junges and Franziska Klügl

Modeling and Simulation Research Center
Örebro University, Sweden
{robert.junges,franziska.klugl}@oru.se

Abstract. There have been a number of suggestions for methodologies supporting the development of multiagent simulation models. In this contribution we are introducing a learning-driven methodology that exploits learning techniques for generating suggestions for agent behavior models based on a given environmental model. The output must be human-interpretable. We compare different candidates for learning techniques – classifier systems, neural networks and reinforcement learning – concerning their appropriateness for such a modeling methodology.

1 Motivation

Methodological questions are more and more in the focus of research on agent-based simulation. The central question hereby concerns what behaviors do we have to create on the agent level so that the intended outcome is produced. However, if it is not fully known which local behavior need to be included in the model, designing and implementing the simulation model might be painful and result in some try-and-error process: modifying the local agent behavior, running and analyzing the simulation, followed by modifying the local behavior again. Such a procedure might be feasible for an experienced modeler who knows the critical starting points for behavior modifications, but not so experienced modelers might get lost.

In this contribution we are addressing this search for the appropriate agent-level behavior by using agent learning. The vision is hereby the following procedure: the modeler develops an environmental model as a part of the overall model, determines what the agent might be able to perceive and to manipulate and describes the intended outcome. The agents then use a learning mechanism for determining a behavior program that generates the intended overall outcome in the given environment. In this contribution we are testing three well-known techniques for their suitability in such learning-driven model development process: Learning Classifier Systems, Reinforcement Learning and Neural Networks.

In the next section we will review existing approaches for learning agent techniques in simulation models explaining why we particularly selected these three techniques. This is followed by a more detailed treatment of the learning-driven methodology and a presentation of the candidate techniques. In section 4 and 5 we

J. Dix and C. Witteveen (Eds.): MATES 2010, LNAI 6251, pp. 185–196, 2010.

describe the used testbed and the experiments conducted with it. The results are then discussed. The papers ends with a conclusion and an outlook to future work.

2   Learning Agents and Simulation

Many different forms of learning have shown to be successful when working with agents and multiagent systems. Unfortunately, we can not cover all techniques for agent learning in this paper, the following paragraph shall give a few general pointers and then give a short glance on related work. In general our contribution is special concerning the objective of our comparison: not mere learning performance but its suitability for a usage in a modeling support context.

Reinforcement learning [1], learning automata [2], evolutionary and neural forms of learning are recurrent examples of learning techniques. Besides that, techniques inspired by biological evolution have been applied in the area of Artificial Life [3], where evolutionary elements can be found throughout the multiagent approach. An example of a simulation of a concrete scenario is [4], in which simulated ant agents were controlled by a neural network that was actually designed by a genetic algorithm. Another approach similar to a learning classifier system (LCS) can be found in [5], where a rules set was used and modified by a genetic algorithm. The interesting point in this last case, is that rule conditions are based on situation descriptions.

Related work approaches the behavior modeling task also from the point of view of usability. This can be seen in [6], where an evolutionary algorithm is applied to behavior learning of an individual agent in multiagent robots. Another example, from [7], describes a general approach for automatically programming a behavior-based robot. Using Q-Learning algorithm, new behaviors are learned by trial and error using a performance feedback function as reinforcement. In [8], also using reinforcement learning, agents share their experiences and most frequently simulated behaviors are adopted as a group behavior strategy. Performance is also analyzed for instance in [9], where reinforcement learning and neural networks are compared as learning techniques in an exploration scenario for mobile robots. The authors conclude that learning techniques are able to learn the individual behaviors, sometimes outperforming a hand coded program, and behavior-based architectures speed up reinforcement learning.

3   A Learning-Driven Methodology

The basic idea behind a methodology using a learning-driven approach consists in the transfer of agent behavior design from the human modeler to the simulation system. Specially in complex models, a high number of details can be manipulated. This may make a manual modeling and tuning process cumbersome specially when knowledge about the original system or experience for implicitly bridging the micro-macro gap is missing. Using self-adaptive agents might be a good idea for supporting the modeler in finding an appropriate agent behavior model. Before we continue with candidates, we give a short idea of the basic modeling process for such a learning-driven development.

3.1   Basic Modeling Process

The starting point of this learning-driven modeling process is the environmental model. In [10] we denoted a more general version of this approach as "environment-driven" design is an analysis of the environmental structure. Based on this, the agent interface and its behavior definition are determined. The steps are in particular:

1. *Identify relevant aspects* (global status, global dynamics and local entities);
2. *Determine the primitive actions of the agent and the reaction of the environmental entities to these;*
3. *Determine what information from the environment must be given to an agent;*
4. *Decide on a learning technique* that is apt to connect perceptions and actions of the agent appropriately for actually producing the agents behavior;
5. *Determine the feedback function for the agents.* This reward has to measure performance of the agents in the given environment and is ideally derived from a description of the overall objective or observed aggregate behavior;
6. *Implement the environmental model* including reward function if needed;
7. *Specify and implement the agents* behavior program or agent interfaces in combination with the chosen learning mechanism;
8. *Test and analyze the overall outcome*, the simulation results and individual trajectories carefully for preventing artifacts that come from an improper environmental or reward model or weak interfaces.

After this process ended, ideally a description of the agent behavior is available that fits to the environmental model and the reward given and thus produces the aggregate behavior intended. Analysis of this model – as indicated in the last step – is essential.

There is a variety of possible learning agent techniques that might be suitable for the aim presented here and requirements such as general applicability or accessibility of the resulting model identified. We selected three standard techniques for further examination: Learning Classifier Systems, Q-Learning and a Feed Forward Neural Network, which we will describe in the next paragraphs.

3.2   Learning Classifier Systems: XCS

The accuracy-based learning classifier system XCS is an iterative online learning system [11]. Behavioral knowledge in XCS is represented by a fixed-size population of condition-action-prediction classifiers. Each classifier predicts the consequences (reward) of executing the specified action given that the conditions are satisfied. This basic framework provides means to represent the knowledge in a way that we can clearly identify the agent behavior model - the conditions and the actions. It is possible to determine the quality of a rule based on the predicted reward and the additional evaluation of the accuracy of this prediction. Conditions are represented using three values: true, false and don't care – allowing for generalized situation descriptions with concentration on the relevant aspects.

XCS has a built-in evolutionary rule discovery component. It approximates prediction values by means of credit assignment mechanisms. A successful learning process in XCS, however, requires two conditions to be satisfied: the underlying problem has to be approximately Markov and random exploration during learning should sufficiently ensure complete problem coverage.

3.3   Q-Learning

Q-Learning [12] is a well-known reinforcement learning technique. It works by developing an action-value function that gives the expected utility of taking a specific action in a specific state. The agents keep track of the experienced situation-action pairs by managing the so called Q-Table, that consists of situation descriptions, the actions taken and the corresponding expected prediction, called Q-Value. Q-Learning is able to compare the expected utility of the available actions without requiring a model of the environment. Nevertheless, the use of the Q-Learning algorithm is constrained to a finite number of possible states and actions. As a reinforcement learning algorithm, it also is based on modeling the overall problem as a Markov Decision Process.

3.4   FFNN - Feed Forward Neural Networks

A Feed Forward Neural Network (FFNN) is an artificial neural network where the information moves in only one direction, forward, from the input nodes, through the hidden nodes and to the output nodes [13]. FFNN is usually using supervised training, yet the application situation here is designed for online reward-based learning in a given environment. Therefore, we modified the overall learning process for producing an appropriate setting for the FFNN. There are three phases that are repeatedly executed. The first phase is an explore simulation with randomly selected actions in given situations. These situation-action pairs are recorded with the reward they produced. After a number of steps, a neural network is trained using the best n situation action pairs. The so trained FFNN is then used in a exploit simulation. The rewards of the selected actions during this exploit phase are recorded in the table. After every explore phase, a new FFNN is trained. We had to notice that the influence of the first weak situation action samples was too high, when barely retraining the network. The results of the explore phase are cumulated.

As a FFNN is a black box, the extraction of the behavioral knowledge is non trivial. There are basically two options. During the exploit run, situation and action pairs are recorded and analyzed. Alternatively – if the number of hidden nodes is not too high – the activation state of the different node can be analyzed showing which particular perceived situation elements were responsible for selecting the action.

This is clearly a very restrictive selection of just three techniques that must be extended in future work using other forms of learning such as evolutionary programming support vector machines, other forms of reinforcement learning, respectively learning automata, etc.

4   Testbed

The scenario we use for evaluating the learning approaches is the same as in [14] where we already describe the integration of XCS-based agents into the agent-based modeling and simulation platform SeSAm. This pedestrian evacuation scenario is a typical application domain for multiagent simulation, and albeit the employed scenario may be oversimplified, we expected that its relative simplicity will enable us to evaluate the potentials of each learning technique as well as to deduce the involved challenges.

4.1   Environmental Model

The main objective of the simulation concerned the emergence of collision-free exiting behavior. Therefore, the reward and interfaces to the environment were mainly shaped to support this.

The basic scenario consists of a room (20x30m) surrounded by walls with one exit and a different number of column-type obstacles (with a diameter of 4m). In this room a number of pedestrians have to leave as fast as possible without hurting themselves during collisions. We assume that each pedestrian agent is represented by a circle with 50cm diameter and moves with a speed of 1.5m/sec. One time-step in the discrete simulation corresponds to 0.5sec. Space is continuous. We tested this scenario using 1, 2 and 5 agents, and the number of obstacles was set to 1, 5, and 10. At the beginning of a test-run, all agents were located at given positions in the upper half of the room.

Reward was given to the agent a immediately after executing an action at time-step t. It was computed in the following way:

$reward(a, t) = reward_{exit}(a, t) + reward_{dist}(a, t) + feedback_{collision}(a, t)$ with $reward_{exit}(a, t) = 200$, if agent a has reached the exit in time t, and 0 otherwise; $reward_{dist}(a, t) = \beta \times (d_t(exit, a) - d_{t-1}(exit, a))$ with $\beta = 5$; $feedback_{collision}$ was set to 100 if a collision free actual movement had been made, to 0 if no movement happened, and to -100 if a collision occurred. The different components of the feedback function stress goal-directed collision-free movements.

4.2   Agent Interfaces

As agent interfaces, the perceived situation and the set of possible actions have to be defined. Similar to [14], the perception of the agents is based on their basic orientation, respectively its movement direction. The overall perceivable area is divided into 5 sectors with a distinction between areas in two different distances. For every area two binary perception categories were used. The first encoded whether the exit was perceivable in this area and the second encoded whether an obstacle was present - where an obstacle can be everything with which a collision should be avoided: walls, columns or other pedestrians.

The action set is shaped for supporting the exiting behavior allowing the agent to ignore the navigation task. We assume that the agents are per default oriented towards the exit. Thus, the action set consists of $A = \{move_{left},$

$move_{slightlyLeft}$, $move_{straight}$, $move_{slightlyRight}$, $move_{right}$, noop, stepback}. For every of these actions, the agent turns by the given direction (e.g. +36 degrees for $move_{slightlyRight}$), makes an atomic step and orients itself towards the exit again. This allows concentrating the learning on the collision avoidance giving the scenario the Markov property.

4.3   Techniques Configuration

The testbed was implemented using SeSAm (www.simsesam.de). Due to an existing integration of XCS as an alternative agent architecture [14] the implementation of a XCS agent in the testbed was basically consisting in assigning the perceptions and actions defined in the testbed implementation to bit string elements of the rule description. The Q-Learning could be implemented by means of the standard high-level behavior language in SeSAm. For the FFNN implementation we used the Joone API (www.joone.org), integrating the management and usage of neural networks as additional primitive language constructs to the SeSAm modeling language.

The XCS comes with a number of 21 configuration parameters ranging from the size of the rule population, via thresholds for the application of the genetic algorithm or diverse initial values for offsprings to discount factors in multistep mode. As in [14], we did not modify these settings, but used the values of the original implementation of XCS [15] following the advice of its developer. This setting of parameters appeared to be reasonable, but might be discouraging the usage of this learning technique.

The Q-Learning technique assumed an initial Q-Value of 0 for all untested situation-action pairs. Additionally, only two parameters have to be settled: we set the learning rate to 1 and the discount factor to 0.5.

The configuration of the FFNN basically concerned the particular setup of the network itself. We use 20 neurons in the input layer (corresponding to the number of elementary perceptions), 10 neurons in the hidden layer, and 7 neurons in the output layer (corresponding to the number of possible actions). The input layer is a linear layer, and the hidden and output layers are sigmoid layers. After each explore phase, the network for 2000 epochs or until the root mean squared error is lower than 0.01. The training set was consisting of the best rule for each situation presented.

5   Experiments and Results

All experiments alternated between explore and exploit phases. During the explore phase, the agents randomly execute an action. In exploitation trials, the best action according to the used learning technique was selected in each step. Every phase consists of 250 iterations. Every experiment took 100 explore-exploit cycles. In contrast to [14], we did not test a large variety of configurations as it was not our goal to find an optimal one, but a more modeling-oriented evaluation of the different techniques.

Table 1. Mean number of collisions - Columns represent the number of agents and number of obstacles

	1 - 1	2 - 1	5 - 1	1 - 5	2 - 5	5 - 5	1 - 10	2 - 10	5 - 10
XCS	0.59	1.1	7.22	0.56	0.89	6.63	0.1	1.79	7.25
	±0.79	±1.23	±2.58	±0.84	±0.82	±3.15	±0.32	±1.46	±3.05
Q-L.	0.22	0.98	8.1	0.75	0.53	8.17	0.14	1.77	9.19
	±0.5	±0.96	±3.71	±0.78	±1	±4.61	±0.38	±1.51	±4.94
FFNN	1.02	1.56	8.59	0.77	1.35	9.51	0.95	1.37	7.83
	±1.79	±1.33	±3.42	±0.95	±1.57	±4.4	±1.19	±1.53	±4.41

In the following we analyze the results of the simulations, first with respect to learning performance and then concerning the usability of the actually learned behavior control for the proposed methodology.

5.1 Performance Evaluation

The metric used for evaluating learning performance is the number of collisions. As we consider a small room for this evacuation scenario, the time to reach the exit does not vary significantly. A collision is not influencing the behavior directly, but the reward the agent got.

Table 1 presents the mean number of collisions for each agent class, at the end of the simulation of each test case. The values are aggregated only over the last 50 exploit iterations (after warm-up period of 10000 steps) to avoid the inclusion of any warm-up data. Means and standard deviation refer to variation within the single runs. One can see that there is no clear tendency that one technique performs better in all scenarios.

Concerning adaptation speed we could observe in all three learning techniques similar dynamics: the number of collisions decreases fast in the beginning, but then the behavioral knowledge converges quite fast.

To have a better illustration of what this means in each technique, we show in figure 1 the trajectories of the agents in exploit phases after a) 10, b) 50 and c) 100 exploit trials. We can see that, since the early exploit trials, XCS and Q-Learning agents already presents a well defined exit-oriented pattern - with small inefficiencies on the way (Q-Learning). The FFNN agents requires more trials to develop such patterns. This happens because the FFNN agent, when facing a collision situation (e.g. in front of an obstacle), must have experienced by exploration, a good solution (positive reward) to avoid that collision. This is not the same case for the XCS and Q-Learning agents, because even if they don't know what is the best action, they know which one to avoid as they also learn from negatively rewarded actions.

5.2 Behavior Learning Outcome

The second objective of this evaluation is the behavior model as the result of the learning process. We base the following analysis on one randomly selected experiment with 5 agents and 10 obstacles.

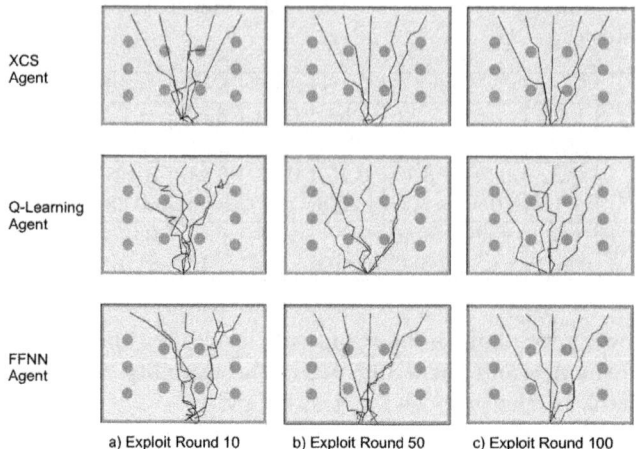

a) Exploit Round 10   b) Exploit Round 50   c) Exploit Round 100

Fig. 1. Exemplary trajectories during exploit trials, for 5 agents and 10 obstacles

XCS Agent. At the end of the experiment, the XCS agent has a rules set with 160 rules, representing his experience after 100 explore and exploit cycles. In this case 71.25% of the rules have a strength value higher than 0, which means that they represent a positive reward experience. Figure 2(a) depicts the strength distribution over the example rule set. Rule strength is hereby a measure of the prediction and fitness, given by: $strength = prediction \times fitness$. Figure 2(b) depicts the experience distribution over the rules set. It presents a small group of experienced rules. This is an effect of the generalization. This small group represents rules that are frequently selected because they generalize the most common situations in this scenario, and therefore are more fitted, which means their reward prediction is more accurate.

Directly considering the rules learned, table 2 outlines the four best XCS rules of an example agent, giving also the fitness and experience information (and the bit string representation of the condition). However, even though the

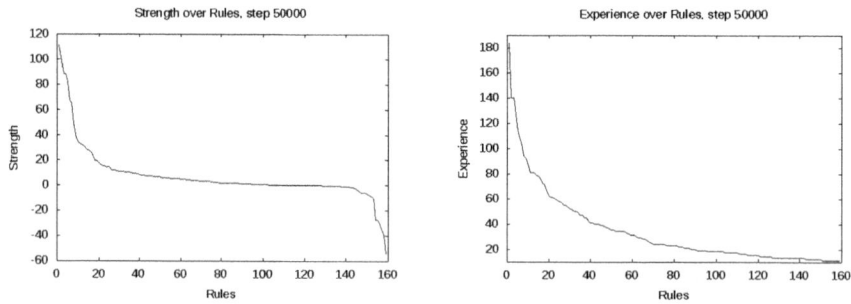

Fig. 2. XCS strenght and experience distribution for an exemplary run with 5 agents and 10 obstacles

Table 2. Best XCS rules for an exemplary run with 5 agents and 10 obstacles (F=Fitness and E=Experience)

Condition (bit string)	Condition Interpretation	Action	F	E
******0******0******	No obst. imdtly. right No obst. near left	$move_{slightlyRight}$	0.71	61
****0*0******0******	No obst. imdtly. ahead or right No obst. near left	$move_{straight}$	0.58	61
00*0*0***0*0*0**	No obst. imdtly. left No exit near left, right or ahead	$move_{slightlyLeft}$	0.56	81
0**0*******00**010**	No obst. or exit left No exit ahead or right Obst. near right	$move_{left}$	0.69	24

generalization has a good impact on the performance, the uncertainties on the reward prediction impact the fitness evaluation. As one can notice from the conditions, the rules are shaped for the particular example agent according to its starting position in the upper right part.

Q-Learning Agent. A Q-Learning agent maintains a table with 1961 situation-action (rule) entries without generalization. In the case with 5 agents and 10 obstacles 44% of the rules either have no experience (they have never been used) or have no reward. Figure 3 shows the distribution of the reward prediction, Q-Value, over the rules set. One can see that there are only a few rules with a high Q-Value. Clearly, the Q-Value alone cannot be a selection criteria for rules forming a behavior model as the ones with the highest Q-Value naturally contain situations where the agent directly perceives the exit. Thus, rules have to be considered for all potentially relevant situations. Although not generalized, the single rules are in principle readable by a human modeler.

FFNN Agent. In the FFNN implementation, the access to the behavior model of the agent is more challenging. There are two possibilities: either analyzing the

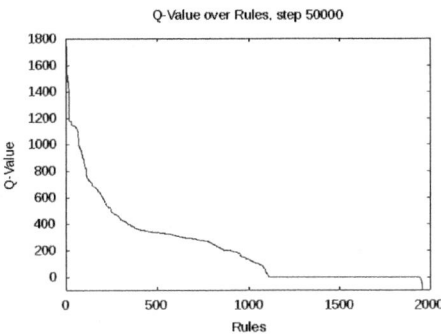

Fig. 3. Q-Learning value distribution for an exemplary run with 5 agents and 10 obstacles

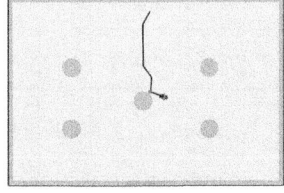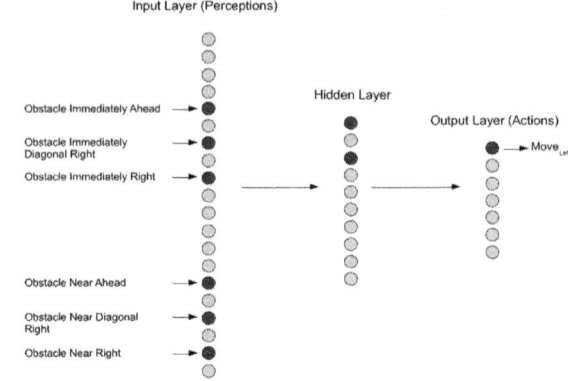

(a) Neural network decision situation

(b) Corresponding Neural network activation

Fig. 4. FFNN exemplary run with 1 agent, 5 obstacles

best rules of final training set – without considering the generalization done by the FFNN or by manually analyzing the activation relations in the net.

The training rules set – in the example containing 45 rules – contains only rule representing a high positive reward which is collected during both explore and exploit phases. In the latter, situation-action combinations used by the FFNN are recorded. Considering the fitness of all rules observed, their fitness is naturally high for all.

More interestedly, yet more effortful to access is the activation state of the network. In figure 4(b), we illustrate the activation for all layer in an example situation. All neurons of one layer are fully connected to the neurons in the next, activation is indicated by (dark) color. This used situation is presented in figure 4(a), where the agent is near the obstacle and can perceive it in the right and front sectors of its perception field. The neural network selects action $move_{left}$.

6   Discussion

The main motivation for this work is investigate the possibilities of creating a learning-based methodology for the design of a multiagent simulation model avoiding a time consuming trial and error process when determining the details of agent behavior. Using a learning technique transfers the basic problem from direct behavior modeling to designing the agent interface and environment reward computation. To do so successfully, a general understanding of scenario difficulties and the available machine learning techniques is necessary.

XCS provides a better interpretability of the rules. For each situation we are able to predict the reward from executing a specific action, how accurate this prediction is (based on the prediction error) and how many times we have executed that action. Combined, these three numbers give relevant information on quality of rules. Besides that, XCS is able to generalize the representation of the rules based on *don't care* bits in the representation of the perceptions.

Q-Learning showed a good overall performance. It requires less time, which means less explore trials, to learn the possible situations in this scenario. The standard implementation of Q-Learning, used in this paper, offers us only the estimated reward for each possible condition-action pair. This full behavior model for the Q-Learning is only partially helpful as a guidance for modeling.

The Feed Forward Neural Network as supervised learning requires good behavior examples, e.g. a proper set of situation-action pairs to train the network. An issue of our integration into a reward-based setting is that only the best rules were used to train the network. Thus negative experience is lost. The neural network will not learn to avoid actions. However, here the reward contained positive and negative elements thus being not fully appropriate for the FFNN approach.

7   Conclusion and Future Work

In this paper we started our investigation towards a learning-driven methodology by evaluating three well-known learning agent techniques. In a simple evacuation scenario, we showed that all the employed learning techniques can produce plausible behavior without one technique showing the superior performance. Yet, the XCS technique outclasses the two others when it comes to the accessibility and usability of the learned behavior model.

Our next steps include the analysis of more elaborate perception and actions, such as including the distance to the exit or splitting actions into turn and move primitives. Thus, to the collision avoidance task the agents have to learn navigation-related activities. An additional plan is to use the best rules to directly construct a new agent model – supporting the evaluation of techniques and finally we will apply learning-based post-processing techniques for working with the situation-action pairs improving the generality of the rules. Beyond that, we will pursue further self-modeling agent experiments: we are considering the application of these learning techniques in other scenarios, such as an evacuation of a train with about 500 agents, complex geometry with exit signs and time pressure. We are also interested in a scenario where cooperation is required, in order to investigate the possible emergence of the cooperation.

References

1. Sutton, R.S., Barto, A.G.: Reinforcement Learning: An Introduction. MIT Press, Cambridge (1998)
2. Nowe, A., Verbeeck, K., Peeters, M.: Learning automata as a basis for multi agent reinforcement learning, pp. 71–85 (2006)
3. Adami, C.: Introduction to artificial life. Springer, New York (1998)
4. Collins, R.J., Jefferson, D.R.: Antfarm: Towards simulated evolution. In: Artificial Life II, pp. 579–601. Addison-Wesley, Reading (1991)

5. Denzinger, J., Fuchs, M.: Experiments in learning prototypical situations for variants of the pursuit game. In: Proceedings on the International Conference on Multi-Agent Systems (ICMAS-1996), pp. 48–55. MIT Press, Cambridge (1995)
6. Maeda, Y.: Simulation for behavior learning of multi-agent robot. Journal of Intelligent and Fuzzy Systems, 53–64 (1998)
7. Mahadevan, S., Connell, J.: Automatic programming of behavior-based robots using reinforcement learning. Artificial Intelligence 55(2-3), 311–365 (1992)
8. Lee, M.R., Kang, E.K.: Learning enabled cooperative agent behavior in an evolutionary and competitive environment. Neural Computing & Applications 15, 124–135 (2006)
9. Neruda, R., Slusny, S., Vidnerova, P.: Performance comparison of relational reinforcement learning and rbf neural networks for small mobile robots. In: Proceedings of FGCNS '08, Washington, DC, USA, pp. 29–32. IEEE Computer Society, Los Alamitos (2008)
10. Klügl, F.: Multiagent simulation model design strategies. In: MAS& S Workshop at MALLOW 2009, CEUR Workshop Proceedings, Turin, Italy, vol. 494 (September 2009)
11. Wilson, S.W.: Classifier fitness based on accuracy. Evolutionary Computation 3(2), 149–175 (1995)
12. Watkins, C.J.C.H., Dayan, P.: Q-learning. Machine Learning 8(3), 279–292 (1992)
13. Mitchell, T.M.: Machine Learning. McGraw-Hill, New York (1997)
14. Klügl, F., Hatko, R., Butz, M.V.: Agent learning instead of behavior implementation for simulations - a case study using classifier systems. In: Bergmann, R., Lindemann, G., Kirn, S., Pěchouček, M. (eds.) MATES 2008. LNCS (LNAI), vol. 5244, pp. 111–122. Springer, Heidelberg (2008)
15. Butz, M.V.: XCSJava 1.0: An implementation of the XCS classifier system in Java. Illigal report, Illinois Genetic Algorithms Laboratory, University of Illinois at Urbana-Champaign (2000)

Price Prediction in Sports Betting Markets*

Juan M. Alberola**, Ana Garcia-Fornes, and Agustin Espinosa

Departament de Sistemes Informàtics i Computació,
Universitat Politècnica de València, Camí de Vera s/n. 46022, València, Spain
{jalberola,agarcia,aespinos}@dsic.upv.es

Abstract. The sports betting market has emerged as one of the most lucrative markets in recent years. In this kind of prediction market, participants trade assets related to sports events according to their expectations. Prices in sports betting markets continually change depending on what is happening in the event. In this paper we propose an approach focused on predicting price movements in order to make benefits regardless of the final result.

We develop an agent who participates in the market focused on the task of learning the price movements in order to make predictions of future prices. Our approach is based on identifying and learn pattern price movements in order to predict the price movements of new events by using an underlying Case Based Reasoning system.

1 Introduction

Prediction markets are speculative scenarios where participants make predictions about future events. Assets regarding all of the possible outcomes of the event are created, and the price of these assets is related with the probability of each outcome. Participants exchange these assets according to their expectations with other participants or with a bookmaker.

In the last few years, sport betting markets have emerged as one of the scenarios in which the most money is exchanged everyday. Sport betting markets are a specific kind of prediction markets where the traded assets are referred to sporting events. Therefore, the attraction of betting on sporting events and the growth in popularity it has experienced, has meant that millions of users make more exchanges in sports betting markets in an average day than other exchanges scenarios such as other financial markets[1].

Sports betting markets usually have a short or very-short duration in comparison with other prediction markets, such as political markets. Markets regarding the probability of landing on Mars in ten years or the probability of a particular candidate becoming the next US president can last months or even years. However, markets regarding the winner of a soccer game or a horse race usually

---

* This work has been partially supported by CONSOLIDER-INGENIO 2010 under grant CSD2007-00022, and projects TIN2008-04446 and PROMETEO/2008/051.

** Juan M. Alberola has received a grant from Ministerio de Ciencia e Innovación de España (AP2007-00289).

last a few hours or minutes. Therefore, prices usually tend to change quickly according to every influential factor related to the event.

Studying how probabilities, and therefore prices, change during the sporting event will allow us to approach sports betting markets in a new fashion more similar to the financial markets. As financial traders buy and sell assets according the prices and their expectations of price increases or decreases, assets regarding sporting events can be traded at a given price in order to make an opposite trade later at a better price, with the goal of making profits regardless of what the final outcome is. Thus, in these markets it is important to predict future price in order to identify the best trading decisions.

Price movements are made by the participants of the sports betting market according the probabilities of the outcomes change during the event. Therefore, participants change prices in a specific sporting event according to what happens in the event.

Based on this idea, we are interested in identifying price movement patterns that can be repeated in different events under the same underlying circumstances. To achieve this goal we develop an agent with an underlying Case-Based-Reasoning (CBR) [8] in which by means of observing past sporting events, the agent is able to predict future price movements for an unknown sporting event and therefore, drawing a price evolution over time.

The rest of the article is organized as follows. Section 2 presents previous works related to our proposal. Section 3 describes the Sports Betting Markets and the trading possibilities according to price movements in order to make profit. Section 4 details the market structure. Section 5 describes the structure of the CBR-agent. In section 6 we evaluate the prediction accuracy of the CBR-agent with real data. Finally, section 7 discusses the contributions of the paper and future work.

2   Related Work

Prediction markets have been studied as powerful mechanisms for predicting the probabilities of future events [5]. Most of the research on prediction markets is focussed on pricing, that is, assessing the most accurate price according the probability of the event. Studies regarding prediction markets, such as the Iowa Electronic Markets, the Foresight Exchange or the Hollywood Stock Exchange demonstrate than these markets provide very accurate probability predictions of future outcomes [11,2]. Other works are focused on stuyding how information is incorporated into the market and therefore, influences the prices [3]. However, to our knowledge little effort has been made towards studying price evolution in prediction markets, with the aim of making a profit regardless the correct outcome.

The problem of predicting future prices and price movements has been broadly studied in the economic field. Since the introduction of computational tools for modeling financial and economic markets, several works have modelled stock markets as time series and have studied the evolution of the assets over time, trying to predict future prices [9,6,12]. However, price evolution in financial markets is not depending on probabilities of specific outcomes.

From the point of view of the use of techniques based on CBR for predicting future prices whatever the context of the problem, few works have been carried out. CBR-based techniques have also been used in a broad range of applications [4,10] but have hardly been applied for the prediction of future prices in financial markets. However, sports betting markets has a critical temporal component which differentiates them from other financial markets and therefore, a CBR approach could identify similar price movement patterns that are repeated in different events, under similar circumstances.

The agent paradigm has been widely used in other competitive scenarios such as the Trading Agent Competition [14], a Fishmarket [13] or artificial stock markets [7]. In these scenarios agents can learn, collaborate and evolve their different strategies in order to compete with other participants. Sports betting markets are scenarios which also require competitiveness and in which the use of agent-based approaches can be very helpful in order to improve the performance of human participants.

3   Sports Betting Markets

Sports betting markets are speculative scenarios about sporting events, where participants exchange assets regarding a specific outcome of the event. For a specific event, there are several markets regarding the winner, the final score, the number of goals or points, handicap markets, etc. Each market has n possible outcomes and each bet can be seen as an $n-way$ bet. The prices of the exchanged assets are related to the probability of the specific outcome happening. Price and implicit probability of an outcome are related by $price = 1/probability$, where probability is represented from 0 to 1.

Trades are made between participants at a given price because they have different expectations about the event. In sports betting markets, users can bet on an outcome (win if this is the final outcome) or against it (win if any of the other outcomes is the final one). Betting on a specific outcome is called *back* and betting against it is called *lay*.

The bookmaker is in charge of receiving the offers of the traders. If a *back* offer and a *lay* offer are compatabile in terms of price and stake (full or partial), the bookmaker matches both offers. If a received offer is not compatible it remains waiting until a compatible offer is received, or until it is deleted by the user or because the market is closed. Therefore, the bookmaker also maintains a list of waiting offers, and continuously shows the best *back* and *lay* prices of these waiting offers in order to allow interested users make offers at these prices.

Let us suppose that user *Alice* wants to bet μ units on placing a *back* bet on a selection (an individual, a team, horse, etc.). This user is betting that the selection will win. *Alice* can accept the best waiting *lay* offer (the *lay* offer which price is the lowest one) or can choose his own price ρ. When user *Bob* wants to place a *lay* bet on this selection (against the selection of *Alice*, that is, the individual will not win), he can also choose his own price or accept the offer of *Alice*.

If *Bob* accepts *Alice*'s offer, *Bob* is placing a *lay* bet on the seletion at price ρ. When the event is over, if *Alice* wins the bet, *Bob* has to pay $\rho - 1$ units for each unit bet on. If *Bob* wins the bet, he keeps the μ units of *Alice*:

$$\text{profit(Alice)} = \begin{cases} \mu^*(\rho\text{-}1) & \text{if Alice wins the bet} \\ -\mu & \text{if Alice loses the bet} \end{cases}$$

$$\text{profit(Bob)} = \begin{cases} -\mu^*(\rho\text{-}1) & \text{if Alice wins the bet} \\ \mu & \text{if Alice loses the bet} \end{cases}$$

3.1   Trading on Sports Betting Markets

Sports betting markets are traditionally used for eliciting the probabilities of final outcomes before the event is started, but can also be approached while the event is being played. As an example, when a soccer match starts it has associated a price ρ for the outcome *0-0 as a final score* because users estimate that the probability of this outcome is ϕ, where $\rho = 1/\phi$. As the match draws to a close and the score remains 0-0, the probability increases and therefore, the price decreases. As sport betting markets have a short or very short duration, the prices change rapidly during the event.

From the point of view of a sports betting market trader, similar to an economic trader, the underlying sporting event and its final outcome is not important, because its goal is to make profits whatever the final outcome is.

In this approach, a sports betting market is seen as a market where the current price of a specific outcome is going to change over time and therefore, the importance relies on detecting if the price will move up or down, how much it will move up or down, when it is going to move and how fast. Therefore, the goal of a sports betting markets trader is to bet on one outcome at a higher price and to bet on the opposite outcome at a lower price.

A trader can make a bet by risking μ units whilst making a *back* bet at a price of ρ_1 for a specific outcome ω. As explained in Section 3, if the bet is finally won, the trader wins $\mu * (\rho_1 - 1)$ units, and loses the μ units if the other outcome is the final one. This trader can make profits if he covers all the bases by betting on the opposite outcome when prices change. In this example the trader can bet μ on the *lay* side at a price of ρ_2. When ending the event, if the final outcome is ω, the trader will win $\mu * (\rho_1 - 1)$ because his first bet has won, but he loses $\mu * (\rho_2 - 1)$ units bet on the second one.

As we can observe, if the price of the *back* bet (ρ_1) is higher than the price of the *lay* bet (ρ_2) the resulting profit will be positive:

$$\mu * (\rho_1 - 1) - \mu * (\rho_2 - 1) = \mu * (\rho_1 - \rho_2)$$

Nevertheless, if the ω outcome is not the final one, the trader will not lose any units, because he loses the μ units risked in the first bet but wins μ units from the second one. Thus, regardless whether ω is the final outcome or not, the trader will not lose any unit:

$$profit = \begin{cases} \mu^*(\rho_1\text{-}\rho_2) & \text{if } \omega \text{ is the final outcome} \\ 0 & \text{otherwise} \end{cases}$$

The same operations can also be made in the inverse order and also the trader can also split the profits between the different outcomes. Due to space restrictions, we do not detail these operations.

As we can observe, the difference in the prices of both trades indicates the amount of profit. Detecting price tendencies and therefore, predicting future prices is the key issue for making profits in these markets.

4   The Market Model

Sports betting markets represent a multilateral market model in which traders send their bets at their own price to the mediator who matches compatible bets. Orders compete for the best *back* and *lay* offers. Therefore, the offers which cannot be matched remain waiting until they can be matched or are cancelled. One of the tasks of the bookmaker is to also show at anytime the best *back* and *lay* prices of these waiting offers. For a specific market there is a list of all the currently *back* and *lay* bids currently waiting, ordered from the highest prices to the lowest.

In this work we use Betfair[1] as the sport betting market studied. Betfair is the world's biggest prediction exchange. According to [1] Betfair processes more than 6 million transactions in an average day (more than all of the European stock exchanges combined). Betfair is based on the New York Stock Exchange model and allows punters to bet at odds set by other punters rather than the bookmaker.

The Continous Double Auction (CDA) is a typical institution of real world exchange markets, such as financial assets, foreign exchange, energy, etc. In this institution, buyers and sellers place their offers at anytime. When a participant accepts a buy or a sell offer, a transaction is made. For modeling a sports betting market, we define a CDA institution where agents can interact for obtaining information of the market at a given moment and also, for placing bets.

In our model, Betfair acts as the mediator between users, matching the compatible bets and showing the best *back* and *lay* prices at a given time. As a wrapper of Betfair, we define the *bookmaker* agent which acts as a gateway between Betfair and the agents. Therefore, when a agent wants to request prices or wants to place offers, it needs to communicate with the *bookmaker* agent. If agents send offers, these will be matched by Betfair or will be queued in the waiting offers queue. If agents are requesting the current prices, the *bookmaker* agent will retrieve them by accessing Betfair. Therefore, from the point of view of other users they do not know if they are trading with humans or agents.

5   The CBR Agent

We can observe that in a tennis match each time the favorite player wins a set, the price of the outcome *winner of the match* gets lower, due to the fact that

---

[1] http://www.betfair.com

the probability of winning is higher. Similarly, the prices of the the *winner* of a basketball match decrease if the favourite team increases the score difference over time. In light of these repeated patterns and the similar movements of prices regarding the state of a sporting event, we propose an agent with an underlying CBR system which captures some features of a current event and finds similarities with other past events. Then, observing the price evolution in these historical events, the agent will be able to predict the more accurate future prices depending on what happens during the event from now on. From now on, we reference this agent as CBR-agent.

We can summarize the tasks that the CBR-agent carries out as follows:

Data acquisition and creation of the case base: the first step is the data acquisition according the requirements of the problem. The CBR-agent interacts with the *bookmaker* agent in order to receive information about sport events. Then, after a data filter process (for excluding samples which may not reveal a real probability at a given moment), the CBR-agent creates the case base which will be used in the CBR cycle.

CBR cycle: once the CBR-agent has created the case base, this is used for solving an unknown problem (in our case predict future prices) given similar past problems. The CBR-agent interacts with the *bookmaker* agent to obtain the information of a sporting event (unknown problem), then the CBR cycle measures the similarity between this problem and a similar past one (one or more). Then, according the future prices of the past problem, future prices are predicted for the unknown problem by adapting the solution of the past one.

In following sections we show an example about prediction in soccer events. By means of this example we detail the processes described above and then we show some results about the system accuracy prediction.

5.1 Experiments

We have carried out the experiments using a real data set from soccer matches played in the 2008-2009 season in the Barclays Premier League. We analyzed this competition because it is one of the most important soccer leagues in the world. Moreover, the large amount of traders that exchange bets at these events means that each event has very high liquidity, and this is important for obtaining more reliable results.

We focus on the price prediction for markets that are the under/over 2.5 goals. These markets show the probability assessed by the participants for scoring in a soccer event less than 2.5 goals (0, 1, or 2) or more than 2.5 goals (3 or more), respectively. We want to learn how the prices evolve depending on the current features of a current game.

5.2 Data Acquisition and Creation of the Case Base

There are several markets that are directly related to the under/over 2.5 goals, whose price evolution should be proportional to the markets studied since they refer to similar final outcomes. These markets are, for example, the markets regarding the exact final score or other markets regarding under/over goals (such as 1.5, 3.5, or 4.5 goals). Other markets are indirectly related to under/over 2.5 goals such as the match odds markets (the winner of the game or a draw) or the next-goal-minute markets. Although the price evolution in these markets may not be proportional to the studied markets (under/over 2.5 goals), it is related to the prices of the markets studied. Finally, other markets such as the number of yellow cards in the game, the number of corners, or the injury time of the event are not related to the studied markets.

Although all the soccer events are completelly different from each other (different players, different teams, weather conditions, dates, and so on), if we consider the prices of the outcomes of different markets, we can find some similarities between an unknown event and a past one. In the example presented in this paper, we define the state of a soccer event at a specific moment according to the next properties:

- The exact moment of the game (in minutes).
- The current score of the game at that particular moment.
- The prices of the under/over 2.5 markets. These show the *back* and *lay* prices for both the under and the over 2.5 goals outcomes.
- Match odds prices. These show the *back* and *lay* prices for the home wins, visitor wins and draw wins.

Taking into account these properties, we can find similarities for two different soccer events and predict future prices.

Every 60 seconds the CBR-agent requests the current values of these properties from the *bookmaker* agent, and then, the CBR-agent stores this information as a sample. Thus, we obtain some samples for a single soccer event. A sample is a quintuple which is described as $\langle m, s, h, v, d, u, o \rangle$ where:

- $0 \leq m \leq 45$ represents the minute of the game. For reasons of simplicity, we study the price evolution in the first half of the event (45 minutes). Thus, this component is an integer.
- $s \in \{0\text{-}0, 1\text{-}0, 0\text{-}1, 1\text{-}1\}$ represents the current score of the game. For reasons of simplicity, we only take into account soccer events that have these current scores.
- h, v, and d are respectivelly the prices refering to the home wins, the visitor wins, and the draw wins from the match odds market.
- u and o are the prices refering to the under outcome and the over outcome from the under/over 2.5 goals market.

Each h, v, d, u and o has two real values $\langle b, l \rangle$ that represent the *back* and *lay* prices for the specific outcome. Each *back* price must be lower than the corresponding *lay* price at any given moment. Otherwise, there would be a possible trade.

The maximum difference allowed between *back* and *lay* prices is represented by ϵ. Therefore, each pair of *back* and *lay* values $\langle b, l \rangle$ fulfills $b < l \leq b + \epsilon$. This ϵ is a specific threshold that we use in order not to consider samples in which at least one pair of *back* and *lay* prices differs more than ϵ.

Since samples are taken every 60 seconds, we create a sequence of samples $x_1, x_2, x_3, \ldots x_n$ for each different event. To simplify notation, if $x_i = \langle m, s, h, v, d, u, o \rangle$, we write m_i to refer to m, and similarly for other components of x_i. It is assumed that the samples are ordered by time, i.e., $m_i < m_j$ whenever $i < j$.

In order to predict the prices of an unknown event in the next δ minutes, we need to find similarities with other past events whose prices are known both at a specific time and after δ minutes. Therefore, we, we need to represent information as a problem description and its solution. In our case, the problem description is each one of the stored samples of a single event and the solution is the state of this event after δ minutes. In the example presented in this paper, we make predictions for the next, 5, 10 and 15 minutes ($\delta = \{1, 5, 10, 15\}$).

Thus, given two different samples of the same event $x_i = \langle m_i, s_i, h_i, v_i, d_i, u_i, o_i \rangle$ and $x_j = \langle m_j, s_j, h_j, v_j, d_j, u_j, o_j \rangle$, such that $m_j - m_i = \delta$, we define a case of the case base as:

$$c^\delta = \langle m_i, s_i, h_i, v_i, d_i, u_i, o_i, d(u_i, u_j), d(o_i, o_j) \rangle$$

Each case represents the information of the event in the moment m_i (initial moment) and the information regarding the event after δ minutes, which in our example is the information regarding the under/over outcomes: $d(u_i, u_j)$ and $d(o_i, o_j)$. We define an operation d on pairs of *back* and *lay* values as follows: $d(\langle b_1, l_1 \rangle, \langle b_2, l_2 \rangle) = \langle | b_1 - b_2 |, |y_1 - y_2| \rangle$. Thus, $d(u_i, u_j)$ and $d(o_i, o_j)$ represent the *back* and *lay* price variations for the under/over markets.

All cases c^δ of all the events that we have two samples x_i and x_j such that $m_j - m_i = \delta$, allow us to create a case base $C^\delta = \{c^\delta \mid c^\delta \text{ is defined}\}$. This case base stores cases of different events, but the information represented in a single case obviously refers to a specific event.

5.3   The CBR Cycle

The case base for a specific δ represents the information of events and their *back* and *lay* prices for the under/over markets in the next δ minutes. Therefore, given C^δ and an input problem $x = \langle m, s, h, v, d, u, o \rangle$, the CBR cycle predicts the *back* and *lay* prices for the under/over markets in the next δ minutes.

The inference process of the CBR system can be summarized in the following steps:

Step 1. Retrieve the cases whose score components are the same and also whose *back* and *lay* prices for the under/over markets in the initial moment are the most similar to the prices of the input problem. For example, given an input problem $x = \langle m, s, h, v, d, \langle b_u, l_u \rangle, \langle b_o, l_o \rangle \rangle$ and a case of the case base $c_r = \langle m_r, s_r, h_r, v_r, d_r, \langle b'_u, l'_u \rangle, \langle b'_o, l'_o \rangle, u^\delta, o^\delta \rangle$, c_r is retrieved if the score is the same than the input problem and if its values are not different from the values of the input problem by more than a threshold ω:

$$s = s_r \wedge | b_u\text{-}b'_u | \leq \omega \wedge | l_u\text{-}l'_u | \leq \omega \wedge | b_o\text{-}b'_o | \leq \omega \wedge | l_o\text{-}l'_o | \leq \omega$$

Step 2. From all cases retrieved in Step 1, we select those whose time component is the most similar. For example, given an input problem $x = \langle m, s, h, v, d, u, o \rangle$

and a case of the case base $c_r = \langle m_r, s_r, h_r, v_r, d_r, u_r, o_r, u^\delta, o^\delta \rangle$, we select those cases where $| m\text{-}m_r | < \pi$.

Step 3. From each case c_r selected in Step 2, where:

$$c_r = \langle m_r, s_r, h_r, v_r, d_r, \langle b_u, l_u \rangle, \langle b_o, l_o \rangle, \langle b'_u, l'_u \rangle, \langle b'_o, l'_o \rangle \rangle$$

for $r = \{1, 2 \ldots R\}$, being R the number of selected cases, we calculate price evolution for the specific price (back,lay) and market (under,over) as follows:

$$e(b, u) = (b_u - b'_u); \; e(l, u) = (l_u - l'_u); \; e(b, o) = (b_o - b'_o); \; e(l, o) = (l_o - l'_o)$$

If a price evolution is positive it means that the specific price is going to decrease in δ minutes; if it is negative, the price will increase δ minutes.

Then, we calculate an average price evolution from all cases $c_1, c_2 \ldots c_R$, for the specific price (back,lay) and market (under,over):

$$A(b, u) = \frac{1}{R} \sum_{r=1}^{R} e(b, u)_r; \quad A(l, u) = \frac{1}{R} \sum_{r=1}^{R} e(l, u)_r$$

$$A(b, o) = \frac{1}{R} \sum_{r=1}^{R} e(b, o)_r; \quad A(l, o) = \frac{1}{R} \sum_{r=1}^{R} e(l, o)_r$$

Consider an input problem $x = \langle m, s, h, v, d, \langle b_u, l_u \rangle \langle b_o, l_o \rangle \rangle$ and price evolutions for the specific price (back,lay) and market (under,over): $A(b, u)$, $A(l, u)$, $A(b, o)$, $A(l, o)$. Then, the predicted back and lay prices for the under/over markets would be:

$$predicted(p, k) = p_k + A(p, k)$$

for each $p = \{b, l\}$ and $k = \{u, o\}$.

Step 4. If the predicted prices are similar to the real ones, the case is then retained in the case base. If one of the four predicted prices is different by more than a specified threshold, the case is not retained, assuming that this case may be an anomalous case. If so, storing it could decrease the prediction accuracy of the entire system. We dynamically change this threshold as the size of the case base increases.

In Step 1, we used a ω threshold of 0.05 for $\delta = 1$ (predictions for the next minute). In other experiments ($\delta = \{2, 5, 10\}$) we used a threshold of 0.20. In Step 2 we used a π value of 1. That is, we took into account only samples whose time component was not greater or lower than the time component of the input problem by more than 1 minute. In Step 1, if no case is retrieved, we increase the threshold to a maximum of twice the initial threshold. If increasing the threshold is not enough to retrive a case, we then consider the values of home, visitor, and draw in order to find similarities with these components. In Step 2, if no case is selected according to this restriction, we increase the π value until we find a case.

6   Results

In Table 1 we can see the price prediction accuracy depending on the number of past events observed. The agent predicts the future prices for 100 sporting events. The table shows in how many of these 100 cases the predicted price was the real one, with some error rate.

We can see that as the agent increases the number of past observed cases, the accuracy of the future price prediction is also increased. We can conclude that future events follow price movement patterns similar to past events. We can see that with 250 cases in the case base, the precision accuracy is around the 90% for an error rate of 0.05. Moreover, for predictions in the next minute this accuracy is almost 100% for the same error rate. Prices are represented in cents and are usually placed between 1.01 and 3 in these markets, thus, this accuracy is high, and probably gets higher if we increase the number of observed cases.

Table 1. Number of cases in wich the predicted price is the real one with error rates

Error Rate	50 cases				150 cases				250 cases			
	Under		Over		Under		Over		Under		Over	
	B	L	B	L	B	L	B	L	B	L	B	L
Prediction for the next minute												
±0.02	73	63	71	64	81	75	72	71	83	78	69	73
±0.03	85	78	81	77	89	85	85	80	91	88	83	82
±0.05	93	93	95	90	96	95	95	91	97	97	95	94
±0.1	100	99	99	99	99	99	99	99	100	100	99	99
Prediction for the next 5 minutes												
±0.02	44	46	42	44	62	60	50	46	68	68	46	49
±0.03	52	66	56	56	72	70	54	62	74	77	65	71
±0.05	74	80	72	76	82	86	78	80	94	87	94	84
±0.1	96	94	88	96	100	96	88	92	100	100	100	97
Prediction for the next 10 minutes												
±0.02	32	41	22	32	54	38	32	35	63	62	44	44
±0.03	43	49	32	41	68	49	43	51	69	67	62	64
±0.05	59	65	41	49	84	73	65	73	91	88	84	80
±0.1	84	86	70	84	100	89	79	95	100	98	96	97
Prediction for the next 15 minutes												
±0.02	43	47	17	23	57	57	43	37	64	66	45	42
±0.03	53	50	37	30	73	67	50	43	74	70	61	64
±0.05	67	67	40	47	91	80	60	57	94	89	87	86
±0.1	97	90	63	77	100	93	73	80	100	98	95	97

Predictions for the next 5, 10 or 15 minutes have a similar accuracy, but predictions for the next minute are slightly more accurate. We can observe that the accuracy is around 70% with an error rate of 0.03. If the error rate is 0.05 the accuracy is around 95%.

Apart from the accuracy precision, it is important to check the price direction accuracy when the predictions are made very quick. In order to draw a price evolution over time we should be able to successfully predict if price increases or decreases at the short-term. In Table 2 we can see a combination of prediction intervals and success rates for four different soccer events during 45 minutes. In this table we show in how many minutes the price direction in the next minute is successfully predicted for the *back* price of the under market.

Table 2. Success rates for price direction prediction in the next minute

Event	Price Direction Accuracy [±0.03]	%
Match 1	34	0.77
Match 2	30	0.68
Match 3	39	0.89
Match 4	30	0.68

We can observe that the market behaviour can be learned due to the success rates for each match are quite accurate. For each different event, the CBR-agent successfully predicts the price direction in practically the 70% of the minutes or even more. Therefore a price evolution from minute 0 to 45 should be quite similar to the real one.

7   Conclusions

In this paper we have seen how sports betting markets can be approached as trading scenarios for making profits regardless of the final outcome of the event. The approach seen in this paper is different from the approaches in which prediction markets have been studied. In these markets, it is important to predict future price in order to identify the best trading decisions.

We focus on predicting future prices by means of detecting future price movements. As the price is related to the probability, and this probability changes as the sporting event is being played, price movements can follow patterns in different events with similar circumstances. Due to the short duration of sporting events, sports betting markets display quick exchanges. Our aim is to identify if the price will move up or down, how much it will move up or down, when it is going to move and how fast can be learned from past events.

From these features, we present a prediction system based on a CBR approach. Observing events, we develop a CBR-agent which is able to find the similarities of a unknown event with other historical ones by using CBR. Therefore, the agent predicts future prices according to its reasoning.

The accuracy of the predictions has demonstated that despite each event being different, under similar circumstances some price movement patterns are repeated. The agent is able to learn these patterns and identifies them in other uncertain events for predicting future prices.

Although we have presented our experiments using a specific sport, other sports should also repeat price movement patterns under the same sporting event circumstances. Thus, the results could be applied to other sports. We also plan to apply CBR prediction for other sport betting markets.

Another area for future work is to identify the most influential factors on the price movements. We can retrieve cases according to different similarity functions and prove which technique make more accurate predictions. The multilateral market model designed should allow us to compare heterogeneous agents with different trading strategies.

References

1. Betfair Corporate, http://www.betfaircorporate.com
2. Chen, Y., Goel, S., Pennock, D.: Pricing combinatorial markets for tournaments. In: STOC '08: Proceedings of the 40th Annual ACM Symposium on Theory of Computing, pp. 305–314. ACM, New York (2008)
3. Debnath, S., Pennock, D.M., Giles, C.L., Lawrence, S.: Information incorporation in online in-game sports betting markets (2003)
4. Gayer, I.G.G., Lieberman, O.: Rule-based and case-based reasoning in housing prices (2004)
5. Guo, M., Pennock, D.: Combinatorial prediction markets for event hierarchies. In: Proceedings of The 8th International Conference on Autonomous Agents and Multiagent Systems, pp. 201–208 (2009)
6. Huang, W., Lai, K., Nakamori, Y., Wang, S.: Forecasting foreign exchange rates with artificial neural networks: A review. International Journal of Information Technology and Decision Making 3(1), 145–165 (2004)
7. LeBaron, B.: Agent based computational finance: Suggested readings and early research. Journal of Economic Dynamics and Control (1998)
8. Mantaras, R.L.D., McSherry, D., Bridge, D., Leake, D., Smyth, B., Craw, S., Faltings, B., Maher, M., Lou, C., Forbus, M.C.K., Keane, M., Aamodt, A., Watson, I.: Retrieval, reuse, revision and retention in case-based reasoning. Knowl. Eng. Rev. 20(3), 215–240 (2005)
9. Moody, J.: Economic forecasting: Challenges and neural network solutions. In: Proceedings of the International Symposium on Artificial Neural Networks (1995)
10. Oh, K., Kim, T.: Financial market monitoring by case-based reasoning. Expert Syst. Appl. 32(3), 789–800 (2007)
11. Plott, C.: Markets as information gathering tools, pp. 1–15 (2000)
12. Raudys, S., Zliobaite, I.: The multi-agent system for prediction of financial time series. In: Rutkowski, L., Tadeusiewicz, R., Zadeh, L.A., Żurada, J.M. (eds.) ICAISC 2006. LNCS (LNAI), vol. 4029, pp. 653–662. Springer, Heidelberg (2006)
13. Rodriguez-Aguilar, J.A., Martin, F.J., Martn, F.J., Noriega, P., Sierra, C., Garcia, P.: Competitive scenarios for heterogeneous trading agents. In: Proceedings of the Second International Conference on Autonomous Agents (1998)
14. Wellman, M., Greenwald, A., Stone, P., Wurman, P.: The 2001 trading agent competition. IEEE Internet Computing 13, 935–941 (2000)

Modelling Distributed Network Security in a Petri Net- and Agent-Based Approach

Simon Adameit[2], Tobias Betz[2], Lawrence Cabac[2], Florian Hars[1],
Marcin Hewelt[2], Michael Köhler-Bußmeier[2], Daniel Moldt[2], Dimitri Popov[2],
José Quenum[2], Axel Theilmann[1], Thomas Wagner[2],
Timo Warns[1], and Lars Wüstenberg[2]

[1] PRESENSE Technologies GmbH, Hamburg
[2] University of Hamburg, Faculty of Mathematics, Informatics and Natural Sciences,
Department of Informatics
http://www.informatik.uni-hamburg.de/TGI/

Abstract. Distributed network security is an important concern in modern business environments. Access to critical information and areas has to be limited to authorised users. The Herold research project* aims to provide a novel way of managing distributed network security through the means of agent-based software. In this paper we present the first models, both conceptual and technical that have been produced in this project. Furthermore we examine the PAOSE development approach used within the project and how it contributes to Herold.

Keywords: Distributed network security, Software agents, Petri nets, Agent-oriented methodologies.

1 Introduction

Computer networks have become more and more omnipresent in recent years. Accompanying this trend, the need for adequate, versatile and flexible distributed systems has risen as well. Distributed systems capitalise on the properties of the different network nodes and use them to provide functionality difficult and inefficient to obtain in classical, centralised systems. A paradigm particularly suited to design distributed systems is agent-orientation. The use of autonomous entities, called agents, which use asynchronous messages for communication or can (to a certain degree) intelligently adapt to unforeseen circumstances makes this paradigm perfect for modelling and implementing distributed systems.

Of course distributing functionality over open networks introduces security risks and issues. Questions that arise are how to protect critical data and how to make sure only authorised users can execute sensitive actions. Classically networks are protected using a perimeter model in which network security components (NSCs) protect the virtual *border* of the network. The problem with this

---

* The Herold research project is supported by the German Federal Ministry of Education and Research (Grant No. 01BS0901). For further information see http://www.herold-security.de

approach is that once the perimeter of the network is breached, the attacker can access the rest of the network almost unimpeded. The Herold research project follows another approach. Instead of relying on a perimeter to protect a network we divide the network into multiple subnetworks, called cells, each protected by their own NSC. The overlapping cells together form the entire network and the NSCs enforce a network-wide security policy in a cooperative effort. This way, if one NSC is breached, only part of the network is open to attacks. The other cells are unaffected.

Further aspects of interest that will be discussed in this paper include for example the use of abstract, global policies that are automatically translated into efficient, localised configurations for NSCs.

To implement our prototype we use the Petri net-based agent architectures MULAN and CAPA. Agents within these architectures possess many properties, like mobility and proactiveness, which make them very versatile and allow and encourage their use within the context of distributed network security. Additionally the PAOSE (**P**etri net-based and **a**gent-**o**riented **s**oftware **e**ngineering) software development approach is especially well suited for these two architectures, so that our work is supported by an elaborate and functional approach.

In this paper we present both a conceptual and technical model of how to realise part of the overall Herold vision. The technical model we will describe is one of the first prototypes developed within the Herold PAOSE cycle and will serve to show the results of using this approach both in regard to the target domain as well as to the versatility of the approach. We will also offer an outlook on possible extensions to our current model.

The paper is structured in the following way. Section 2 distinguishes our approach from related work. In Section 3 we will outline the theoretical and technical background of our work. Section 4 describes the conceptual view of the overall Herold vision and the current Herold model, while Section 5 examines parts of the implementation. The paper concludes in Section 6 and gives an outlook on future work.

2   Related Work

Herold lies at the intersection of multi-agent systems, policy-based management, and network security. Different approaches have been proposed in the literature that also address these or related domains. Herold differs from previous work in its unique combination of an agent- and policy-based approach to network security, the automatic transformation of global policies to NSC configurations (i.e., "refinements"), and provisioning network security as a cooperative effort.

Different approaches on agent-based network management have been proposed in the literature [7,1,10,5]. In principle, Herold is closely related to such approaches while, however, focussing on network security and solely relying on stationary agents. In particular, Herold differs from most previous approaches for being policy-based, addressing the localisation of policies, and transforming policies to NSC-specific configurations.

Closely related to Herold, Uszok et al. [13] have presented an approach to the representation, conflict resolution, and enforcement of policies for the agent framework *KAoS (Knowledgeable Agent-oriented System)* [2]. Besides using a different policy language, focussing on network security, and having a different architecture, Herold can be considered a generalisation of this approach as the KAoS approach does not address refinements of policies.

Ponder2 [12] is a prominent example of a policy-based management system that supports refinements of policies. In contrast to Herold, it relies on a Peer-to-Peer architecture instead of an agent-based architecture. Moreover, its concept of refining policies significantly differs from Herold's policy transformations: Having policies defined in terms of hierarchical "domains," Ponder2 allows to refine policies by adding additional objects to these domains or by moving policies down in the domain hierarchy. In contrast, Herold refines policies by mapping them to NSC-specific configurations defined in a different language than the policy itself (using NSC-specific transformations).

3   Background

Our agents follow the MULAN architecture described in [11]. MULAN stands for **Mul**ti-agent **n**ets, a name that perfectly describes the main idea behind the approach. Every aspect of agents in MULAN is modelled with reference nets, a high level Petri net formalism described in [9]. Following the nets-within-nets idea examined, for example, in [14], tokens of reference nets can again be reference nets, thus allowing for a hierarchical nesting of nets, which can interact with one another. With the help of this formalism it is possible to model the different layers of the MULAN reference architecture. The lowest level is represented by agent behaviour. Behaviour is modelled through so-called protocol nets, which are tokens in the next layer, the agent layer. The agent nets are located in their runtime environment, the platform nets, which themselves are located in system nets. This way it is possible to model a complete multi-agent system using four levels of interacting nets-within-nets. CAPA (Concurrent Agent Platform Architecture) is an extension to MULAN focussing on interoperability and communication, which was described in [6]. It provides full compliance with the standards of the Foundation for Intelligent Physical Agents (FIPA). It does so by providing a standardised message format for the MULAN agents and by replacing the upper Petri net layers of the MULAN reference architecture. These layers are now implicitly defined by actual communication relations between different platforms. The Petri net editor and simulator RENEW serves as the build- and runtime environment for systems using MULAN and CAPA. A description of RENEW can be found in [9] or on the website **www.renew.de**.

The PAOSE approach has been described, for example, in [3] and [4]. The accompanying development methodology is especially suited for software development within the MULAN and CAPA architectures, but is general enough to be used in many other contexts. The aspect most relevant for this paper is rapid prototyping, which gives the approach some agile properties. In general

Paose exhibits concepts and ideas from many other approaches. First steps within Paose use subsets of UML to define coarse designs, which are directly translated into Petri net models. These models only need to be slightly modified to provide the desired functionality, so that they almost directly correspond to prototypes within the approach. These prototypes are then recycled in further iterations. In this way the Paose methodology contains aspects of UML, model driven approaches and agile software development.

4   Conceptual View

Before going into the details of our conceptual model we must first describe the overall vision and approach behind Herold. Generally speaking the Herold project aims to provide a novel, agent-based approach of managing and controlling NSCs, both active (e.g. firewalls) and passive (e.g. intrusion detection systems). Security attributes and rules are defined in an abstract global policy that covers the entire network. This policy is enforced locally and cooperatively by the NSCs under the control of a Herold system. The global policy is created and maintained by different network administrators cooperatively and is automatically transformed into technical configurations for the NSCs. These technical configurations only contain the information relevant and necessary for the NSC they are deployed on. Information and rules that are irrelevant to a certain NSC, for example information about network events that, due to network topology, cannot possibly occur within the scope of this NSC, are removed from the configuration for this NSC. This so-called localisation of policies ensures efficiency in policy enforcement by keeping the policies at the smallest size needed. This approach entails that the NSCs, which are distributed within the network, are responsible for the security of their own compartment, or cell, of the network. This cell-based approach to network security improves security compared to a more classical perimeter approach, in which NSCs are located at the border of the supervised network and form a single line of defence against attackers. In the perimeter approach an attacker that breaches or circumvents one NSC can, in the worst case, access the entire network. With the cell-based approach an attacker can only access the (small) part of the network that lies within the cell of the NSC breached and is controlled by no other NSC.

The control and configuration of the NSCs are handled by autonomous software agents, which interact to cooperatively ensure the enforcement of the global policy. Regarding the NSCs as nodes of a distributed system it is possible to naturally map agents and agent concepts into the Herold system. These agents provide means of defining the global policy, allowing different administrators to edit the global policy concurrently, transforming the abstract global policy into technical configurations, localising the global policy for each NSC under their control and finally deploying the localised and technical configurations onto the NSCs. Basically, the agents are responsible for accepting the global policy as an input from the administrators, keeping it consistent for all users and transforming and deploying it correctly.

The ambitious goal of designing and implementing the Herold approach described above covers several iterative models. We will now describe the first complete Herold model in its conceptual idea. Based on this concept and in accordance to the PAOSE approach the following section will present how part of the functionality of our concept has already been implemented in a prototype. The model supports the key concepts of managing NSCs through agents and localising policies for individual NSCs. The localisation is handled with the concepts introduced in [8] and will not be further discussed in the scope of this paper. There are three general aspects of our model which have to be described: the network model, the policy model and the use cases. We will now examine these three aspects.

Network Model. The model assumes a connected network topology, where each node has a unique address. While the network topology is not described explicitly, the Herold users provide a description of the NSCs that are used to execute the global policy. The description of a NSC includes its network interfaces, the associated addresses, a routing table, and information on how to configure the NSC. This information is used when localising the global policy for the respective NSC. As the Herold system is not aware of the network topology with this model, some types of NSCs may not be covered by this model. Handling such NSCs is deferred to more elaborate models with a network model that includes information on the topology of the network. Besides the descriptions of the NSCs, the network description additionally covers groups to organise the network components and the assignment of network components to groups.

Policy Model. The users of the Herold system share a single, common global policy that is always active. The policy is defined in terms of 5-tuples with unique addresses and (logical) groups as defined by the network description. The tuples consist of two pairs of source and target address and port and the action. Semantically, the policy contains a rule with an *allow* or *deny* action for each possible 5-tuple. The groups, however, allow to syntactically describe the policy more concisely. The Herold system localises the global policy for each managed NSC and transforms the localised policy to a NSC-specific configuration format. The Herold system then deploys the configurations to the respective NSCs.

Use Cases. The model includes use cases on editing the global policy and network descriptions, on policy transformations and on configuration deployment. Herold users edit a single global policy and a single network description. Multiple users may edit the policy and the network description concurrently, which requires an explicit design decision on how to cope with issues arising from concurrent editing (e.g., the lost update problem). The use cases are:

— *Use cases concerning the global policy* (View the current list of rules and the status of the system; add/delete/modify/move a rule)
— *Use cases concerning the network description* (View the current set of NSCs; add/delete/modify a NSC; view the current set of groups; add/delete/rename a group; add/remove network components in a group)

The NSCs, as external systems, are actors that interact with Herold in a single use case, namely the deployment of the NSC-specific configurations.

As mentioned before this model is just one step on the way to the overall Herold vision. However it already incorporates the key aspects of Herold: Cooperative creation of a global policy, localisation of this global policy and automated transformation into configurations for NSCs. The core of the Herold approach is already present within this model and it is possible to extend and enhance this model towards the overall vision.

A quite interesting aspect of the Herold project in general is how the PAOSE approach plays into the development of the Herold system. The approach allows us to follow a fast iterative process, which produces many prototypes each incrementing and enhancing the last one. In a way the conceptual model described in this section can be seen as only one prototype on the way to the overall vision. But not only the iterative process naturally supports the development of Herold. The self-organisational aspects of the approach and the division of the target context into three dimensions (roles, interactions, ontology) naturally support the development of systems that have a distributed context, like Herold.

5   Implementation

We will now present the implementation of a subset of the functionality provided by our conceptual approach. We have chosen this subset of our model for two main reasons. On the one hand this subset is small and simple enough to be presented in the scope of this paper, on the other hand the prototype implementing this subset highlights the very important prototyping aspect of our PAOSE approach, discussed above. It is the first prototype created for this model and is referred to as *model zero*.

Model zero introduces the key functionality of the Herold application, in its simplest form. The model covers system administrators (acting as users) who interact with a global policy, described as a list of rules. From these interactions, the resulting policy is localised and deployed to a NSC.

The network submodel of model zero assumes a space of unique addresses with subnets with perfect routing, but without any further network topology and no explicit network description. The network submodel has no concept of network locations or NSCs and also does not support the grouping of components. The policy submodel assumes a single, global policy that is always active and that talks about communication relations that are characterised by protocol, source and target addresses and source and target ports. Every policy is assumed to be total, i. e. it implies an *allow* or a *deny* judgement for each of the possible communication relations per protocol. Since it is impossible to specify all individual rules, the policy may be written as an ordered list of rules where each rule is written as a pattern that can match many possible communication relations. The list is evaluated with a "first match wins" semantics. To make the policy total, there is an implicit last rule that matches everything and specifies

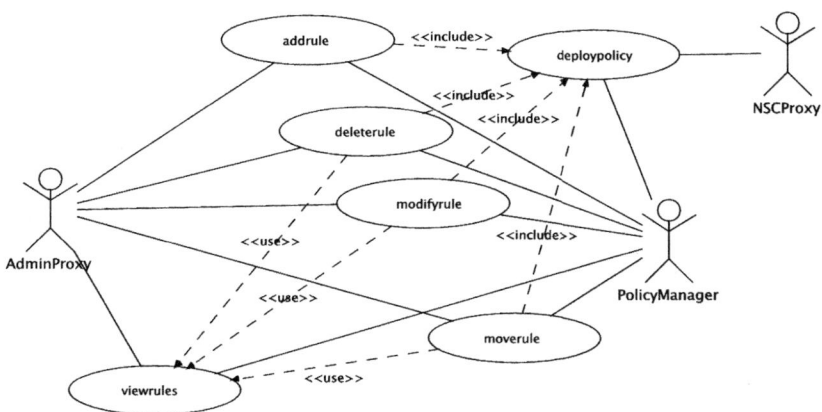

Fig. 1. Model zero - Use case diagram

a default decision for this policy. Since the network model is non-local, there is no localisation of policies. In a way the policy can be seen as the configuration of a single, omnipotent NSC.

For model zero a subset of the overall model containing six use cases has been identified. Figure 1 depicts the use case diagram.

deploy policy. In this use case the current global policy is configured and deployed into a NSC. This is the only use case in model zero that is not directly called by an actor, but is included in all of the other use cases that in some way change the global policy. It is called whenever the global policy has been successfully changed and before the lock on the global policy is lifted.

add rule. This adds a new rule to the policy at a given evaluation order position.

delete rule. The delete rule use case removes a rule from the global policy.

modify rule. This use case modifies one rule of the global policy. The parameters within this interaction are both the old and new rule.

move rule. The move rule use case can be seen as a special case of the modify rule use case, in which the actual rule itself is left unchanged and only the position of the rule within the global policy is modified.

view rules. This use case returns all the rules of the current global policy.

The use cases involve three actors, namely:

Admin Proxy. This represents a system administrator. He has administrative control over the global policy and can thus initiate the different use cases.

Policy Manager. This actor represents an entity, which is in charge of managing the central list of rules.

NSC Proxy. This actor represents the NSC within the use cases. It is only involved in the deploy rule use case, since all other operations only work with the global policy managed by the policy manager.

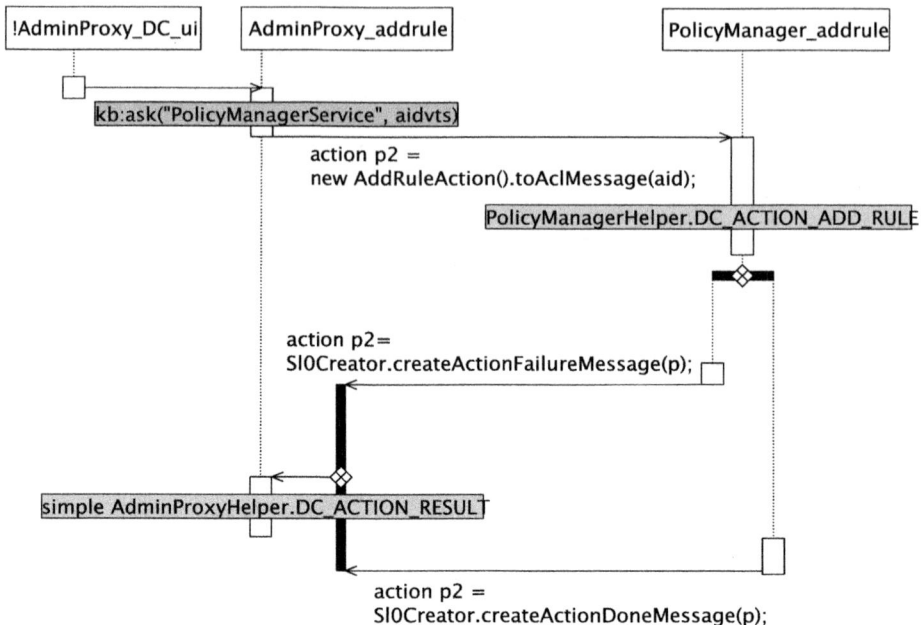

Fig. 2. Interaction protocol for the add rule use case

From these use cases it is possible to automatically generate the artefacts needed for the next modelling steps using the RENEW toolset. In the case of MU-LAN and CAPA the use cases are realised through interactions between agents, which themselves correspond to the actors. These interactions are defined through agent interaction protocols, from which the actual agent behaviour protocols can be generated. Behaviour outside of these interactions (e.g. internal decision making) is modelled through decision components which generally serve as the internal behaviour of agents. An agent's knowledge is defined in it's knowledge base that is defined during modelling but can change during execution.

We will now exemplary discuss one of these interactions in detail. We have chosen to illustrate the add rule use case/interaction for this example, since it shares much of its structure with other use cases, as is discussed below. Figure 2 shows the agent interaction protocol for this use case.

The interaction is started by the *AdminProxy_DC_ui*, which represents the user interface for an administrator. The other two actors in this diagram represent the agent protocols, which model the behaviour of the agents which correspond to the admin proxy and policy manager actors of the use case. The first action the *AdminProxy_addrule* protocol executes is to look up and find the address of the policy manager from the knowledge base. Once this is done a message is sent to the policy manager containing the request to add a rule, as well as information about the new rule. This is then passed internally over to the decision component of the policy manager agent. Within this decision

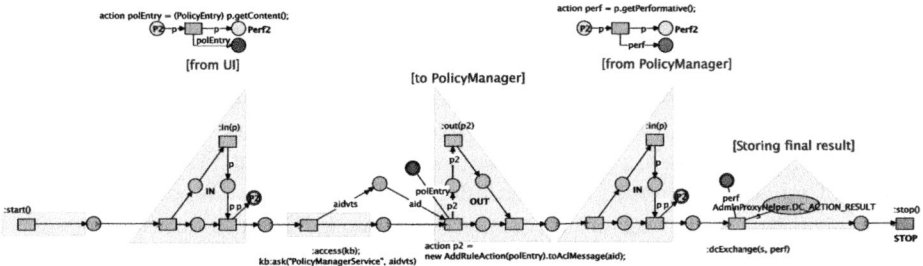

Fig. 3. Agent protocol for the admin proxy actor in the add rule use case

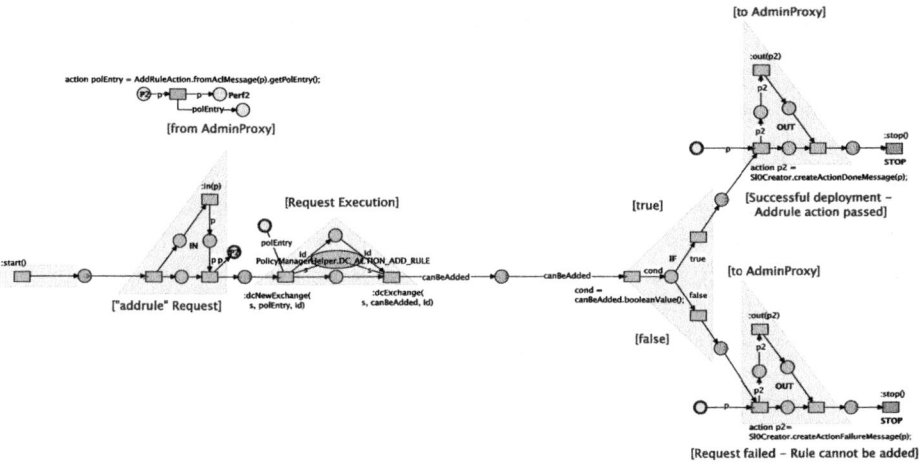

Fig. 4. Agent protocol for the policy manager actor in the add rule use case

component the new rule is evaluated and added to the global policy. If this has succeeded, the deploy rule interaction is called and the new policy deployed in all known NSCs. The decision component replies to the protocol with either a failure or done, depending on whether problems occurred at any step. This result is then sent as either an ActionDone or an ActionFailure message to the admin proxy protocol and passed to a decision component, which stores the results of interactions for later inspection. This concludes the interaction/use case. From this agent interaction protocol the stubs for the agent protocols can be automatically generated using the RENEW toolset. These stubs only need a minimal amount of change in their inscriptions until they are complete and model the functionality described above when executed. The resulting final two protocols can be seen in Figures 3 and 4.

5.1   Assumptions and Simplifications

Mainly, our assumptions and simplifications are related to both the *interaction protocols* and the *concurrent* access to the policy pool.

Even though we did not elaborate on all the use cases, one can straightforwardly see that they all rely on the same pattern: identify a single entity and make it execute a functionality on your behalf. This pattern is well captured in the standard FIPA request protocol. A functionality requester, the *initiator*, contacts a functionality provider, the *participant*, to request the provision of a functionality. After examining the request, the participant first notifies the initiator of whether it agrees to providing the functionality or not. Also, in case an error occurs while examining the request, the initiator is notified as well. In case the participant agrees to executing the functionality, it does so and sends the initiator the result. The final result can then be communicated either as a simple notification, a reference to a generated object or a notification of failure.

Given the simplicity of our model, we assumed that an agent enacting the participant role will always accept a functionality whenever contacted. As well, we minimised any message examination error. Thus, we shortened the request protocol and removed the acceptance phase.

Another careful consideration during the modelling exercise is with respect to *concurrency* control, i.e., how to provide concurrent access to the global policy. Indeed, despite the simplicity of the current model, concurrency remains one of its pillars. Although we pondered over several possible solutions, we finally chose a *pessimistic lock* approach for the sake of simplicity. Only *write* operations (add rule, move, modify and delete rules) are considered for lock. Thus, at any time one can view the current set of rules in the policy. The scope of the lock is the entire policy. In the future, we envision to narrow the scope down to a subset of rules and if necessary to a single rule. In doing so we will easily cope with, for example, partial policies, while improving the performance of our models.

5.2   Step-by-Step Modeling

In this section we briefly take the reader through the different steps that led to the Petri net models, which control the behaviour of the agents. As mentioned earlier these steps fall into the PAOSE guidelines.

1. *Use cases:* Identify the actors and draw the use case diagrams.
2. *Ontology objects:* Ontology objects help define the concepts referred to in the content of agent messages.
3. *Interaction diagrams:* Elaborate on the interactions defined in the use case diagrams.
4. *Interaction models:* Using a RENEW plugin, we automatically generated the Petri net models corresponding to the interaction models (*agent protocols*).
5. *Decision components:* We draw the nets that support internal decision makings for each agent.
6. *Knowledge Bases:* We configure the knowledge base for each agent.

Going through this process as a cycle yields multiple prototypes, each improving upon the functionality and stability of the previous version. In the model zero prototype, we packaged the necessary aspects to model the key functionality of the Herold application. Note that this model bears many simplifications and can only serve as a proof of concept. Further prototypes will extend model zero in various regards, like network modelling, localisation and policy management, until a satisfactory version of our overall model is achieved.

6 Conclusion

In this paper we presented our work within the Herold research project. We examined the overall Herold vision and presented our conceptual approach to realising this vision. We detailed the important aspects of the conceptual model and then proceeded to describe one of the prototypes implementing a first, important subset of the overall, conceptual functionality. The description detailed the submodels and the general use cases of the prototype. For one of these use cases the actual implementation was exemplarily presented. Afterwards the prototype and some design decisions were discussed.

Further prototypes are already being developed. They incorporate more concepts described in the conceptual model and in the overall vision. Aspects of the overall vision being addressed are:

- **Policies:** One aspect lies in handling the global policy. For example the support of partial policies is planned, which do not cover the entire space of possible events. These would have to be completed internally, but would make handling of policies easier for the user. Another point here would be the provision of a policy pool and policy templates, which would make the generation of policies easier. The support of obligation policies in addition to the current authorisation policies and the relationship of the policy model to the network model are also being examined.
- **Network model and localisation:** Another aspect regards the network model and the localisation. The overall vision includes an explicit, expressive network model in order to localise the global policy in the most efficient way. This network model needs to be expressive enough to describe realistic settings, but still easy to use. The network model and the related complex localisation algorithms are important aspects of the Herold project and will be addressed in the near future.
- **Transformation into configurations:** Another aspect that has not been discussed in detail in this paper is the transformation from the (abstract) policy to the actual technical configuration files for the NSCs. This affects the policy model, since the transformation into different specific configuration languages has to be supported.

By following the PAOSE development approach the Herold project is supported by an approach that naturally maps concepts of the target domain into the development cycle. The fast prototyping encouraged by the approach allows us to iteratively enhance the produced systems. In conclusion the overall Herold project aims at providing a surplus within the domain of distributed network security. The first steps within this endeavour have been presented in this paper.

References

1. Bieszczad, A., Pagurek, B., White, T.: Mobile Agents for Network Management. IEEE Communications Surveys 1(1), 2–9 (1998)
2. Bradshaw, J.M., Dutfield, S., Benoit, P., Woolley, J.D.: KAoS: toward an industrial-strength open agent architecture. In: Software Agents, pp. 375–418. MIT Press, Cambridge (1997)
3. Cabac, L., Dörges, T., Duvigneau, M., Reese, C., Wester-Ebbinghaus, M.: Application Development with Mulan. In: Proceedings of the International Workshop on Petri Nets and Software Engineering (PNSE'07), pp. 145–159 (2007)
4. Cabac, L.: Multi-Agent System: A Guiding Metaphor for the Organization of Software Development Projects. In: Petta, P., Müller, J.P., Klusch, M., Georgeff, M. (eds.) MATES 2007. LNCS (LNAI), vol. 4687, pp. 1–12. Springer, Heidelberg (2007)
5. Du, T.C., Li, E.Y., Chang, A.-P.: Mobile Agents in Distributed Network Management. Communications of the ACM 46(7), 127–132 (2003)
6. Duvigneau, M.: Bereitstellung einer Agentenplattform für petrinetzbasierte Agenten. Diploma thesis, University of Hamburg (2002)
7. Goldszmidt, G., Yemini, Y.: Delegated Agents for Network Management. IEEE Communications Magazine 36(3), 66–71 (1998)
8. Großklaus, A.: Policybasierte Konfiguration von verteilten Netzwerksicherheitskomponenten. Diploma thesis, University of Hamburg (2007)
9. Kummer, O.: Referenznetze. Logos Verlag, Berlin (2002)
10. Puliafito, A., Tomarchio, O.: Using Mobile Agents to Implement Flexible Network Management Strategies. Computer Communications 23(8), 708–719 (2000)
11. Rölke, H.: Modellierung von Agenten und Multiagentensystemen – Grundlagen und Anwendungen. Logos Verlag, Berlin (2004)
12. Twidle, K., Lupu, E., Dulay, N., Sloman, M.: Ponder2 – A Policy Environment for Autonomous Pervasive Systems. In: Proceedings of the 2008 IEEE Workshop on Policies for Distributed Systems and Networks (POLICY '08), pp. 245–246. IEEE Computer Society Press, Los Alamitos (2008)
13. Uszok, A., Bradshaw, J., Jeffers, R., Suri, N., Hayes, P., Breedy, M., Bunch, L., Johnson, M., Kulkarni, S., Lott, J.: KAoS Policy and Domain Services: Toward a Description-Logic Approach to Policy Representation, Deconfliction, and Enforcement. In: Proceedings of the 4th IEEE International Workshop on Policies for Distributed Systems and Networks, pp. 93–98. IEEE, Los Alamitos (2003)
14. Valk, R.: On Processes of Object Petri Nets. Technical Report FBI-HH-B-185/96, University of Hamburg, Department of Computer Science (1996)

Author Index

GPSR Compliance

*The European Union's (EU) General Product Safety Regulation (GPSR)
is a set of rules that requires consumer products to be safe and our
obligations to ensure this.*

*If you have any concerns about our products, you can contact us on
ProductSafety@springernature.com*

In case Publisher is established outside the EU, the EU authorized
representative is:

Springer Nature Customer Service Center GmbH
Europaplatz 3
69115 Heidelberg, Germany

Batch number: 09478804

Printed by Printforce, the Netherlands